The Drama of a Rural Community's Life Cycle

The Drama of a Rural Community's Life Cycle

Its Prehistory, Birth, Growth, Maturity, Decline, and Rebirth

S. ROY KAUFMAN

WIPF & STOCK · Eugene, Oregon

THE DRAMA OF A RURAL COMMUNITY'S LIFE CYCLE
Its Prehistory, Birth, Growth, Maturity, Decline, and Rebirth

Copyright © 2020 S. Roy Kaufman. All rights reserved. Except for brief quotations in critical publications or reviews, no part of this book may be reproduced in any manner without prior written permission from the publisher. Write: Permissions, Wipf and Stock Publishers, 199 W. 8th Ave., Suite 3, Eugene, OR 97401.

Wipf & Stock
An Imprint of Wipf and Stock Publishers
199 W. 8th Ave., Suite 3
Eugene, OR 97401

www.wipfandstock.com

PAPERBACK ISBN: 978-1-7252-6989-7
HARDCOVER ISBN: 978-1-7252-6990-3
EBOOK ISBN: 978-1-7252-6991-0

Manufactured in the U.S.A.   09/08/20

Scripture quotations contained herein are from the New Revised Standard Version Bible (NRSV), copyright © 1989 by the Division of Christian Education of the National Council of Churches of Christ in the U. S. A., and are used by permission. All rights reserved.

Figure 1. From *Remember Your Relatives,* Reneé Sansom-Flood and Shirley A. Bernie, original map drawn by Benedictine Sister Leonarda Longen, edited by Heritage Hall Archives. Used with permission of the Business and Claims Committee of the Ihanktownan Dakota Oyate (Yankton Sioux Tribe), Wagner, South Dakota.

Figure 2. From *The European History of the Swiss Mennonites from Volhynia,* Martin Schrag, and used with permission of Frank Stucky and the Harley Stucky Estate.

Figure 3. Originally published in *Mennonite Life,* and used with permission of Mennonite Library and Archives, North Newton, Kansas.

Figure 4. From *Mennonite Historical Atlas,* 2nd edition, William Schroeder and Helmut T. Heubert, used with permission of Centre for Mennonite Brethren Studies, Winnipeg, Canada, and the Heubert Estate.

Figures 5, 7, 9, and 10. Courtesy of Heritage Hall Archives, Freeman, South Dakota, with special thanks to Marnette Ortman Hofer, Archivist, for her help in preparing all the illustrations, and for all her support and assistance in the preparation of this book.

Figure 8. From *Looking Back,* used with permission from Salem-Zion Mennonite Church.

Figures 11, 12, and 16. Compliments of County Wide Directories, Larchwood, Iowa, edited by Heritage Hall Archives.

Figure 15. Cover of *A Moment on Our Journey of Faith*, used with permission of Salem Mennonite Church.

Contents

List of Illustrations | vii
Introduction | ix

Part I: Components/Actors in the Drama | 1

1. The Story of the Land and Its First Inhabitants | 3
2. The Imperial History and Its Intrusion into the Land | 21
3. The Prehistory of the Agrarian Cultures
   That Came into the Land | 42

Part II: A Rural Community's Life Cycle | 69

4. The Community's Birth in Immigration
   and Displacement (1874) | 71
5. The Community's Growth to Maturity (1875 to 1925) | 97
6. The Community in Its Maturity (1925 to 1975) | 130
7. The Community's Decline under an
   Industrial Agriculture (1975 to 2025) | 159

Part III: Toward the Rebirth of the Community | 191

8. The Community's Movement toward
   Revitalization (2000 to 2050) | 193
9. The Re-formation of an Agrarian Culture | 219
10. The Role of Religious Faith in the Formation
    of an Agrarian Culture | 239

Bibliography | 263
Index | 271

List of Illustrations

Figure 1	Yankton Treaty Cession of 1858	37
Figure 2	Migrations of the Swiss Volhynian Mennonites	50–51
Figure 3	Mennonite Travel Route from Prussia to Russia	56
Figure 4	Hutterite Migrations in Eastern Europe	61
Figure 5	Settlements of the Germans-from-Russia in the Freeman Area	90
Figure 6	Sod House	94
Figure 7	Early Pioneer Homestead	104
Figure 8	First Salem Church, 1880; Zion Church, 1881	106
Figure 9	Tieszen House/Barn; *Grosse Kirche*, 1879	110
Figure 10	South Dakota Mennonite College, 1903	122
Figure 11	Hutchinson County, South Dakota	150
Figure 12	Turner County, South Dakota	151
Figure 13	Small Farm of the 1950s	156
Figure 14	Salem/Salem-Zion Membership	173
Figure 15	Salem Mennonite Church Buildings	174
Figure 16	Salem Mennonite Church Prayer Walks	175

Introduction

THIS IS THE STORY of a rural community. It is the story of a specific local rural community, the one surrounding the small town of Freeman, in southeast South Dakota. It is the story of the land and the people who came to live upon this land and built this rural community. While it includes the people who first came to this land—the Native Americans, it is specifically the story of the European settlers who came to this land in the 1870s—the *Germans-from-Russia*.[1] More specifically, it is the story of the three Anabaptist groups—Low German Mennonites, Hutterian *Prarieleut*, and Swiss Volhynian Amish—who came from Ukraine in 1874 and settled in the area around Freeman. These three groups share a common faith heritage but each had their own dialect and customs and ethnic identity.

The story of a rural community is the story of the agrarian cultures that comprise it. Agrarian cultures grow out of the symbiotic relationship between human communities and the landscape and natural environment through the agricultural practices that are employed. The landscape or natural environment is shaped by the human community as it engages in agriculture, in this case, as the prairie of the Great Plains was broken and trees were planted. But the human community is also shaped by the constraints and opportunities of the natural environment, in this case, as immigrant communities from Russia came to settle on the land of southeast South Dakota.

Given the specificity of land and community interaction, it is not surprising that even most small rural communities comprise a number of very local agrarian cultures, in this case, the three Anabaptist/Mennonite groups that settled around Freeman, South Dakota. There would be at least three more Russian-German sub-cultures around Freeman of other

---

1. The terms *Germans-from-Russia* and *Russian-Germans* will both be used in this book to refer to ethnic Germans who immigrated from Russia to the United States.

religious backgrounds and also several of other ethnicities who participated integrally in the development of this rural community. The focus here will be on the Anabaptist/Mennonite sub-cultures with which I am most familiar. I am a native of the Freeman community and was reared in the Swiss Volhynian agrarian culture of the Anabaptist/Mennonite faith, so that is the story I know best. While I will refer to the other cultures of the community, this will mostly be the story of how these Anabaptist/Mennonite cultures helped to shape and were shaped by the rural Freeman community and its landscape.

I have felt for some time that the Freeman community represents an ideal example of the life cycle of an agrarian culture. The land around Freeman was virgin prairie when immigrant settlers came here in 1874 to build their life on this land. In addition, the settlers who came here were already established agrarian cultures with a long history and strong ethnic and faith heritage. So what we have here are established agrarian cultures immigrating to a virgin prairie and being *born anew* in this landscape. After an initial struggle and much hardship in its *birth*, the community *grew up* and came to a kind of *maturity* in this place. And then, in the last fifty years or so with the industrialization of agriculture, the community has entered a long *decline* we might think of as its *old age*. It remains to be seen whether the next stage will be the *death* of the community or its revitalization or *re-birth*, taking on a different life as it moves into the future.

While the agrarian cultures that built this community were not alone and worked together, their joint histories parallel one another both in coming to this land and in the building of this community. The whole *life-cycle* of the community is exhibited in the 150-year span of the community's life. I have no idea whether 150 years is a normal life span for a rural community, but it is in any case the lifetime of this community. Whatever happens next in this community will likely be the story of other, succeeding agrarian cultures, however much it might (hopefully) be rooted in those original cultures. So the boundaries of the community's life, from birth to death, are fairly well defined within this 150-year span from 1874 to 2024, and within what has become essentially a two-county geographic area in southeast South Dakota. The bulk of this book, in Part II, will examine the life of the community through its birth, growth, maturation, and decline.

But of course, the story of this community does not begin in 1874, either for the land or for the people who came to settle on this land in that year. The land has a millennia-long, indeed an eon-long, story that is crucial to understand as the story of the land and its people is told. In the same way, the community of people who came to settle on this land have a centuries-long pre-history as agrarian cultures that must also be understood as the story of this rural community is told. Particularly since the beginning of the modern era, the story of the land and its people has been shaped by the particular human institutional intrusions to which the land has been subjected—the history of the imperial powers that have laid claim to the land and its resources. These stories and themes will be explored in Part I of this book.

While the story of the Freeman, South Dakota, rural community may have a particular interest for the people living in that community, this story is told with the intention of having a much wider significance and broader audience. The story of the Freeman community is seen as paradigmatic for rural communities and agrarian cultures generally. There are, it is hoped, lessons to be learned from this story about what makes a rural community tick, what makes it sustainable and healthy, what prolongs its life or leads to its revitalization or causes it to die. Part III will explore these lessons, and particularly the role religious faith has in the formation of an agrarian culture.

Already it should be evident that this book is not the work of either an historian or a sociologist, though it utilizes insights and methods from both of those disciplines. However, I am not trained as either an historian or a sociologist. I am a pastor who spent my entire forty-year pastoral career serving rural congregations in rural communities of the Great Plains. I was reared and nurtured in an agrarian culture; I have lived in agrarian cultures; and I am a passionate advocate for agrarian cultures and rural communities as the most promising context for living humanely and sustainably here on Earth. I am also deeply committed to the Anabaptist tradition of Christian faith, with its long agrarian history and its commitment to alternative communal living as its missional calling in the world. Mennonite churches have had a keen sense of being alternative communities of faith with values and an ethos different from the dominant cultures in which they have emerged and in which they have lived.

In the light of all this, this book might best be understood as an interpretive history of the Freeman community. I make no pretense about being objective, a disinterested observer. I am prepared to make judgments about the choices I and my community have made that have led both to our successes and to our failures. I will of course seek to be accurate and provide documentation in presenting facts and events relevant to the story being told. However, as with any story of a life or a community, only a few selected facts and events will be referenced, and I make no apology if these are the facts and events that seem to confirm my perspectives and biases about rural communities and agrarian cultures.

Having served five struggling rural congregations through my pastoral career, all of which grew smaller during my tenure, I am keenly aware of the forces arrayed against rural communities and traditional cultures all around the world. I have no illusions about the challenges that confront agrarian cultures in the modern world. They confront the impositions of government bureaucracies, corporate domination, and technocratic demands. However, these forces are nothing new. While rural communities are clearly oppressed by these forces, they can be empowered to move beyond seeing themselves as victims. I believe that rural communities and agrarian cultures have within themselves the resources needed to resist and withstand all the pressures and threats brought against them. This book and the story it tells are designed to describe some of the dynamics that enable rural communities and agrarian cultures to survive and thrive even in the midst of the imperial forces that have always exploited and oppressed them.

PART I

Components/Actors in the Drama

1

The Story of the Land and Its First Inhabitants

SYNOPSIS

For millennia and eons, the land of Earth is being prepared for the human presence that will in the fullness of time come to inhabit each place. Geological forces shape and form the land, creating the particular biome of each place. Climatological forces continue to shape the land, defining both the opportunities and the constraints of the life forms that emerge and take their place in the landscape through the eons. There is something ultimate in the shaping of the land—something spiritual, something divine, something that always confronts us with mystery and wonder. And so, the land makes itself ready to receive the human presence.

Land and people live in reciprocal relationships. The land shapes the human community, defining both the possibilities and the constraints that exist for the human community. And the human community shapes the land, particularly since the dawn of agriculture, the domestication of plants and animals beginning some ten thousand years ago. Agricultural landscapes begin to emerge, changing sometimes radically the appearance of the land. But always, even in the most intensive agricultural environments, there remains that reciprocal relationship of the land and the people who come to live in that particular place.

In order to survive and thrive, human communities need to learn carefully both the possibilities and the constraints that the land they inhabit may offer them. Misjudging the characteristics of the land is a sure course to disaster, for both the land and the human community that lives upon the land. Generations of experience are required to learn the expectations of the land, and that is true especially for an agricultural environment that brings such profound and often radical changes to the landscape. Every agrarian culture might be seen as an experiment into how land and human community may live together in sustainable ways.

The first human communities on the Great Plains of North America lived lightly on the land. Their presence was hardly felt. Artifacts of their lives are sparse. Their history is largely unrecorded, lost in the mists of time. They mostly followed the rivers and waterways of the land, bearing witness to the importance of water to the land and the human community. Unknown to us are the families and tribes and peoples who made their lives and their homes upon this land and its prairies. Yet what these aboriginal peoples of North America learned through their millennia of living on this land must not be lost. Theirs was an intimate and spiritual connection to the land and its life, a profoundly deep connection to the places they inhabited.

FINDING THE CONTEXT OF OUR LOCAL PLACE

It is a truism to observe that everything happens on a space-time continuum. Every incident, every event, every story, every thing, every life is located in a specific time and place. In order to understand the significance of something, it is important to ground it or root it in the specific time and place in which that something occurred.

This is particularly important for those like myself who see things and understand life from the perspective of Christian faith. At the heart of Christian faith is the incarnation, the belief that Creator God became uniquely human in a specific person at a specific time and place. Christians believe that God became human in the person of Jesus Christ, who lived for some thirty years early in the first century of the Common Era in the land of Palestine. The thing about the incarnation is that it makes every time and every place holy, sacred, special, God-inhabited! If Creator God valued this world and this life enough to enter it personally in that life at that time and place, that also means Creator God values every specific time and place as a God-inhabited space-time! That's what makes it so important to root and ground this story in its specific time and place.

But of course, specificity is always relational and relative to everything else that exists. Nothing exists in isolation from everything else. I already identified this as the story of the Freeman, South Dakota, rural community from its birth nearly 150 years ago until today. So our first task is to define the context of this particular place and time.

THE EARTH AND NORTH AMERICA

To begin on the grandest scale, we find our home on Planet Earth, which first began to coalesce around the Sun some 4.6 billion years ago. This may seem to us at first like far too vast a canvas to comprehend. Yet the truth is that the Earth is but a tiny speck against the vastness of the Universe. Our Sun is only one of billions of stars in the Milky Way Galaxy, whose expanse we can only begin to glimpse in the night sky above us. And likewise, the Milky Way Galaxy is but one of billions of galaxies we can see with the aid of telescopes. And if 4.6 billion years seems like a long history here on Earth, it too pales next to the fourteen billion or so years that have passed since the Universe had its beginnings. Yet it was here on Planet Earth that the long journey of life as we know it occurred, first in the prokaryotic life invisible to the naked eye more than three billion years ago, and then in all the myriad forms of life visible to us in the Phanerozoic Eon that began about 600 million years ago. Wherever and whenever on Earth we live, this is our story. This is what has shaped us and made us what we are.[1]

We begin to narrow the field of vision when we observe that we live on the North American continent, or the *New World*, as we white people of European origin conceitedly call it. It is no surprise that the first chapter of Genesis should speak of God's creative act on the third day of creation as the separation of dry land from the sea. While the sea certainly teems with life intricately woven with our own life, we are creatures of the land as humans. And the land, as we have come to know, rests on large continental plates that over millennia move upon Earth's crust. Two hundred million years ago there was one large continental landmass that split apart until eventually the continents assumed the shapes they have today.[2]

---

1. Jakeš, *Living Planet Earth*, 9–20.
2. Jakeš, *Living Planet Earth*, 68–89.

Turtle Island, as Native Americans call the North American continent, began to assume its current shape and position relative to the other continental land masses during the Cretaceous Period (145 to 65 million years ago) of the Mesozoic Era. Prior to this time, the North American craton, as the continental plates are called, was often covered by a shallow sea, accounting for the quartzite rock formations underlying parts of southeast South Dakota, as well as the many Cambrian aquatic fossils found in the rocks. Three hundred million years ago, plate tectonics began to raise the Appalachian Mountains to our east, and much later, beginning some 165 million years ago, the Rocky Mountains began to form to our west. Between these mountain ranges lay that vast area that eventually became the prairie grasslands of the Great Plains.[3]

THE GREAT PLAINS

The Great Plains, huge and varied as they are, do bring us to the biome and ecosystem of our target area of Freeman, South Dakota. Prairie grasslands, like those found in the Great Plains, are among the more recent innovations of life on Earth. With about ten thousand species worldwide, grasses first appeared only about sixty million years ago. The Great Plains has about 140 grass species in forty-one genera.[4] A global overview of Earth's major biomes reveals that grasslands are the largest biome geographically.[5] Since the advent of agriculture some ten thousand years ago, grasslands were among the areas adapted to agricultural use in both grazing and field cultivation.

While the continents were shaped in large measure by the geological forces of continental drift along with earthquakes and volcanos, the Great Plains themselves have been shaped more by climatological forces. By most current definitions, the Great Plains extend from mid-Alberta and Saskatchewan in Canada to Texas, and from the Rocky Mountains to the eastern borders of North and South Dakota and the Missouri River,[6] though some sources also include parts of Minnesota and Missouri and

---

3. Savage, *Prairie*, 32–46.
4. Savage, *Prairie*, 64.
5. Savage, *Prairie*, 5.
6. Lavin et al., *Atlas*, 12–13. Maps of the Great Plains fitting this description can be found throughout this atlas.

most of Iowa.⁷ The former definition encompasses an area of 973,500 square miles, 13 percent of the area of the United States and Canada.⁸ Thus the Great Plains have been formed to a large extent by the sediments eroded from the Rocky Mountains over the millennia since their formation, with a downward slope from west to east of a kilometer.⁹

The transformation from rocky mountain to prairie soil is long and complicated. It involves rain and frost, and erosion by both wind and water. Moisture and frost gradually fracture rock into small pieces, which is then carried off by wind and water. Water also activates chemical processes that break down rocks into clay and smaller particles.[10] These sediments in turn are colonized by a rich microbial life and eventually by plants, whose roots hold the soil and whose life cycle adds nutrients to the emerging soil. The plants in turn are eaten and utilized by different forms of animal life, and gradually a prairie ecosystem emerges. Two forms of underground life are particularly important for the formation of prairie soils—earthworms and ants.[11] Indeed, the full richness of prairie life is to be found underground, in the soil.[12]

SOUTHEAST SOUTH DAKOTA

When we narrow the focus still further to the local area around Freeman and southeast South Dakota, we find that the land was shaped by still another climatological event—the Ice Age of the Pleistocene Epoch of the Cenozoic Era that began some two million years ago. These most recent ice ages the Earth has experienced were labeled from oldest to most recent the Nebraskan, Kansan, Illinoisan, and Wisconsin glaciations, indicating their most southern reach, though today it is understood that the ice ages were too fluid for these names to be dated with any accuracy.[13] Roughly the northern third of the North American continent was covered with

---

7. Savage, *Prairie*, 9. Maps of the Great Plains fitting this description can be found throughout the book.
8. Lavin et al., *Atlas*, 13.
9. Savage, *Prairie*, 8.
10. Gries, *Roadside Geology of South Dakota*, 7.
11. Savage, *Prairie*, 103–9.
12. Savage, *Prairie*, 92.
13. Gries, *Roadside Geology of South Dakota*, 14–16.

ice at the greatest extent, probably in the Kansan glaciation.[14] The glaciation's western edge roughly followed the present course of the Missouri River though North and South Dakota, meaning that the landscape of southeast South Dakota was altered by the glacial ice.[15]

The larger Freeman community contains glacial debris from the Gary sub-stage of the Wisconsin Ice Age which began some sixty thousand years ago.[16] The Gary drift sheet covers the broad James River valley from north to south through South Dakota. The subsequent Altamont stage also left debris on the eastern side of the Gary drift sheet. Parts of the Freeman community along Turkey Ridge have debris from the Altamont stage which follows the Vermillion River.[17]

Turkey Ridge itself, which forms the southern border of the larger Freeman community and extends from south of Freeman down to Spirit Mound north of Vermillion, is a unique geological feature of southeast South Dakota.[18] Running southeast from Freeman, Turkey Ridge rises some four hundred feet above the surrounding prairie and has a rock core of Niobrara chalk with an overlay of Pierre shale, rock layers dating back to the Cretaceous Period. It formed the divide between two pre-glacial rivers, showing the way the glaciers altered the course of pre-glacial rivers from east to southeast.[19] Glaciers were unable to plane down Turkey Ridge, and only left a thin veneer of glacial debris on the surface as they overrode it.[20]

With this, we have managed to define the geographical area of the larger Freeman community which is the subject of this book. It is bounded on the west by the James River, on the east by the Vermillion River, and on the south by Turkey Ridge. These two rivers reflect the drainage pattern established by the melting glaciers, which only receded from this area ten thousand to fifteen thousand years ago.[21] The north boundary is more indeterminate, but might be understood as the apex where the watersheds of Wolf Creek and the West Vermillion River converge. In

14. Savage, *Prairie*, 53.
15. Savage, *Prairie*, 9.
16. Gries, *Roadside Geology of South Dakota*, 15.
17. Gries, *Roadside Geology of South Dakota*, 57.
18. Gries, *Roadside Geology of South Dakota*, 57–60, 63, 88–89.
19. Gries, *Roadside Geology of South Dakota*, 18–19, 57, 89.
20. Gries, *Roadside Geology of South Dakota*, 57.
21. Gries, *Roadside Geology of South Dakota*, 15–18.

terms of current political boundaries, this includes the eastern third of Hutchinson County and the western three-fourths of Turner County. This area, comprising about 720 square miles, or twenty townships in these two counties, is the land that will be the subject of this book.[22]

The town of Freeman was founded in 1879 after the agrarian cultures, which are the subject of this book, settled in this area. The location of Freeman, central to the rural community that developed in this area, is largely the accident of the construction of the Chicago, Milwaukee, and St. Paul Railroad in 1879 from Marion Junction to Running Water, Nebraska.[23] Freeman's location not only happened to be central to the several agrarian cultures that settled in the area and built the community. It is also very nearly at the top of the three watersheds described in the last paragraph. Water in the west half of Freeman runs into the James River watershed, and in the east half of Freeman water runs north into Silver Lake and then into the West Vermillion River. If Freeman, which occupies one square mile, had been built on the section two miles south of its present location, part of Freeman would have also drained into the Turkey Ridge Creek watershed. It is one of those fascinating historical/geographical coincidences that shape the identity of a rural community. All three watersheds can be seen on the hill about a mile and a half south of Freeman.

THE HOLOCENE EPOCH

The native flora and fauna of the Great Plains changed dramatically over the many millennia, as we see in the fossils at Ashfall Fossil Beds State Historical Park at Orchard, Nebraska, about one hundred miles southwest of Freeman. Here we find the fossilized remains of animals common to the Great Plains during the Miocene Epoch (twenty-four to five million years ago) that perished at a waterhole, suffocated by ash from a volcanic eruption that occurred about twelve million years ago. Here you can see "scores of animals—rhinoceroses, zebra-like horses, saber-toothed deer, camels, turtles."[24] The volcanic eruption that laid down all the ash in Nebraska occurred in what is now Idaho, but now that volcanic hot-spot is under Yellowstone National Park. Large volcanic eruptions

---

22. See Figures 11 and 12, Hutchinson and Turner County maps, in chapter 6.
23. Freeman Centennial Steering Committee, *Freeman Facts*, 9.
24. Bryson, *Short History*, 207.

from this hot-spot have occurred about every 600,000 years, and it was about that long ago that the last eruption there occurred. So perhaps we are due for another such cataclysmic eruption in our time.[25]

The point to be made is that the flora and fauna of the Great Plains have always been in flux, from the age of the dinosaurs until today. But for our purposes, perhaps we should look at what the Great Plains looked like at the dawn of the Holocene Epoch, which began about ten thousand years ago. This is also incidentally about the dawn of human history in other parts of the world. And it may also be about the time Homo sapiens first made its appearance on the Great Plains.

Ten thousand years ago the landscape of the Great Plains appeared much as it does today geographically. The mega-fauna including the wooly mammoth that had populated the Great Plains even fifteen thousand years ago had quite suddenly disappeared, whether because of climatic changes at the end of the ice age or hunting by the first human inhabitants of the land. So, ten thousand years ago the bison we associate with the Great Plains were already at the apex of the prairie eco-system.[26] The prairie eco-systems of the Great Plains have been fairly stable and sustainable for these past ten thousand years. In terms of the geological time frames we have been discussing, this hardly represents the blink of an eye in time. But in terms of the human presence here on Earth, ten thousand years encompasses the entire span of human history and then some. The alarming thing is that this entire prairie eco-system has almost all been dismantled and destroyed beyond repair only in the past two hundred years, since the arrival of European colonizers in America.

Today it is impossible for us to imagine what southeast South Dakota would have looked like prior to the European invasion in terms of flora and fauna. While most native species of plants and animals survive here or there, now is not at all like then. Imagine vast herds of bison that covered the hills from time to time in their migrations, along with herds of pronghorn and elk and deer. Imagine the range of carnivores that followed these herds—bear, cougar, wolf. Imagine the vast tall-grass prairies that met our ancestors—a vast sea of grass taller than a man. Imagine all the birds, those that live on the prairie and those that migrate, those that nest in the lakes and potholes and sloughs left by the glaciers, and those on the rivers and streams carved by glacial run-off. Imagine the color of the prairie in

---

25. Bryson, *Short History*, 209, 228.
26. Savage, *Prairie*, 59–60.

full summer bloom, when the forbs of the prairie appear in force. Imagine the lightning-ignited prairie fires that burned and revitalized the prairie every few years.[27] Here and there along the rivers and streams, imagine the small bands of humans, the first inhabitants of this land, preceding by centuries the First Nations tribes whose names we know.

Here was a world of beauty and peace, an eco-system of living things in balance. Yes, there were the fires and storms, the droughts and floods, the harshness of long cold winters and the searing heat of the dry summers, the unfettered winds of the vast, flat, treeless prairie. But all the forms of life on the prairie adapted to these challenges and created a vital and sustainable ecosystem capable of surviving all but the most severe and sustained threats.

The part of the prairie which is the focus of our interest, southeast South Dakota, is on the boundary between the Central Tall Grasslands and the Northern Mixed Grasslands,[28] between the forest steppe and the steppe.[29] This area is geographically described as the Glaciated Central Lowlands of the Great Plains.[30] Water is the critical constraint in this area. Average precipitation is between twenty and twenty-five inches a year,[31] and there is no significant underground reservoir like the Ogallala Aquifer that underlies much of the Great Plains further south.[32] It is this shortage of water that created the perception of this area as the Great American Desert, described by Walter Prescott Webb, the great early historian of the Great Plains—a perception that persisted until after European settlement began following the Civil War.[33]

The soil of the area is the typical deep soil of the grasslands, built and held by the extensive root systems of the prairie grasses. Prairie soils are classified as mollisols—thick, dark, rich soils. Reflective of the boundary characteristics of the grasslands in this area, the mollisols here are on the boundary between the moist, warm soils of Iowa and Minnesota to the east and the dry, warm soils characteristic of the High Plains to

---

27. Savage, *Prairie*, 85.
28. Savage, *Prairie*, 23.
29. Lavin et al., *Atlas*, 31.
30. Savage, *Prairie*, 9.
31. Lavin et al., *Atlas*, 41.
32. Lavin et al., *Atlas*, 32.
33. Webb, *Great Plains*, 152–60.

the west.[34] In another classification of soils, the soil of southeast South Dakota is described as Chernozem, characterized as dark brown to black, "a clay loam soil formed from the glacial drift."[35] These soils are enriched by minerals and ground-up rock left behind by the glaciers.[36]

It is generally assumed that the first human inhabitants of North America crossed the Bering Strait into Alaska from Asia late in the Ice Age of the Pleistocene, and represented Paleolithic cultures.[37] These were hunter/gatherer cultures rather than agricultural societies, and undoubtedly some of these early human communities crossed the land of South Dakota, following the rivers and streams of the state. These Stone Age peoples of North America seemed to disappear from this region by about 5000 BCE.[38] Much later, beginning around 500 CE and continuing on for several hundred years, there is evidence of the Mound Builder cultures from the Mississippi River valley present in South Dakota. The Prehistoric Indian Museum at Mitchell, South Dakota, fifty miles northwest of Freeman, has revealed a large agricultural village of lodges dating back to about 1000 CE.[39]

The first named Native American nation to sojourn in South Dakota is the Arikara, who moved into the central Missouri River valley from Kansas and Nebraska sometime in the sixteenth century. The Arikara established a sophisticated agricultural economy supplemented by the hunting of game and continued through the eighteenth century. Early in the nineteenth century the Arikara villages in South Dakota were abandoned when the Arikara joined the Mandan nation in North Dakota.[40] The Dakota nations who made South Dakota their home subsequent to the Arikara were already influenced by the European colonization of North America, so their story will be picked up in the next chapter.

---

34. Savage, *Prairie*, 102–3.
35. Schell, *History of South Dakota*, 8.
36. Savage, *Prairie*, 99.
37. Schell, *History of South Dakota*, 15.
38. Schell, *History of South Dakota*, 15.
39. Robinson, *Village on the Bluff*, 42. Description of the Prehistoric Indian Village site.
40. Schell, *History of South Dakota*, 16–18.

WHAT THE LAND TEACHES US

If my description of the Great Plains during the Holocene Epoch is not too idyllic and idealized, the point to be made is that barring cataclysmic geological or climatic events like volcanic eruptions or glaciations, Earth's ecosystems tend to create stable and sustainable biomes that flourish and teem with many diverse life forms. It is Nature's way, the way God creates! Throughout the long story of life on Earth, we see these times of stable biomes that thrive between the eras of cataclysmic change, which are also, despite their threat and destructiveness, an integral part of God's creative process. While so brief in relation to geological time, the Holocene Epoch of the past ten thousand years represents a stable period of Earth's geological and biological life that has enabled the human story to unfold. Our species as one of millions has been blessed to come to maturity in such a time as this—the Holocene Epoch, characterized by the stable ecological systems we have been describing.

Humans have made the most of this opportunity. Modern humans have in the past ten thousand years moved into all of the major biomes of Earth and made them their home. From the polar regions to the tropics, from mountain heights to coastal lands, from deserts and grasslands to the forested woodlands of the temperate zones, humans have made their home in every biome and adapted their lives successfully and sustainably to those diverse settings. Since the past ten thousand years have also seen the emergence of agricultural societies and agrarian cultures, it must also be acknowledged that many traditional agrarian cultures have adapted themselves to the constraints of the ecosystems in which they are living even as they modified these environments with their agricultural practices. Native American societies that predate Columbus are examples of this.

What we learn from this long story of the land's preparation for the human presence is that humans are intended to mimic the processes of Nature in every environment they inhabit. I believe this to be God's intention for the human family, a fulfillment of the human calling to care for the Earth given in Gen 2:15. We are designed by God to take Nature as our guide and teacher in learning how to live sustainably here on Earth. In the process, we are given the high calling of participating with God in the unfolding of life and creation.

Nevertheless, for those who do not share this theological perspective, it also seems to be true that human experience teaches us the wisdom of taking Nature as our guide and teacher. Years ago, a book was published with the title *Topsoil and Civilization*, in which the authors examine all the ancient civilizations of the world. Early on, they quote an anonymous source who said "civilized man has marched across the face of the earth and left a desert in his footprints."[41] Their book goes on to substantiate the bold assertion of this quote. They say that historians "seem not to have recognized that the destinies of most of man's empires and civilizations were determined largely by the way the land was used. . . . Seldom do they note that the conquerors or colonizers had often ruined their own land before they started to take that of their neighbors. . . . They forget that many of the poor and weak nations once had plenty. They do not note that most of the poor people of the earth are poor mainly because their ancestors wasted the natural resources on which present generations must live."[42]

This should give us pause when we consider that the flora and fauna of the Great Plains have been almost entirely obliterated in the past 150 years of use by European colonizers. This is particularly true of the Corn Belt and the heavily cropped lands from North Dakota to Texas, and barely less true of the heavily grazed lands of the High Plains.[43] There are hardly any native prairies left, particularly in the Corn Belt, on whose western edge the Freeman community is built.[44] All the lands of this region are heavily eroded. Industrial methods of agriculture using large machinery heavily dependent on fossil fuels and petroleum products have created a largely inert soil requiring ever more intensive technological interventions in order to remain fertile. Though not true of the Freeman community itself, many agricultural enterprises in the Great Plains are dependent on irrigation from underground reservoirs like the Ogallala Aquifer that are rapidly being depleted.[45] The long-term sustainability of this agricultural system is questionable.

The reality is that land and people always live together in symbiotic, reciprocal relationships, or else both land and people suffer destruction. Human communities living on the land inevitably shape the landscape on which they live, to be sure. In the agricultural practices of every agrarian culture, there is some artificial introduction of plant or animal species

---

41. Dale and Carter, *Topsoil and Civilization*, 6.
42. Dale and Carter, *Topsoil and Civilization*, 7.
43. Lavin et al., *Atlas*, 131–35.
44. Lavin et al., *Atlas*, 142–54; Savage, *Prairie*, 113–15.
45. Lavin et al., *Atlas*, 34–35, 134–36.

into the environment and some reshaping of the landscape through the cutting down or the planting of trees, the erection of fences for livestock, and the tilling of soil for the planting of crops.

Still, in a healthy symbiosis, the land also shapes the human community. The land establishes the opportunities and the constraints under which the human community may flourish. The land establishes the parameters of the human reconstruction of the landscape beyond which there is only destruction for both land and community. In this way, Nature must always be the teacher of the agrarian culture, informing the culture of the best and most sustainable ways of interacting with the land and its ecosystem. We must be about *Learning to Listen to the Land* and *Meeting the Expectations of the Land*, as the titles of two fine anthologies of agrarian thought suggest.[46] We must be about *Becoming Native to This Place*, the title of one of Wes Jackson's fine books.[47]

Thankfully, there are by now any number of efforts to redirect the human agrarian enterprise in these ways. One of those efforts is being made by Wes Jackson, whose book was just referenced. Jackson, as the director of the Land Institute at Salina, Kansas, has for several decades been involved in the effort to breed perennial grain crops to replace the annual grains raised on the Great Plains.[48] Perennial grains would mimic the polyculture of the grasslands of the Great Plains and preserve the prairie soils.

There are also many other practical experiments in sustainable farming. Lyle and Garnet Perman, who farm and ranch in northern South Dakota with their son's family, have a unique ambition. Most farmers would say they want to leave their land as good as they found it. The Permans want to restore the land to its pre-colonial condition, before the plow and barbed-wire tamed the land. So they are gradually seeking to restore the prairie grasslands for their beef cattle.[49] Two other examples of pioneering practitioners of a new agriculture are Mark Shepherd, who describes his Wisconsin farm in *Restoration Agriculture*, and Joel Salatin, whose Virginia farm is described in *Folks, This Ain't Normal*. Shepherd's

---

46. Jackson et al., *Meeting the Expectations*; Willers, *Learning to Listen*.

47. Jackson, *Becoming Native*.

48. Jackson, *New Roots for Agriculture*, which describes the work of the Land Institute.

49. Kaufman, "Award-winning Farm Family."

farm features an integrated permaculture approach to agriculture and Salatin's farm is an integrated farming system.[50]

In addition to these more advanced pioneers in appropriate agricultural technology are the hundreds of small farms across the country who band together and learn from each other about sustainable farming and rural community in organizations like the Land Stewardship Project in Minnesota, Dakota Rural Action in South Dakota, and the Center for Rural Affairs in Nebraska.[51] Even land grant universities, long known as unapologetic advocates for industrial agriculture, are now experimenting with sustainable agriculture, as in the Leopold Center for Sustainable Agriculture at Iowa State University in Ames, Iowa.[52] And then there are all the local non-profits, like the Rural Revival organization in Freeman I am a part of, described later in this book, that seek to rebuild community by working for a local food system and new models of land tenure for how land is passed from one generation to the next.

LAND MADE READY FOR THE HUMAN PRESENCE?

I have been speaking in these last pages about the land being alive, something to which we relate in symbiotic ways, something that shapes human communities, something that is to guide and teach us about how we may best live in every particular place on Earth. I would even be prepared to speak of the land making itself ready for the human presence through the long geological and climatological history of the land being shaped and assuming the landscape it has in this Holocene Epoch. It was as though the land was preparing itself for the advent of this mature human creature that entered it over the past 100,000 years, but especially in these last ten thousand years of human history.

I should first explain what I intend by this kind of speech about the land. It is a way of speaking about the creative process in a non-theological, figurative manner. As a pastor, I am personally more comfortable speaking about God preparing the land for the human presence, and that is really what I intend when I speak this way. Still, there are advantages to using the more figurative language of the land as being alive. It may help

---

50. Shepherd, *Restoration Agriculture*; Salatin, *Folks, This Ain't Normal*.

51. See websites for Dakota Rural Action; Center for Rural Affairs; Land Stewardship Project.

52. See website for Leopold Center.

us understand our need to see the land itself, or Nature, if you will, as our conversation partner in the task of learning how to live appropriately here on Earth. Yes, ultimately it is God who is our teacher and guide in this, but in this case, God is active and present in the land, in Nature itself. It is by paying heed to the land that we learn the ways of God. Nor, with this kind of speech, do I wish to imply a kind of pantheism in which God is identified with Nature. It is important for me to understand God as the author of the creative process, and who in God's being transcends the material world of Nature, however much God is also revealed and found within the world of Nature.[53]

The other question to be addressed is the appropriateness of using such highly anthropocentric imagery as *the land making itself ready for the human presence!* Such language has indeed been used in highly negative and harmful ways in the past, as rationale and justification for the exploitation of the world of Nature by human agencies enthralled with the power and wealth to be gained from such exploitation. It seems to presuppose the superiority of the human, and the human right to use the Earth for self-centered human aims. This has indeed been the perspective of all the powers of human civilization, from the first emergence of the city as a center of power removed from the world of Nature.

Perhaps it is indeed impossible to redeem the form of speech in question. Yet I for one feel it is worth the effort to make the attempt. This form of speech is for me rooted in the biblical and Christian understanding of both the world of Nature and the nature of humanity as God's creation. The biblical record seems to root the human creature solidly in the world of Nature. We were created along with all other creatures of the land on the sixth day of creation in Gen 1, and we were formed by God "from the dust of the ground" (Gen 2:7). Yet we were also created as humans, male and female, in the image of God, according to God's likeness (Gen 1:26).

It is this ambiguous character of the human which justifies the notion that God might be preparing creation somehow for the human presence. But it is valid only if we understand our calling within that creation. Being imbued with God's image, we are called to reflect God's image within God's creation, to represent the character of God revealed throughout the Bible, within creation or the world of Nature, and supremely in the life,

---

53. Philosophically, what I am describing is panentheism, based on Whiteheadian Process Philosophy, and described by theologians Hartshorne, *Divine Relativity*, and Cobb, *A Christian Natural Theology*.

death, and resurrection of Jesus Christ. We are called to represent God within creation, and in this way to participate with God in the unfolding of life and creation. That is why it is so crucial for us to allow the land, the world of Nature, to teach us the ways of God. Though we may bear God's image, we are also creatures of the land that God has made, dependent upon it, foolish and destructive unless we live within the opportunities and constraints that the land offers to us. Without Nature as our teacher, we know virtually nothing about how to live within the element that sustains our lives. Yet, despite this, we must ponder whether our nature that both roots us in the land and invites us to reflect God's image within creation does not somehow endow us with a unique place within creation.

Reflecting on the complexities of the Universe and its fourteen-billion-year unfolding, philosophers of science are struck with the fine tuning required for a galaxy and a star and a planet like the Milky Way and the Sun and the Earth to emerge, to say nothing about such a planet bearing the profusion of life the Earth has borne, culminating in creatures like ourselves capable of conscious thought. It can of course be a matter of chance, but then there would have to be an infinite number of universes in order for this one to come out just right. Or, there might indeed be a divine Creator who has guided and shaped this long journey that culminated in a creation like ourselves, conscious of ourselves and God and able finally to participate with God in the further unfolding of life and creation. It is as though God wished for one mortal creature who would have the ability to partner with God in the unfolding of life.

What I have just described is the Anthropic Principle. It is defined this way by John Polkinghorne, a British physicist and Anglican priest: "A collection of scientific insights indicating that the possibility of the evolution of carbon-based life [and we might add, human consciousness, the *anthropic* aspect of the principle] depended upon a very delicate balance among the basic forces of nature and (perhaps) also on very specific initial circumstances for the universe."[54] Given this principle, people like Polkinghorne confess a divine agency in the unfolding of the Universe and life as more plausible than the many universes chance would require.

However, the Anthropic Principle might also be seen as a confirmation of the unique place of humankind within creation. If we do indeed represent within the natural world some kind of culmination in the creative process, if we might be in some way an end toward which the

---

54. Polkinghorne, *Faith of a Physicist*, 195.

unfolding of this Universe has been moving, then we might be justified in speaking of the land preparing itself for the human presence. And if all this is true, what it suggests to me is that the Creator wanted in the end a partner in the creative process, a creature capable of participating with God in the ongoing unfolding of life and creation. And that would be every human person, every human community. Is this a high calling, or what?

In any case, we have found a world very well prepared for our maturation these past ten thousand years of the Holocene Epoch. All the diverse lands of Earth have indeed been made ready for our coming, and have enabled us to establish communities of human life throughout the Earth. So there are just two more questions. How well have we represented God's image in our stewardship of this world? And, how long will it last, or how might we enable it to last?

AN APOCALYPTIC ERA

We live in a time of apocalyptic fervor. Popular media are full of visions of the end of the world as we know it. Some of these are religious, like the Left Behind series. Most of them are secular, envisioning some form of a future dystopia—technological experiments gone wrong, warfare, or environmental disasters like earthquakes or volcanoes. Editing this book in the early months of 2020 as the pandemic of the coronavirus spreads across the world disrupting the global economy, to say nothing of the daily life of all the Earth's people, we are reminded again how vulnerable we all are in this globalized world. And the more dependent we are on this global system, the more vulnerable we all are.

There are indeed an unending number of ways in which the world as we know it could come to an end. There are the possibilities of asteroids striking the Earth, volcanic eruptions or earthquakes that would cause a new mass extinction of life such as ended the age of the dinosaurs. As mentioned earlier in this chapter, the volcanic hotspot under Yellowstone National Park is due to erupt sometime soon, and when it does, it may well be the end of human life in our country for generations to come. Life has been possible on Earth these past ten thousand years only because Earth has been kind to us and so far spared us the cataclysmic environmental changes that would end our civilization.

And then we face also the humanly-caused disasters of environmental decay and accidents and pollution and exploitation, global warming and climate change, nuclear war or accidents, technological aberrations of genetic or atomic or molecular manipulations, economic and political collapse. The list goes on and on. Over these we do have some control. We can at least resolve to live our own lives and build our own communities with the land, Nature, as our teacher and guide. We can at least seek to accurately re-present the image of God, reflect God's character of love, in the ways we live together here on Earth. That isn't much, to be sure. It doesn't guarantee any kind of future outcome. We don't know what the future holds and have no control over it. But the choices we make can affect the trajectory of the future in life-affirming directions. And that, perhaps, is all that God or the land expects of us mere mortals.

2

The Imperial History and Its Intrusion into the Land

SYNOPSIS

IN CONTRAST TO THE apparently benign presence of the aboriginal inhabitants of the land, the European presence from its inception was experienced as an imperial intrusion. The North American continent was *discovered* by European states, all with imperial ambitions—Spain, Portugal, France, and England. In the late fifteenth century, no less a personage than the pope of Rome declared the *Doctrine of Discovery*, granting the kingdoms of Spain and Portugal the right to lay claim on any non-Christian lands and peoples. So-called pagans who converted could be spared, but if not, they were to be enslaved or killed. The Doctrine of Discovery is being used to this day as a legal argument to deny aboriginal claims to the land. The argument goes like this: *We found it; it's ours!* Never mind that others had found the land long before Europeans came to these shores!

The Age of Exploration in the fifteenth and sixteenth centuries was at its root a race by European imperial powers to lay claim to as much of the world as the flags of their nations could cover. It was at first a search for easy wealth like gold treasure, but along the way any other exploitable resources or peoples were fair game. Before long, European colonies were also established in North America, leading to a permanent colonizing presence on the land known to aboriginals as Turtle Island. The end result is that today every square inch of land on Earth and the sea extending from the land, with the exception of some of Antarctica, is claimed by one or another sovereign nation. No land on Earth is exempt from this claim!

Anyone wishing to understand traditional or agrarian cultures all around the world has to come to terms with this imperial history, for every traditional and agrarian culture is bound to be exploited or oppressed by the imperial claims of nation-states over the land. This is true even when agrarian cultures themselves become the agents of imperial control and colonization, as so often happens. This has indeed been the experience of the rural community treated in this book. The dynamic of relations between imperial centers of power and the traditional and agrarian cultures on which they depend always favor the imperial centers of power. There is no exception to this rule. All agrarian and traditional cultures can hope to do is to fly beneath the radar of imperial power and thus subvert or undermine it, in this way preserving the rural, agrarian life.

The imperial history of the Great Plains began in the late seventeenth century. After LaSalle explored the upper Mississippi in 1682, France claimed the entire Mississippi drainage area, establishing a colony in Louisiana. At the Treaty of Paris in 1763, Louisiana was ceded to Spain. The French empire builder Napoleon regained control of Louisiana from Spain in 1801 and wanted to keep it for France. However, fearing an Anglo-American alliance if he did so, he sold Louisiana to the United States in 1803 as the Louisiana Purchase, sealing the geopolitical fate of the Great Plains.

TRADITIONAL AND CONTEMPORARY MODELS OF LAND USE

The land of Earth—its fruitfulness and its life and its resources—used to be a Commons, like the water we drink and the air we breathe, available to all alike, the free gift of a gracious Creator. As physical beings, all humans depend on the gifts of the land (and sea), just as our bodies require water to drink and air to breathe. As human societies spread out and began to live in the varied ecosystems of Earth, they adapted to the land in each place and were shaped by it, so that eventually humans differentiated into many ethnic groups and some generalized racial types, though humans of all races remain part of one human species and can inter-breed.

The Imperial History and Its Intrusion into the Land

These human communities and societies eventually formed larger clans and tribes and even nations, all of whom were associated with particular regions or areas of the world. Nationhood or nationality in this ancient sense is quite different from the meaning given it today. Then it described a coalition of related ethnic groups who lived in particular regions, but without clearly defined political or territorial boundaries, whereas today nationality refers to all the diverse people of any ethnicity born within a particular geographical area or territory over which a particular governmental power claims sovereignty.[1]

It doesn't seem as though any of these ancient communities, clans, tribes, and nations had definite political boundaries. They were simply known to inhabit particular areas. And they might indeed, in any of these social forms, migrate from one land to another, as we see the children of Israel doing in the Old Testament. Yet these human communities rarely if ever laid claim to a particular piece of real estate or territory to assert sole ownership of it. The land, in traditional human societies, like the air we breathe and the water we drink, was understood to be a Commons, freely available to all.

This is not to say that there was not at times conflict over land and resources, either between individuals in a community, or between various societal groups. Often these conflicts would erupt into violence and even warfare between groups. Yet these were usually disputes over land tenure issues, over who had the right to access and use a particular area or its resources, and not matters of ownership or real estate or sovereignty per se. The notion of *owning* or *laying claim* to a particular piece of real estate would have then seemed absurd, as it still seems to traditional human communities today. The land, like the water and the air, was too clearly the gift of a generous Creator to be possessed by any human or human agency.

What a contrast this is to our world today! Outside of Antarctica, there is not a square kilometer of land that is not claimed by one of the nearly two hundred sovereign nation-states that rule our world and declare their sovereignty over a particular area of land. Much of Antarctica is also claimed by one or another power, as are extended areas of the sea by nations with coastal boundaries. Nor is this all just a matter of benign political sovereignty. These nation states allow individuals and corporations to buy and sell the land and to do pretty much as they please with it,

---

1. Jeschke, *Rethinking Holy Land*, 25.

with only minimal environmental or social justice considerations limiting the exploitation of the land and its resources.

What we have witnessed in recent centuries is the commodification of all natural and human resources for economic use and exploitation. This surely extends to all the land and natural resources of Earth, but increasingly it extends also to the other remnants of the natural commons—water and air. Few people in many parts of the world have access to free water. Even in rural areas, rural water associations control the water and its delivery to homes, just as urban centers control and meter the use of water. As residents of Flint, Michigan, have discovered, this commodification of water does not assure access to safe water. Water for human use is increasingly purchased from corporations who find the sale of bottled water a profitable business. As the air has become increasingly polluted in some urban areas, even the air we breathe is being commodified for the benefit of the corporate world. How many of us would put up without air conditioning?

THE AGRICULTURAL REVOLUTION AND THE RISE OF CIVILIZATION

How did we get from the world of traditional human societies to the world in which we live today? It started with the Agricultural Revolution that began about ten thousand years ago in the Middle East and then spread across the world. As plants and animals were domesticated by humans for human use, human communities for the first time could settle down and live in permanent settlements. Until then, human communities were hunter/gatherer societies that had nomadic lives and moved seasonally at least to gather Earth's bounty or to follow the migrating herds of animals.

By itself, the development of agriculture may not have had such a devastating effect on human history and the natural world. Agrarian cultures that developed with agriculture learned to live fairly sustainably within the constraints and the opportunities provided for them by their natural environment and the ecosystem in which they lived. These agrarian cultures surely made many mistakes, but in an era of low technology, Nature turned out to be a wise if harsh mistress, helping these agrarian cultures to develop sustainable agricultural practices and ways of life.

Still, the problem arose with the success of the Agricultural Revolution. The domestication of plants and animals not only allowed local communities to settle for the first time in villages. It also produced an excess of agricultural production. This in turn allowed the villages to grow larger and to become more complex, with some members of the community no longer involved in agriculture, but now becoming merchants or craftsmen or smiths or miners. As these early villages grew more populous and complex, some of the community members also became priests and rulers and educators and servants of all of the above. And before you knew it, more than six thousand years ago, full-fledged cities emerged, with full-fledged class and caste systems.

These cities were obviously dependent on the agricultural villages around them. Because they were impersonal and complex and stratified or hierarchical societies, they also had an advantage of power over these surrounding agricultural villages with their simple, face-to-face communal structures. And so began the process by which agrarian cultures came increasingly under the control of the urban centers where they lived, and upon whom they depended as the market for their produce. We might recognize this as a form of imperialism, which William Appleman Williams defines as "the loss of sovereignty—control—over essential issues and decisions by a largely agricultural society to an industrial metropolis. Superior economic power subjects an inferior political economy to its own preferences."[2] In other words, the city *(metropolis* literally means *mother city* in Greek) ends up determining how the agrarian cultures that sustain it will operate, how they will function and use their land.

It was not long before this hegemony of the city over the countryside evolved into the development of civilization. The first civilizations of the human family rose before the end of the fourth millennium BCE in the alluvial plains of the Tigris and Euphrates Rivers in Mesopotamia (modern Iraq), the Nile River in Egypt, the Indus River in India, and the Yangtze and Huang Ho or Yellow Rivers in China.[3] The first empire is usually thought to be that of Sargon I, ruler of Agade in Mesopotamia around 2350 BCE.[4] Empires are notable for the way they bring disparate cultures or nations under their power, functioning as colonial powers that are able to exploit these diverse communities and their resources with their superior power. What this means is that the institutional structures of the city, the state, and the empire—the powers agrarian

---

2. Williams, *Empire*, 7.

3. Barraclough, *Harper Collins Atlas*, 52.

4. Garraty and Gay, *Columbia History*, 60–61; Barraclough, *Harper Collins Atlas*, 54–55.

cultures have confronted throughout history and still today—were all already in place well before 2000 BCE, the time we normally think of as the beginning of documented history.

While agrarian cultures must share responsibility for the way Earth has been exploited through the past ten millennia, it can fairly be said that it occurred primarily through the power and influence of the cities, civilizations, and empires made possible by the Agricultural Revolution. It was typically these structures and powers of human civilization that have forced agrarian cultures to use the land in destructive and unsustainable ways, leading to the truth of the saying, "civilized man has marched across the face of the earth and left a desert in his footprints."[5]

THE AGE OF EXPLORATION AND THE DOCTRINE OF DISCOVERY

In order to understand the interplay of agrarian cultures and institutional powers in the North American continent, it is helpful to understand the motives driving European kingdoms to engage in the exploration and colonization of the Americas and the rest of the world. The Age of Exploration is generally understood to have begun in what may seem to us the unlikely kingdom of Portugal in the fifteenth century. There Prince Henry the Navigator and King John II authorized expeditions down the western coast of Africa in search of a sea route to the Far East—India and China. By 1488 Bartholomeu Dias had rounded the Cape of Good Hope, and a decade later Vasco de Gama had reached India. These sea expeditions were made possible by technological advances in sailing techniques making it realistic to sail into the open sea and then return to the point of departure.[6]

For the Portuguese, as for the other European countries who followed their lead in explorations across the sea, the motivation was primarily commercial. The rise of the Ottoman Empire and the fall of Byzantium in 1453 had rendered the overland trade routes to the Far East problematic if not impossible.[7] With the Portuguese kingdom dominating the southern and eastern routes to the East around Africa,

---

5. Dale and Carter, *Topsoil and Civilization*, 6; see also Kaufman, *Healing God's Earth*, chs. 3 and 5 for a fuller discussion.

6. Garraty and Gay, *Columbia History*, 622.

7. Wells, *Outline of History*, vol. 2, 616.

other European kingdoms, initially Spain under Ferdinand and Isabella, undertook to explore a western route to the Far East across the Atlantic Ocean. So it was that Christopher Columbus *discovered* the *New World* of North America, making landfall first in the Bahamas in 1492 in the first of four voyages across the Atlantic, though Columbus himself apparently lived under the illusion that he had indeed already crossed to the East and didn't realize a whole vast continent lay before him.[8]

While the Portuguese contacts in the East were primarily mercantile and while they showed little interest in conquest or colonization, the same cannot be said for the Spanish. Their explorations of Mexico and Central and South America led to the early military conquest of first the Aztec civilization in Mexico in 1519 to 1521 by Hernán Cortés, and then the Inca civilization of Peru in 1531 to 1538 by Francisco Pizarro. These conquests of indigenous civilizations of the Americas brought Spain much wealth. Although Florida and the southern coast of North America were also claimed by Spain, their explorations in the South and Southwest gave them no new treasures or wealthy peoples to conquer. Thus both conquest and colonization marked the Spanish entry into the Americas.[9]

The success of both Portuguese and Spanish ventures across the seas inspired other European powers to join the fray. John Cabot explored the eastern coast of North America for England as early as 1497, and Jacques Cartier explored the St. Lawrence River in Canada for the French between 1534 and 1541.[10] Initially, all these explorations were still motivated by seeking another route to the Far East. However, early in the seventeenth century, colonies began to be established in the Americas. The first English colony was in Jamestown, Virginia, in 1607, and the French established a colony in Quebec in 1608. The pilgrims came in 1620 to Plymouth, Massachusetts, and the Massachusetts colony was established in 1630, followed by Connecticut, Rhode Island, and Maryland in the next decade.[11]

As it turned out, the British were most successful in establishing a colonial presence in North America. Perhaps this was due in part to the religious dimension of the British colonies. Massachusetts was established as a Puritan colony, the heir of the Puritan movement to bring reforms to

8. Garraty and Gay, *Columbia History*, 622.
9. Garraty and Gay, *Columbia History*, 623.
10. Garraty and Gay, *Columbia History*, 623.
11. Garraty and Gay, *Columbia History*, 663–69.

the Anglican Church of England early in the seventeenth century. When their movement met with resistance in England, they welcomed the opportunity to form a model Christian community in America.[12] In the same fashion, Maryland was formed by Roman Catholics who were also seeking religious freedom in a new land.[13] The religious element in the formation of the British American colonies may well have helped in the establishment of successful colonies in America. However, it also aided and abetted in the American sense of Manifest Destiny that has shaped so much of American life—the idea that America was indeed a promised land for people of particular Christian faiths, and therefore that Americans were destined by God to conquer and possess and rule the land from sea to sea.

In this context, we must also observe that while the British may not have been as bent on conquest as the Spanish were in Central and South America, the British American colonies had no conscience against displacing the aboriginal inhabitants of North America. While European and Native cultures were not always hostile to one another in British North America, both warfare and disease decimated the Native population of North America, which may have been at least as high as eighteen million prior to 1492 and declined to less than a quarter million by the end of the nineteenth century.[14]

The European presence in North America was further compromised morally by the introduction of the slavery of African peoples, especially in the southern colonies that favored the establishment of large plantations. Slaves from Africa were brought to Virginia and Maryland in the 1660s, and slaves were a part of South Carolina from its founding in 1663.[15] By 1708, black slaves comprised half the population of South Carolina, and by 1740 they were two-thirds of the population.[16]

As European kingdoms vied with one another to stake their claims on lands across the sea, they sought the sanction of religious authority for their actions, as political powers often do. In the context of the Christendom to which all European kingdoms belonged, and prior to the Reformation, the supreme religious authority was the Pope in Rome. Ever since

---

12. Garraty and Gay, *Columbia History*, 666.
13. Garraty and Gay, *Columbia History*, 669.
14. Dismantling the Doctrine of Discovery, "Fact Sheet."
15. Bostick, *History of Slavery*, 5–6.
16. Bostick, *History of Slavery*, 19.

the fourth century when the emperor Constantine made Christianity the official religion of the Roman Empire, the Catholic Church was called to play the uneasy role of sanctioning the use of political and military power on behalf of the rulers of Europe. Christian rulers, for their part, often saw their actions aiding the expansion of Christian faith through the use of political and military power. It was part of the mentality that inspired the Crusades in the Middle East from the eleventh to the thirteenth centuries.

In any case, the kings of Portugal and Spain sought papal approval for their explorations and the wealth it gave them. One papal bull granting this, *Dun Diversas*, was promulgated on June 18, 1452, by Pope Nicholas V. It charged the Portuguese king, Alfonso V, to "invade, capture, vanquish and subdue . . . all Saracens [Muslims] and Pagans and all enemies of Christ . . . to reduce their persons to perpetual slavery . . . and to take away all of their possessions and property."[17] Here was religious sanction for the Portuguese slave trade that was even then beginning as they explored the west coast of Africa. Another bull, *Romanas Pontifex*, published three years later on January 8, 1455, went on to declare that all the territory of such people might also be claimed for a Christian sovereign. This bull, though addressed to King Alfonso of Portugal, extended the same rights to all other Christian sovereigns of Europe.[18] Somewhat later another pope, Alexander VI, was called to adjudicate competing claims between Portugal and Spain. The papal bull *Inter Caetera*, published in 1493, granted Spain lands west of the 38° of longitude, later extended to 46°37', and Portugal lands east of this line. This latter provision is why Brazil, discovered in 1500 by Pedro Cabral, became a Portuguese colony, since the eastern part of Brazil lies east of this line.[19] This bull also established the principle that one Christian nation did not have the right to lay claim to land already claimed by another Christian nation.[20]

Together the three bulls described above form the basis for the Doctrine of Discovery—"a philosophical and legal framework dating to the 15th century that gave Christian governments moral and legal rights to invade and seize Indigenous lands and dominate Indigenous Peoples."[21]

17. Dismantling the Doctrine of Discovery, "Fact Sheet."
18. Dismantling the Doctrine of Discovery, "Exhibit Timeline."
19. Hale, *Age of Exploration*, 56–58.
20. Gilder Lehrman Institute of American History, "Doctrine of Discovery, 1493."
21. Dismantling the Doctrine of Discovery, "Fact Sheet."

This doctrine was used to disenfranchise, commit to genocide, and enslave indigenous people all around the world, including here in North America. It was used in the 1823 decision by Chief Justice John Marshall in *Johnson v. McIntosh*. In this unanimous opinion of the United States Supreme Court, Marshall observed that "Christian European nations have assumed 'ultimate dominion' over the lands of America during the Age of Discovery, and that—upon 'discovery'—the Indigenous people had lost 'their rights to complete sovereignty, as independent nations,' and only retained a right of 'occupancy' in their lands."[22] The court argued that the United States inherited its rights under the Doctrine of Discovery from Great Britain upon achieving independence in 1776.

In its baldest form the Doctrine of Discovery grants so-called Christian nations the right to lay claim to any portion of the Earth it can find and upon which it can plant its flag if it is unclaimed by another Christian state. It then has the right to use that land and its resources and people in any way it sees fit. It is sobering to view a world map at the end of the nineteenth century and to see the way in which European powers, including Great Britain, France, Germany, Portugal, Spain, the Netherlands, Belgium, Italy, Russia, and the United States had carved up the world and its peoples.[23] Many of the geopolitical conflicts that continue in the world today, especially in the Middle East, are the consequence of those ill-fated colonial adventures perpetrated by *Christian* nations in the past and still being advanced today.

These outrageous claims of national sovereignty over the lands of the Earth are a far cry from the ancient understanding of the Earth belonging to God. "The earth is the LORD's and all that is in it, the world, and those who live in it" (Ps 24:1). And to God's own people, those whom God chose and to whom God promised land, God says, "The land shall not be sold in perpetuity, for the land is mine; with me you are but aliens and tenants" (Lev 25:23). Always, in the Bible, there is a frank recognition that there is nowhere in the world we can go that someone else has not already occupied. When Abram arrives in Canaan as the promised land of his sojourn, the Bible declares, "At that time the Canaanites were in the land" (Gen 12:6). Always we are called and have to learn how to live with the people who were already there before us!

---

22. Dismantling the Doctrine of Discovery, "Exhibit Timeline."
23. Barraclough, *Harper and Collins Atlas*, 244–45.

IMPERIAL HISTORY OF THE GREAT PLAINS

As in chapter 1, we now move from a general consideration of the imperial intrusion into North America to the imperial presence on the Great Plains, the area of this book's interest. It is generally assumed that *history* properly begins when *civilized people* enter the scene of a particular area and era. Again, chapter 1 should serve to remind us that the geo-physical and aboriginal history of a place is as integral to its story as the subsequent story of the entry of so-called civilized nation states. This part of the story is significant primarily for what it helps us understand about the interactions of indigenous cultures with imperial power, as well as the subsequent relationship between the agrarian cultures who settled as colonial agents of imperial power and those powers themselves.

Spain was the first European empire to lay claim to much of North America. As already noted, the Spanish had conquered the Aztecs in Mexico by 1521, and subsequently colonized Mexico. Their empire eventually extended as far north as Santa Fe, New Mexico, which was established by 1599.[24] There were also Spanish explorations onto the Great Plains proper. Álvar Núñez, Cabeza de Vaca, and several companions who had been captured by Indians spent the years from 1527 to 1530 wandering through southern Texas.[25] And from 1540 to 1542, from the southwest, Francisco Vásquez de Coronado led a military expedition as far north as Kansas, truly into the heart of the southern Great Plains, on a search for a reputed city of gold called Quivira. These and other explorers all noted the vast herds of buffalo on the Great Plains.[26]

Despite their success in colonizing Mexico, the Spanish were never able to make any sustained settlements in the Great Plains region, despite their claim to sovereignty over it. Walter Prescott Webb, the pre-eminent historian of the Great Plains, devotes a lengthy chapter 4 of his book to this failure. He says that while the Spanish colonial system worked well in Mexico, where the indigenous population was conquered and then used as agricultural labor, that system was ill-suited to the Great Plains region.[27] He also notes that the Spanish introduction of the horse to America, such a vital tool in their conquests, also represented their undoing in the southern Great Plains when the horse was adopted by

---

24. Webb, *Great Plains*, 115.
25. Lavin et al., *Atlas*, 57.
26. Lavin et al., *Atlas*, 57.
27. Webb, *Great Plains*, 87–94.

Native American tribes who with the horse were able to challenge Spanish hegemony and prevent colonization there.[28]

Despite Spanish claims of sovereignty over the North American land mass, Spain was unable politically and North America was too massive geographically to make good on its claims. Of course, Spain colonized Mexico and portions of the American southwest, and Spain also successfully defended their claims in Florida, discovered in 1513 by Ponce de Leon and explored by Hernando de Soto in 1539. The first permanent European settlement in North America was St. Augustine, Florida, in 1565.[29] And Florida remained a Spanish possession until 1821, except for a brief period of twenty years (1763 to 1783) when it was ceded to England.[30] But Spanish claims to sovereignty notwithstanding, the British established the thirteen colonies all along the East Coast of North America in the seventeenth and eighteenth centuries. And it was the French, pioneers in exploring the Great Lakes region, who were the first European power to assert real sovereignty over the Great Plains region.

The first French settlement in North America was established in Quebec by Samuel de Champlain in 1608. The French expanded west through the Great Lakes region in the decades following.[31] In 1682, La Salle (his full name was Rene-Robert Cavelier, Sieur de La Salle), by then a veteran French explorer of the Great Lakes, led a party down the Illinois River to the Mississippi, and from there to the mouth of the Mississippi on the Gulf of Mexico. There he raised the French coat of arms and claimed all the lands drained by the Mississippi River for France. This included virtually all the land from the Appalachian to the Rocky Mountains and from the Great Lakes to the Gulf of Mexico, and thus included also the entire Great Plains. He named this vast area Louisiana after his king.[32]

French colonization in North America, perhaps by virtue of French aims, but certainly because of the unique environment of the Great Lakes region with its lakes and rivers, took a different course than either British or Spanish colonization in America. The French established trading posts throughout the region and developed a thriving fur trade, which utilized both French trappers and also Native American tribes. While

28. Webb, *Great Plains*, 114–18.
29. Garraty and Gay, *Columbia History*, 660–662.
30. Hicks et al., *Federal Union*, 147, 196.
31. Schell, *History of South Dakota*, 24.
32. Dicks, "A Territory with Many Flags," in Jennewein and Boorman, *Dakota Panorama*, 73.

French colonization in the Americas was not without its racial tensions, perhaps it can be said that the French were more inclined to engage Native American cultures, especially in trade.[33] And of course, French and Indian fraternization led to the formation of the hybrid Métis culture which continues to exist and play a major role in the politics of the prairie provinces of Canada—Saskatchewan and Manitoba.

In the eighteenth century, French explorers moved overland west from the Mississippi River valley and began exploring the lands of South Dakota. As early as 1679, Daniel Greysolon, the Sieur Dulhut (Duluth), explored the headwaters of the Mississippi and may have come as far as Big Stone Lake in northeast South Dakota. Also before 1700, Pierre Charles Le Sueur, based along the Minnesota River, may have explored as far as the Big Sioux River around Sioux Falls.[34]

However, the first major exploration of South Dakota is credited to the La Verendrye family. From his base at Lake Winnipeg in Manitoba, the father, Pierre, explored the upper Missouri River regions in 1738. In 1741, he sent two of his sons, François and Louis-Joseph to continue explorations along the Missouri River. The brothers buried a lead plate proving their presence at Fort Pierre, South Dakota, on the Missouri River on March 30, 1743. The plate was discovered by school boys on February 17, 1913, and can be seen at the South Dakota State Historical Museum in Pierre. The two brothers also explored most of western South Dakota as far as the Black Hills.[35]

The imperial fortunes of the Great Plains shifted again in 1763. That year, in the Treaty of Paris ending the French and Indian War, France ceded all their territory east of the Mississippi River to Great Britain, which after the American Revolution of 1776 became a United States territory. About the same time, on November 3, 1762, France ceded their territory west of the Mississippi to Spain.[36] So suddenly, the French colonial power that had dominated the exploration of the Great Plains for nearly a century lost their entire North American land base. Now, under Spanish rule, the fur trade in the Great Plains shifted to the Missouri River valley and its tributaries. St. Louis became the center for this trade

33. Lavin et al., *Atlas*, 57–58.
34. Schell, *History of South Dakota*, 25.
35. Schell, *History of South Dakota*, 27–29.
36. Dicks, "A Territory with Many Flags," in Jennewein and Boorman, *Dakota Panorama*, 73–74.

in the second half of the eighteenth century, as well as the Spanish capital of the upper Louisiana territory.[37]

The dawn of the nineteenth century saw the final flurry of imperial changes for the Great Plains. On October 1, 1800, in the Treaty of San Ildefonso, Louisiana Territory (the area west of the Mississippi River) was returned to the French. However, Napoleon Bonaparte, the French emperor, feared an Anglo-American alliance against France, so in a surprise move, he agreed to sell Louisiana Territory to the new United States, in order to forestall the Anglo-American alliance.[38] And of course the American president, Thomas Jefferson, had already had his eye on the vast territory of Louisiana, which would more than double the size of the new United States.

So, for about $15 million, the United States purchased Louisiana from the French in 1803, thus sealing the future of the Great Plains as part of the United States.[39] In fact, however, Spanish administration of Louisiana continued until December 20, 1803, when control of the territory was turned over to the United States. In a ceremony of transfer of power in St. Louis on March 9, 1804, the flag of Spain was lowered, and then the flag of France was briefly raised and then lowered, before the flag of the United States was raised, to signify the transfer of sovereignty from Spain to France to the United States.[40]

The United States wasted no time in exploring its vast new addition. On January 18, 1803, Thomas Jefferson commissioned the Lewis and Clark Expedition, which left St. Louis on August 30, 1803, reached the West Coast, and returned to St. Louis in August 1806.[41] Lewis and Clark followed the Missouri River on their expedition, and so traveled through South Dakota from Sioux City to the North Dakota border. Indeed, the Missouri River would be the primary mode of transportation for the exploration and development of the area until the coming of the railroad late in the nineteenth century. The fur trade, which the French had begun

---

37. Dicks, "A Territory with Many Flags," in Jennewein and Boorman, *Dakota Panorama*, 74.

38. Dicks, "A Territory with Many Flags," in Jennewein and Boorman, *Dakota Panorama*, 74–75.

39. Hicks et al., *Federal Union*. 309–11. A map of the Louisiana Purchase is on page 310.

40. Dicks, "A Territory with Many Flags," in Jennewein and Boorman, *Dakota Panorama*, 75–76.

41. Schell, *History of South Dakota*, 38–43.

so many years earlier, reached its peak in the first half of the nineteenth century. In addition to beaver and other small mammals, the fur trade in this period also included buffalo robes. Buffalo were hunted partly for the economic value of their hides, but also to eliminate the economic base for the First Nations who depended on the buffalo for their livelihoods.[42] First Nations living along the Missouri River were also key players in the fur trade.[43]

THE FORMATION OF DAKOTA TERRITORY AND STATEHOOD

The nineteenth century saw the final disenfranchisement of American First Nations, as the United States expanded and settlers came in, first from the Appalachian Mountains to the Mississippi River, and then into the newly purchased territory of Louisiana. The Arikara in South Dakota and the Mandan in North Dakota were the resident tribes along the Missouri River at the beginning of the nineteenth century. The Arikara, part of the Caddoan linguistic family, were agriculturalists, and when the horse entered the country, they were active in trading horses, especially to the Dakota nations who were migrating westward. Eventually, disease and warfare decimated the Arikara villages, and by the early 1830s they joined the Mandan in North Dakota.[44]

The Dakota nations of the Siouan linguistic family may have had their origins in the Great Lakes region as agricultural peoples. They were pushed westward into Wisconsin and Minnesota and finally onto the Great Plains in colonial times due to pressure from other tribes who were also driven by pressure from colonial America. These groups gradually began moving onto the Great Plains in the eighteenth century.[45] There are in all seven Dakota nations, known as *Oceti Sakowin*, or the Seven Councils Fire. There are four Santee or Eastern Dakota nations, two Nakota nations including the Yankton Sioux in southeast South Dakota, and the Lakota or Teton Sioux of the Plains.[46] All of these nations became known to white people as the Sioux nations. Given the dominance these Dakota

---

42. Champagne, *Native America*, 163.
43. Schell, *History of South Dakota*, 49.
44. Schell, *History of South Dakota*, 16–18.
45. Champagne, *Native America*, 161–63.
46. US-Dakota War, "*Oceti Sakowan.*"

nations came to have in this area that was to become Dakota Territory, these are the nations that eventually ceded to the United States the lands of this area in exchange for reservations.

There were three main treaties that affected the lands and nations of this area. There was the Treaty of Traverse des Sioux, negotiated in July, 1851, just north of St. Peter, Minnesota. This treaty ceded most of southern and central Minnesota and parts of Iowa and eastern South Dakota to the United States in exchange for a ten-mile-wide reserve along the Minnesota River from Mankato to Big Stone Lake in South Dakota.[47] The later Treaty of Laramie concluded at Fort Laramie, Wyoming, on April 29, 1868, opened up overland routes to the West Coast and set aside all of western South Dakota as the Great Sioux Reserve, though that only lasted until gold was discovered in the Black Hills in 1874.[48]

The cession most relevant for our story in this book is the treaty with the Yankton Sioux nation signed on April 19, 1858. It ceded all lands north and east of the Missouri River to the Big Sioux River and with a northern boundary roughly from Pierre to Watertown; in other words, all of what became southeast South Dakota, roughly a quarter of the state. In return the Yankton Sioux nation received a reserve in what is now Charles Mix County in South Dakota, along the Missouri River west of Yankton.[49] The terms of this treaty and a map of the cession can be found in *Remember Your Relatives*.[50]

---

47. Schell, *History of South Dakota*, 72.
48. Schell, *History of South Dakota*, 88–89, 125.
49. Schell, *History of South Dakota*, 69–72.
50. Sansom-Flood and Bernie, *Remember Your Relatives*, 44–52. See Figure 1, Yankton Sioux Cession.

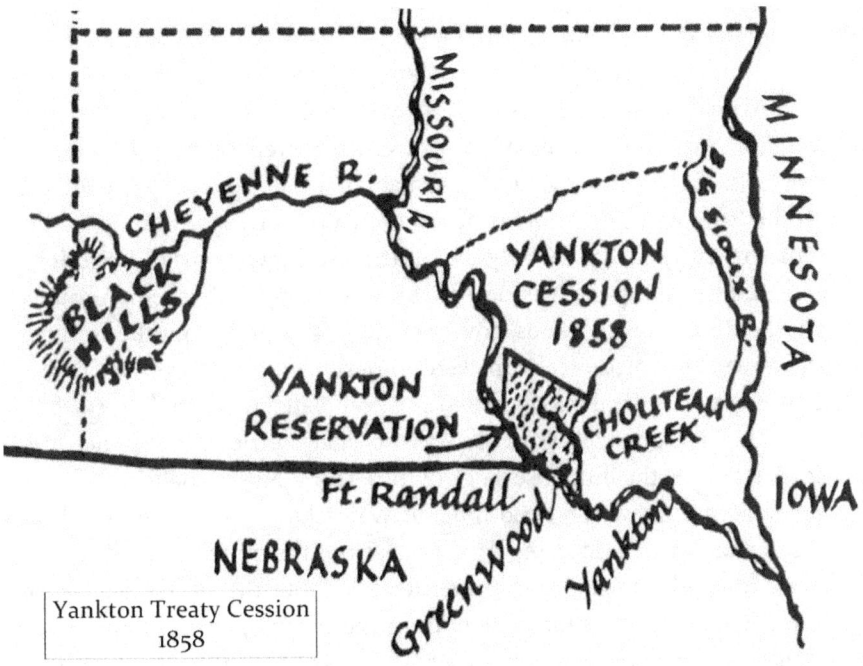

Yankton Treaty Cession 1858

After all the dust settled, there were nine Dakota reservations in what became South Dakota—Pine Ridge and Rosebud in the southwest, Cheyenne River in central South Dakota west of the Missouri, Standing Rock also west of the Missouri on the North Dakota state line, Lower Brule and Crow Creek both in central South Dakota along the Missouri River, Sisseton in northeastern South Dakota, Flandreau on the eastern border of South Dakota, and Yankton along the Missouri River in southeast South Dakota.[51]

We should observe that the terms of the treaties establishing these reserves and granting cessions to the United States were uniformly broken by the United States government. The treaties were made to pacify the peoples of the First Nations and were often entered into by leaders of the First Nations under duress. Subsequent acts by the federal government continued to disenfranchise First Nations. In particular, the Dawes Allotment Act of 1887 sought to privatize Indian lands in the hands of individual members of the respective tribes.[52] The effect of this act was to

---

51. See Champagne, *Native America*, 162, for a map showing these reservations.
52. Schell, *History of South Dakota*, 310.

allow white settlers to purchase reservation land from tribal members, so that by the 1920s as much as 80 percent of many reservation tribal lands passed into the hands of land speculators and crop farmers.[53]

Always, white settlers stood ready to enter lands ceded by the various First Nations as soon as the various treaties were signed. This was the case with the Yankton Cession, when about a thousand settlers gathered on the Iowa and Nebraska border in the winter of 1859, waiting for the senate to ratify the treaty.[54] By this time the Dakota towns of Vermillion and Yankton along the Missouri River were being established. Throughout the decade of the 1860s, government surveys to lay out the counties and townships of the cession were undertaken. The survey of Turner County was begun already in 1859 and completed by 1867.[55]

The Homestead Act of 1862 was the legal vehicle by which the United States made the immense lands of the Great Plains available to settlers. Favorable terms were offered to Civil War veterans in the years following the Civil War, and many Americans from the more crowded eastern states took advantage of the Homestead Act. But the United States was also aggressive in seeking settlers from European countries who shared their white, European origin and culture and adhered to the American ideals of individual freedom and religious liberty for white, European, *civilized* people.

Under the Homestead Act, a quarter section (160 acres) of land could be claimed under three arrangements. The homestead provision granted eligible persons (twenty-one years of age, head of family, and citizen or alien intending to be a citizen) title to 160 acres in exchange for minor title fees, evidence of tilling at least ten acres, and evidence of residing on the land for five years. The pre-emption provision allowed someone squatting (residing) on the land for six months to purchase the quarter section of land for a small fee ($1.25 an acre). The timber claim provision allowed someone to claim 160 acres upon proof that they had planted ten acres of trees on it (residence was not required).[56] The entry of railroads into the area in the 1870s also fostered the introduction of settlers and the establishment of towns.[57] The government often granted

53. Schell, *History of South Dakota*, 313.
54. Schell, *History of South Dakota*, 71.
55. Stoddard, *Turner County*, 11–13.
56. Schell, *History of South Dakota*, 170–74; Koller, "This Was Homesteading in Dakota," in Jennewein and Boorman, *Dakota Panorama*, 221–23.
57. Schell, *History of South Dakota*, 161–68.

The Imperial History and Its Intrusion into the Land

railroads wide rights of way in public lands, and the railroads were free to sell excess land to homesteaders after the railroad was built.[58]

United States expansion westward usually began with the formation of a vast territory. After a number of years of tutelage in self-government as a territory, all or part of the territory became one of the states of the union. In the late 1850s, as Sioux Falls was being established on the Big Sioux River and began to challenge the leadership of Yankton on the Missouri River, applications were made to Congress for the formation of Dakota Territory. Congress authorized the formation of Dakota Territory on March 2, 1861, with Yankton as its capital.[59] Originally, Dakota Territory was huge, encompassing not only all of today's North and South Dakota, but most of Montana and Wyoming as well.[60] By 1882, Dakota Territory was reduced to the area of the states of North and South Dakota.

The formation of Dakota Territory formalized the settlement of southeast South Dakota that had already begun. However, settlement was put on hold for a number of years by the Indian uprising that began along the Minnesota River in August 1862 and continued until 1866. The Santee Sioux nation in Minnesota was protesting the intrusion onto and loss of the reservation land promised to them along the Minnesota River in the 1851 Treaty of Traverse des Sioux. These were also the years of the Civil War, so the nation was preoccupied with that conflict. The 1870s saw a renewed and intensified settlement of Dakota Territory, and it was at this time that the Germans-from-Russia who are the subject of this book made their way onto the Great Plains.[61]

Agitation and plans for statehood in South Dakota began early in the 1880s and continued throughout that decade. Both North and South Dakota achieved statehood within the United States in 1889 as the thirty-ninth and fortieth states of the Union.[62] Statehood may represent the coming of age of the territories of the Great Plains as First Nations were effectively disenfranchised and white settlers introduced into the area. The imperial aims of the United States, succeeding the imperial dreams

---

58. Koller, "This Was Homesteading in Dakota," in Jennewein and Boorman, *Dakota Panorama*, 222.

59. Schell, *History of South Dakota*, 72–77.

60. See map in Jennewein and Boorman, *Dakota Panorama*, 152, to see the full extent of Dakota Territory.

61. Koller, "This Was Homesteading in Dakota," in Jennewein and Boorman, *Dakota Panorama*, 224.

62. Schell, *History of South Dakota*, 219–22.

of the powers who previously laid claim to the Great Plains, were now accomplished. The land, which before was empty and desolate in the imperial view, was now made fruitful through the development of agriculture and rural communities. The land and its people were colonized. Civilization had triumphed!

WHAT DOES IT ALL MEAN?

As a young person growing up in the Freeman, South Dakota, community in the 1960s, I confess that I was totally oblivious to this imperial history of the Great Plains, as well as to the First Nations people who were and still are our neighbors in this state, comprising 8.9 percent of the state's population.[63] There have, by this time, been many informal family and community histories written about this community. Rarely have any of these approaches to our history sought to examine in any depth this imperial history of our country, the Great Plains, and our state. Broader histories of the state do pay attention to this imperial history. However even there, the writing tends to reflect the dominant culture's understanding of aboriginal people and their experience in the disenfranchisement and cultural destruction they suffered.

As I have looked more carefully at this imperial history of our land, I have often been amazed at the juxtaposition of events occurring in the secular world—this imperial history, and our own history as a community. Perhaps if we had been more cognizant of this juxtaposition, we may have been more reflective about the choices we were making along the way, and more deliberate in the kinds of relationships we chose to forge as a community.

In any case, keeping this imperial history of the land in mind enables us to understand the displacement and disenfranchisement and cultural destruction that occurred among the First Nations of North America with the arrival of the European powers. This imperial history also helps us keep in mind our own experience as colonial agents on behalf of these imperial powers. We often were little more than pawns in the chess games of political and geographical hegemony being played out by the imperial powers. While our agrarian cultures were coveted by these powers for their agricultural expertise, the powers were always prepared to exploit and manage these local agrarian cultures as well for their own advantage.

---

63. Wikipedia, "Demographics of South Dakota."

Perhaps the most dramatic example of this can be seen in the pattern of settlement established by the United States. Declaring that the land belonged to the state as public land and therefore available to be colonized, the United States decided on private property as the mode by which the land would be made available through the Homestead Act. This destroyed and made impossible the communal village life familiar to many of the agrarian cultures that came to the Great Plains. Not only that, but it also made the private land-owners beholden to the state through taxation and regulation, and put private land-owners in competition with one another, weakening further the communal bonds upon which agrarian cultures thrive.

I don't think this was the result of some sinister plot in order to gain control over the rural population. I think it was simply the working out of the values and presuppositions on which the dominant cultures of urban civilization have been based. But the point is that the better we are able to understand the dynamic between agrarian cultures used in imperial colonization and the powers that rule them, the better agrarian cultures will be able to subvert and undermine the domination those imperial cultures exercise over agrarian cultures. That's why it is so important to study and come to understand the imperial history of the land!

3

The Prehistory of the Agrarian Cultures That Came into the Land

SYNOPSIS

Most of the German Mennonite immigrants who came to the Great Plains from the Ukraine in 1874 brought with them only what they could carry. They had been for the most part landless in the Ukraine and were destitute upon their arrival here in America. Yet, seen from a different perspective, these immigrants brought with them an extraordinary wealth. They brought with them an agrarian culture and heritage that had been honed and shaped by generations of sojourning in the lands of Europe, from Switzerland and the Netherlands to Russia, with stops all along the way. In the process, they had learned how to make the land fruitful to sustain their lives and the lives of the noblemen at whose pleasure they worked the land. This is after all what it means to have or to be an agrarian culture—a culture shaped by the *agros*, the field or land upon which one lives and which one works. Agriculture, in its root meaning, is human culture shaped by the field or land upon which those humans live.

These agrarian cultures also carried a heritage of faith. These Mennonite communities in the Ukraine were the heirs of the Anabaptist movement of the sixteenth century. Born in the throes of the peasant rebellions of the 1520s, these communities had discovered in Christian faith the spiritual resources that enabled them to build sustainable communities able to resist in nonviolent ways the depredations of the imperial powers under which they lived. Despite, and perhaps in part because of the severe persecution they and their faith compatriots experienced, these Anabaptist communities had developed alternative, agriculturally-based communities of faith as a missional response to the oppressive imperial powers under which they lived. They were content to live as second-class citizens at the pleasure of lords and nobles who owned the land and coveted their agricultural expertise. Though this required frequent uprooting, they wanted not only to avoid persecution, but also the taxation and conscription that came with land-holding and citizenship.

What this means is that the German Mennonite immigrants who came to the Great Plains in 1874 were tightly-knit communities, interrelated genetically and ethnically and by faith convictions. In contrast to current individual or family immigration patterns, these immigrants came to Dakota Territory as villages that were also church congregations. They did not immigrate as individuals or families, but as communities. Perhaps this alone is what enabled them to survive their first years as pioneers on the prairies of the Great Plains.

The Mennonites who came to the Freeman community went to Ukraine in the Russian Empire in the years following 1770. In those years the Russian Empire was expanding to the Black Sea through a series of victories over the Turkish Ottoman Empire. The Russian czarina, Catherine the Great, who was a German princess, invited German agriculturalists to come settle in the Ukraine and participate in the colonization of that rich agricultural area, with the promise of being able to live in German colonies, keep their German language, and be exempt from Russian military service. Germans of Reformed, Lutheran, and Catholic faith, as well as Anabaptists, responded to this invitation, and many of these German communities settled on the Great Plains of North America a century later.

THE CHARACTER OF AGRARIAN CULTURES

Wendell Berry, the preeminent agrarian thinker and writer of our time, writes about the crisis of culture in the agricultural crisis of our time.[1] Berry insists that the current agricultural crisis is not technological but cultural. It represents a failure of culture and human community, not a failure of technique. Berry speaks of the wisdom required by agriculture involving "several generations—enough to establish complex local

---

1. Berry, *The Unsettling of America*, ch. 4.

cultures with strong communal memories and traditions of care."[2] "A good farmer . . . is a cultural product; he is made by a sort of training, certainly, in what his time imposes or demands, but he is also made by generations of experience. This essential experience can only be accumulated, tested, preserved, handed down in settled households, friendships, and communities that are deliberately and carefully native to their own ground, in which the past has prepared the present and the present safeguards the future."[3]

This chapter will explore the *pre-history* of several of the local agrarian cultures that moved to the Great Plains in the 1870s and together established the rural community of Freeman, South Dakota. Much of the American West seems to have been settled by established American citizens from the East who moved to the West to take their chances on a new frontier. Sometimes they came with a community of like-minded and related friends and family, but more often they seem to have come as individual families seeking their fortunes in a new land, in keeping with the individualistic ethos of the emerging American society.

By contrast, Freeman and other rural communities like it on the Great Plains came here as *communities*, as groups of people who often had a long and complicated pre-history of living together in other places of the world. They came, in other words, as agrarian cultures with a long history of agricultural experience, often in a variety of environmental settings.

In the Introduction, I spoke about agrarian cultures growing out of the symbiotic relationship between a human community and the natural environment in which it lives. This implies, as Berry says, that a community will live in a place long enough to become "native to their own ground."[4] A mature agrarian culture, in other words, takes a couple of generations to develop, as a particular human community shapes and comes to be shaped by the particular natural environment in which it finds itself.

At the same time, the most successful agrarian cultures seem to be those who do not have to start from scratch, forming a human community while also being shaped and molded by the natural environment. Throughout history, agrarian cultures have uprooted themselves voluntarily or involuntarily and moved from one place to another. In their new

---

2. Berry, *The Unsettling of America*, 45.
3. Berry, *The Unsettling of America*, 45.
4. Berry, *The Unsettling of America*, 45.

place, it takes a couple of generations to adapt to the new environment, but they also bring with them a heritage of agrarian experience in another place that facilitates their adaptation to the new place. These cultures are shaped and molded by their new environment and experience considerable change in their folkways, agricultural practices, and relationships to the other local cultures around them as well as the dominant culture of their new place. But their agricultural adaptation to their new environment is eased by the history and heritage they bring with them.

The history and heritage of every local agrarian culture involves both agricultural practices and wisdom and also a core ethnic identity that shapes and forms their life together. This ethnic identity involves the presumed origin of the group. Often that identity is also shaped by a shared faith heritage that expresses the values and commitments of the community. The ethnic component is never pure, and the faith heritage evolves over time as well. Every community incorporates new blood through marriage, relationships with neighboring communities, or shared faith commitments (conversions), even while the community continues to preserve the *myth* of its presumed ethnic and faith origins. Still, ethnic identity and faith heritage, along with the agricultural practices of the community, are the primary shapers of every local agrarian culture. The cultural identity of the agrarian community is what bears the generational wisdom enabling the community to adapt and thrive in new environments.

THE AGRARIAN CULTURES OF THE FREEMAN COMMUNITY

The rural community of Freeman, South Dakota, was formed primarily by German people who came to America in the 1870s from Russia. I would identify about a half dozen specific local agrarian cultures who participated in the formation of the Freeman community. Three of these, representing strains of Anabaptist faith but of varying ethnic origin, are most well-known to me and will be the primary focus of this book. However, there were also several other Russian-German groups, particularly of Reformed and Lutheran faiths, who came to the area at the same time and were very active in the formation of the Freeman community. Their story parallels in many ways the history of the Anabaptist groups during the past two or three centuries. I will endeavor to make reference to these groups throughout the book, but the more in-depth analysis will focus on the three groups of Anabaptist faith.

Two of the groups in the formation of the Freeman community represent my own ethno-cultural-faith heritage. My father was from the Swiss Volhynian, or *Schweitzer* group, which settled in the area east and south of Freeman in 1874. *Schweitzer* refers to the dialect some of this group picked up while sojourning in the German Palatinate for a century,[5] but the core ethnicity of this group was Swiss, and many of the members of this Anabaptist group can still trace their ancestry back to Switzerland. My mother descended from the Low German group that settled north and east of Freeman, mostly between the towns of Freeman and Marion. This group spoke Low German as their mother tongue, and their origin was likely in the Netherlands, so they were Dutch Anabaptist, or Mennonite.

The third Anabaptist group in the Freeman community is the *Prairieleut* (Prairie People) of the Hutterite movement, who spoke a Hutterish dialect. The Hutterites had their origin in the Moravian Anabaptist movement of the sixteenth century. The *Prairieleut* had abandoned communal living already in Russia and so settled on individual farms west of Freeman, but near many of their relatives who established the famous communal Hutterite colonies, many of them along the James River.

In addition to these three groups of Anabaptist faith, a Lutheran group from Heilbronn in the Crimea settled southwest of Freeman in 1875 and 1876. Several Reformed groups came from Russia as well. The Johannestal group settled west of Freeman, the Kassel group settled between the towns of Freeman and Menno, and the Klein Kassel group settled north of Freeman.[6]

THE AGRARIAN ROOTS OF THE ANABAPTIST MOVEMENT

The three Mennonite sub-cultures of the Freeman community all have their roots in the Anabaptist movement of the sixteenth century. The Anabaptist movement arose in the time of the Reformation, which began

---

5. Emil J. Waltner, *Banished for Faith*, 149–50.
6. Rath, *Black Sea Germans*, 88, 92–93, 404. See Figure 5, Settlements of the Germans from Russia in the Freeman Area, in ch. 4, for the location of the various local cultures described in this section.

with Martin Luther's attempts in Germany to reform the Catholic Church beginning in 1517.

The beginning of the Anabaptist movement has generally been understood to occur in Zurich, Switzerland, in 1525, where Ulrich Zwingli was instituting reforms that resulted in the Reformed Church. Several Zurich residents and some outsiders felt that Zwingli's reforms were not advancing far enough or fast enough. In particular, they advocated for a believer's baptism and questioned the current practice of infant baptism, refusing to baptize their own children. On January 21, 1525, Conrad Grebel, Felix Manz, George Blaurock, and some others, met together and baptized each other on their confessions of faith as believers in Christ, thus initiating the Anabaptist movement.[7] *Anabaptist* means simply *re-baptized* or *baptized again*, and was the name given to the movement by their adversaries, as a pejorative term.

While this was indeed an actual historical event, and while it is useful for every movement to have a defining origin story, the actual emergence of the Anabaptist movement is much more complicated and convoluted. This is true of any major historical movement as well. The danger of the defining origin story is that it distorts the reality of a movement's character. In this case, it led to the assumption that Anabaptism had a single origin (monogenesis) in Switzerland when in fact there were multiple origins (polygenesis) of the movement in different lands and at different times both before and after 1525.[8] This origin story allowed a normative definition of Anabaptism to emerge that was primarily theological in character. "The Anabaptist Vision" promoted by Harold S. Bender defined the character of the movement in terms of discipleship, the church as an accountable community, and an ethic of love and nonresistance.[9] Furthermore, this origin story led to the assumption that the first Anabaptists were educated and urban, highly motivated for mission, and that within a few generations, Anabaptism devolved into closed, rural communities withdrawn from the world—*Die Stille im Lande* (The Quiet in the Land).

What this origin story of Anabaptism overlooks, and what more recent Anabaptist historiography has recognized, is that the early sixteenth century was a time of tremendous social and political upheaval, and that

---

7. Dyck, *Mennonite History*, 33–34.
8. Snyder, *Anabaptist History and Theology*, 400–404.
9. Bender, *The Anabaptist Vision*, 13–23.

this social unrest influenced all the choices of those involved in religious reforms. The Anabaptist movement emerged concurrently with the Peasants' War of 1524 and 1525. As many as 300,000 peasants throughout central Europe—Germany, Switzerland, France, and Austria—rose up violently against their noble overlords. As many as 100,000 peasants were killed, unable to adequately defend themselves against the well-armored armies of the noblemen.[10]

It is well known that Anabaptism had its greatest appeal among the peasant population of Europe, and the reason is not difficult to understand. Anabaptism expressed a radical egalitarian communalism grounded in biblical faith that empowered rural peasants to nonviolently resist and subvert the oppression under which they were living. Seeing the futility of violent resistance in the Peasants' Wars, Anabaptist communities might have understood themselves and can be seen as missional alternatives in the development of agrarian communities able to live under the radar of imperial power and to survive the frequent persecution that caused them to be spread throughout Europe, voluntarily or involuntarily.

Despite their nonviolent faith, Anabaptist communities were seen to be as real or even greater a threat to imperial power than peasant mobs armed with pitchforks and shovels, so they were persecuted severely with banishment, imprisonment, torture, and death, as witnessed in the *Martyr's Mirror*.[11] With their faith and heritage to sustain them, Anabaptist communities had found a way to resist and challenge imperial power while also bearing a missional witness to another way of life. Despite their reputed quietism, agrarian Anabaptist communities were cells of missional leaven that spread and bore fruit wherever they fled or were forced to flee.

THE EUROPEAN PILGRIMAGE OF THE GROUPS WHO CAME TO SOUTH DAKOTA

All three of the Anabaptist groups who came to the Freeman, South Dakota, area in 1874 had a long pilgrimage in Europe that can be traced

---

10. Snyder, *Anabaptist History*, 32–33.

11. van Braght, *Martyr's Mirror*. See, for example, the stories and illustrations of Anneken Hendricks in Amsterdam and Wolfgang Binder in Bavaria, both executed in 1571, 872–75.

from their place of origin to different parts of the Ukraine in Russia in the nineteenth century. This is the story of three small agrarian communities of faith who against all odds retained and built upon their ethnic and faith heritage over a period of more than three centuries. An attempt will be made in what follows to sketch the sojourns of each of these three groups, how and why they ended up in the Ukraine, how they learned to know about each other there, and began to influence each other. The story of this chapter will be complete when we find these three groups in the Ukraine and when their fortunes there changed and they began the search for a new homeland. In each case, we will seek to understand the dynamics that led them to the Ukraine. We will also explore their character as agrarian communities of faith.

The Swiss Volhynian Journey

The Swiss Volhynian Amish who came to Dakota Territory in 1874 trace their ethnic and faith heritage back to Switzerland and the Swiss Brethren, as the Anabaptists of Switzerland referred to themselves. They gained the additional name of Volhynian from their sojourn in the northwestern Ukrainian province of that name where they lived in the years prior to their emigration to America. While many family names have been added to this group through marriage and conversion through the years, the core of this group can trace their ancestry back to Switzerland, mostly to the Canton of Berne. The Kaufman name, for example, is traced back to the village of Grindelwald, at the foot of Jungfrau.[12]

In most cases, there is no documented evidence about when after 1525 these Swiss families joined the Anabaptist movement and became Swiss Brethren. Nor, except perhaps with a few exceptions, do we know when our ancestors left Switzerland, as there were frequent expulsions and flights from Switzerland by small groups throughout the sixteenth and seventeenth centuries.[13] We do know there was a large expulsion of Swiss Brethren in 1671, with some seven hundred immigrating to the Palatinate in Germany, and others fleeing to the Alsace in France,[14] and this is where many of the Swiss Brethren who later ended up in Volhynia were settled at the beginning of the eighteenth century.

12. Schrag, *European History*, 17; Emil J. Waltner, *Banished for Faith*, 138.
13. Waltner, *Banished for Faith*, 139–42.
14. Waltner, *Banished for Faith*, 143; Schrag, *European History*, 21, 39.

MIGRATIONS OF THE SWISS (VOLHYNIAN) MENNONITES

Switzerland
Zurich 1525
Canton Bern 1526

The Emmenthal Valley in Canton Bern is probably the ancestral home of most Swiss Volhynians. Because of persecution they migrated in 1650 with a large migration in 1670 and another migration in 1711.

ALSACE 1525 and again 1643 — Goering, Graber, Rothe, Kaufman. Many fled Alsace during Louis XIV's persecution of Protestants including Mennonites.

MONTEBELIARD (Florimont and Belfort) — Mennonites came in 1670-1791. Large migration came in 1671. Included: Kaufman, Graber, Gerig, Stucki, Lichti.
Early 1700's—1713 Menn's came from Alsace and Switzerland including Stucki, Graber, Gerig, Kaufman, Lichti, Flückiger, and others.
Moses Gerig passport of Feb. 8, 1791 included: Gerig, Graber, Lichti, Kaufman, Rothe.

THE PALATINATE (Pfalz) Arrived in the Palatinate 1650 and remained to 1786. Areas of Germany located on both sides of the Rhine River with Heidelberg as the political center.
The Mennonite families moved into the area west of Worms near Kirchheim-Bolanden (present village of Weierhof is located near Marnheim). Family names include: Krehbiel, Miller, Schrag, and Zerger.

GALACIA—1784-1786—Located near Lemberg, Austria (territory was acquired in the First Partition of Poland. This area is under the sovereignty of Russia and was renamed L'vov). There were 3 villages: **Falkenstein** 1784—6 family names included: Bachman, Krehbiel, Schrag, Mundelheim, Ewy, and Merk. **Einsiedel** 1786—18 family names included: Albrecht, Mauer, Mueller, Schmidt, Sutter, Zercher, and Rupp. **Rosenberg** 1788—3 families.

Einsiedel, Austria stopped temporarily and possibly moved to Podolia on the lands of Prince Czartoryski.

HUTTERITE BRUDERHOF REDITSCHOFF near Wischenka, Russia. Families include: Mueller, Berthold, Zerger, Schrag, Krehbiel, Schmidt, and Sutter. Schrag women married 2 Hutterite men.

MICHALIN settlement near Machnovka 1791? (Invited by Prince Protocki) by Mennonites that came from Graudenz on the Vistual Delta. In 1797 Swiss families of Krehbiel, Mueller, Schrag, and Zerger joined them.

The Prehistory of the Agrarian Cultures That Came into the Land

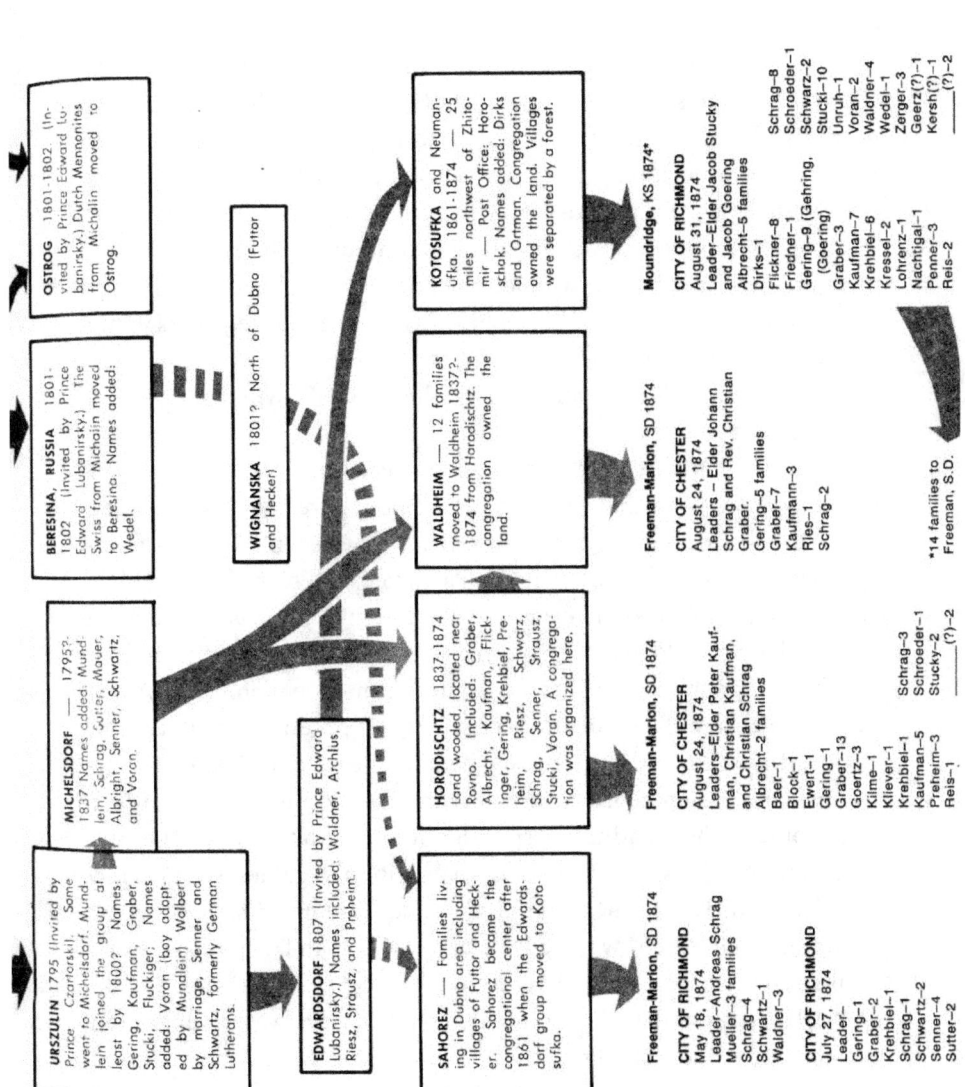

It was late in the seventeenth century that a conflict emerged among the Swiss Brethren, in part due to the severe persecution faced by these communities. While many Swiss Brethren were willing to make some compromises in order to avoid persecution, Jacob Ammann and those who followed him insisted on a stricter withdrawal and an internal communal discipline using the ban to enforce conformity to the community's values. The conflict between Jacob Ammann and Hans Reist and their followers led to a split among the Swiss Brethren and the emergence of the Amish as followers of Jacob Ammann in 1693. This split affected communities of Swiss Brethren not only in Switzerland itself, but also in the Palatinate and the Alsace, with some congregations siding with the Amish and others in the same larger community choosing the more moderate path that later was called the Mennonite Church.[15] Ammann was based in Alsace when he began his work, so the congregations in that area nearly all became Amish.[16] Indeed, the Swiss Brethren congregations that moved to the Ukraine and became the Swiss Volhynians were all of the Amish persuasion.

The Swiss Brethren who moved to the Palatinate in 1671 were welcomed by Prince Karl Ludwig, who was seeking to rebuild his lands devastated in the Thirty Years' War (1618 to 1648). Anabaptist groups found some degree of religious liberty in the Palatinate, and many congregations prospered and remained there for more than a century. It was there that the Swiss Volhynians adopted the Schweitzer dialect they brought with them to America.[17] In the early eighteenth century some Mennonite and Amish communities from the Palatinate began emigrating west to America, about the time the groups we are discussing here went east to the Ukraine.[18]

Late in the eighteenth century, Mennonites, Amish, and other German people in the Palatinate responded to an invitation from the Austrian emperor, Joseph II. The Austrian empire had gained the province of Galicia in the 1772 partition of Poland (an area now in southwestern Ukraine), and Joseph II wanted industrious German farmers to settle in the area. In the 1780s, more than three thousand German families from the Palatinate went to Galicia. Included among them were twenty-eight Anabaptist families, of whom about a half dozen were Amish families

15. Schrag, *European History*, 23–24.
16. Dyck, *Mennonite History*, 114.
17. Schrag, *European History*, 25.
18. Dyck, *Mennonite History*, 146.

who made this move between 1784 and 1786. These Anabaptist groups settled in three villages south of Lemburg (now L'vov, Ukraine)—Falkenstein, Einsiedel, and Rosenberg.[19] Except for the Amish families, most of these Galician Mennonites emigrated to Kansas and Minnesota in the 1880s.[20]

Tensions emerged between the Mennonite and Amish contingents among the Swiss Anabaptists in Galicia. The community was visited in 1793 and 1795 by Hutterite missionaries from the colony that had been established already in northeastern Ukraine.[21] In 1796 the Amish contingent of the Galician Anabaptist community, about a half dozen families, left to join the Hutterite colony at Wischenka.[22] It was a short-lived adventure, and the Amish left a year later and some joined a Low German community at Michalin, Ukraine, in 1797,[23] before rejoining the emerging Swiss Amish settlements in Volhynia in 1801. An interesting sidenote here is that two Swiss Amish girls married Hutterite boys when their families spent time in the Hutterite colony. One, Katherine Schrag, married the Hutterite colony minister's son, Andreas Waldner. When he died some twenty years later, Katherine and her three sons and five daughters returned to her Amish people in Volhynia, thus introducing the Waltner name into the Swiss Volhynian community.[24]

A second contingent of Swiss Amish people found their way to Volhynia via the Alsace and Montbeliard in France. Anabaptist groups that had become well-established in the Alsace, especially in the years following the expulsion of Anabaptists from Switzerland in 1671, were driven out of the Alsace when it became part of France. In 1713, King Louis XIV expelled most of the Anabaptists from the Alsace. Many found refuge at Montbeliard, France, in the independent duchy of Prince Leopold-Eberhard.[25] In 1791, a small party of Swiss Amish at Montbeliard were invited to settle on lands of a Polish prince, Czartoryski. This prince was related by marriage to the rulers of Wurttemberg, who

---

19. Schrag, *European History*, 29.
20. Smith, *Smith's Story*, 208–9.
21. Emil J. Waltner, *Banished for Faith*, 163–65.
22. Schrag, *European History*, 33–35.
23. Schrag, *European History*, 37–38.
24. Waltner, *Banished for Faith*, 165, 174.
25. Schrag, *European History*, 39.

governed Montbeliard.[26] About a half dozen families made this journey. They visited the Galician Mennonite community briefly, and then settled in Podolia south of Volhynia for some years on Prince Czartoryski's lands before the partitioning of Poland required them to be resettled in the villages of Urszulin and Michelsdorf, in what is today eastern Poland, a few miles northeast of Lublin.[27]

Some families left these villages in 1807 to establish the village of Edwardsdorf in Volhynia, west of Dubno, Ukraine. The remaining families left in 1837 to establish the village of Horodisch in Volhynia.[28] Eventually four main Swiss Amish villages emerged in Volhynia that came to America in 1874—Horodisch, Sahorez and Kotosufka (new villages supplanting Edwardsdorf), and Waldheim. All of these villages are near the cities of Rovno and Dubno except for Kotosufka which was northwest of Zhitomir.[29]

Nearly all the people in these four villages, about one thousand people in all, immigrated to America in 1874, about half to the area around Freeman and the other half to Moundridge, Kansas. No organized Swiss Volhynian presence continued in the Ukraine. None of these Swiss Amish people went to eastern Europe at the invitation of the Russian Empire, but the area of Volhynia where they eventually settled came under Russian rule in 1795 in the final partition of Poland, so they may be considered a part of the Germans-from-Russia.

Typical family names among the Swiss Volhynians going to Volhynia include: Flickinger, Gering, Graber, Kaufman, Krehbiel, Miller, Schrag, Schwartz, and Stucky. A number of these family names have variant spellings. Family names added to the Swiss Volhynian community in Volhynia include Albrecht, Ortman, Preheim, Ries, Senner, and Waltner.[30]

---

26. Schrag, *European History*, 46.

27. Schrag, *European History*, 46–47.

28. Schrag, *European History*, 48.

29. Schrag, *European History*, 49–56, including maps showing location of villages. See also Figure 2, Migrations of the Swiss Volhynian Mennonites.

30. Schrag, *European History*, 54–56. Author's note: This and the other lists of family names that follow in this chapter are representative, and not complete. My apology to those whose names have been omitted.

The Low German Mennonites of South Dakota

The Anabaptist movement in Holland began in the 1530s through the work of Melchior Hoffman, Obbe and Dirk Philipps, and others.[31] While the Anabaptists in the Netherlands eventually achieved religious toleration, they were heavily persecuted in the early years when Holland was under the rule of the Catholic Hapsburg Emperor of Spain, Charles V.[32] With Anabaptist communities under threat and without adequate leadership, the former Roman Catholic priest Menno Simon converted to Anabaptism and gave leadership as well as his name to the Anabaptists in the Netherlands.[33]

Persecution drove some Anabaptists east along the coast of the Baltic Sea to the Vistula River Delta in what was then East Prussia and now is Poland, beginning in the 1530s.[34] Here, especially in the free city of Danzig, the industrious Mennonite farmers thrived, draining the swamplands of Prussia with expertise they had gained in their native Holland. However, growing militarism in Prussia with its attendant threats of war taxes and conscription by the 1780s led the Mennonites of Prussia to seek a new homeland.[35]

At this time, the Russian empress, Catherine the Great, who ruled from 1762 to 1796, was seeking people of her ethnic German heritage to colonize lands the Russians had taken from the Turkish Ottoman empire in the 1780s. Catherine was a German princess who had married into the Russian royal family, and she invited her own German people to colonize these lands around the Black Sea. She had already invited Germans to colonize the area around the Volga River in the 1760s.[36] In 1788, she renewed the terms of German colonization, promising freedom of religion; freedom from taxation and conscription by the Russian Empire; and freedom to keep their own culture, schools, and language, all of which amounted to self-rule within the German colonies of Russia.[37]

The first Mennonite colony in Russia, Chortitza, was established in 1788 by immigrants from Prussia. A second large colony, Molotschna, was

31. Dyck, *Mennonite History*, 75–79.
32. Dyck, *Mennonite History*, 86.
33. Dyck, *Mennonite History*, 80–81.
34. Dyck, *Mennonite History*, 94.
35. Dyck, *Mennonite History*, 127.
36. Stumpp, *German-Russians*, 10.
37. Dyck, *Mennonite History*, 127.

established along the Molotschna River, under Catherine's successor, Czar Alexander I, in 1804. Both of these colonies were in southern Ukraine near the Black Sea.[38] These colonies prospered greatly throughout the nineteenth century, establishing a strong Mennonite cultural life. There were 120,000 Mennonites in Russia after World War I, including many who had by then been exiled to Siberia, and by then eighteen thousand had emigrated to North America in the 1870s.[39] This was still a fraction of the total number of Germans in Russia, which totaled nearly 1.8 million in 1897.[40]

Travel Route often taken by Mennonites traveling from the Danzig area to Chortitza and Molotschna. Map adapted from the Mennonite Historical Library

The normal route for Prussian Mennonites immigrating to the Ukraine brought them through the province of Volhynia, so it is not surprising that some of them also settled in that area.[41] The first Prussian Mennonite village in this part of Ukraine appears to be Michalin, between

---

38. Dyck, *Mennonite History*, 128–30.
39. Dyck, *Mennonite History*, 137.
40. Stumpp, *German-Russians*, 20.
41. See Figure 3, Mennonite Travel Route from Prussia to Russia.

Zhitomir and Berdichev in 1791.⁴² This is the same community that welcomed the Swiss Amish after their failed attempt to join the Hutterite colony. The settlers at Michalin were invited by the local prince, Potocki, and apparently this community settled on individual farms rather than in villages like most of the other Anabaptist settlements in Volhynia.⁴³ A disagreement with the prince around 1800 led a number of this community to move to Volhynia proper, where they established the village of Karlswalde, along with other Prussian Mennonites moving east.⁴⁴ The Karlswalde group along with a number of nearby and associated villages, accepted the invitation of Prince Lubanirsky to settle on his lands, just south of Ostrog in Volhynia.⁴⁵

A number of families from Mennonite villages in Volhynia went to the Molotschna colony in 1835 hoping to improve their lot. However, the prosperous Mennonites in the Molotschna refused to allow these newcomers from Volhynia to purchase land, and instead invited them to be their servants! After enduring this for thirteen years, this group returned to Volhynia in 1848 and established the village of Heinrichsdorf, not far from Michalin. This group had close fellowship with the Karlswalde group, sharing the services of Elder Tobias Unruh. Most of this group emigrated to Avon, South Dakota, in 1874 where they continued to have close relations with the Anabaptist groups around Freeman.⁴⁶

The Mennonite Low German groups who came to Dakota Territory in 1874 had diverse origins in the Ukraine. The first Mennonite to come to Dakota Territory in 1873 was Daniel Unruh, a wealthy landowner from Crimea, originally from Molotschna, who came with his large family and a party of dependent workers and settled along Turkey Ridge Creek southeast of Freeman. A group of immigrants from the Molotschna colony settled west of Marion. Quite a number from Karlswalde and associated villages in Volhynia settled in the area around Silver Lake north of Freeman, between Dolton and Marion. A number of families from Michalin also came to the area around Marion.⁴⁷

42. Schrag, *European History*, 37.
43. Abe J. Unruh, *Helpless Poles*, 56–58.
44. Unruh, *Helpless Poles*, 58–59; Schrag, *European History*, 38.
45. Unruh, *Helpless Poles*, 59–60; Schrag, *European History*, 38.
46. Boese, *Prussian-Polish Mennonites*, 42–43.
47. Boese, *Prussian-Polish Mennonites*, 77–78.

Typical family names reflecting Low German heritage include: Adrian, Becker, Berg, Boese, Buller, Deckert, Dick, Dirks, Engbrecht, Ensz, Epp, Ewert, Fast, Friesen, Goossen, Jantzen, Ratzlaff, Richert, Schartner, Schmidt, Schultz, Tieszen, Unruh, Voth, Wiens, and Willms.[48] Some of these family names have variant spellings.

The Hutterian *Prairieleut* of West Freeman

The Hutterite movement had its origins in Moravia in the late 1520s, as Anabaptism spread through Tyrol, Austria, and South Germany through the efforts of missionaries like Hans Hut (d. 1527). Hut already emphasized the New Testament ideal of sharing of goods.[49] Archduke Ferdinand, an ardent Catholic ruler, severely persecuted Anabaptists in these regions. Anabaptists were able to find a measure of respite in Moravia, today a region of Czechoslovakia, under the protection of Leonhard, one of the lords of Lichtenstein. As many as twelve thousand Anabaptists may have found their way to Nicolsburg (now Mikulov, on the Czech/Austrian border) by 1527.[50]

There was always pressure on these Anabaptists to take up the sword against the invading Turkish empire. While some Anabaptists relented and took up the sword, others known as Stabler (staff-bearers) refused.[51] In 1528, Leonhard of Lichtenstein expelled these Stabler (about two hundred adults) who eventually found refuge in Austerlitz (now Slavkov, Czechosolvakia). But on their way out of Nicolsburg, these Anabaptist refugees spread a cloak on the ground and put all their earthly possessions onto it in order to hold all things in common. This event in 1528 is understood to be the founding moment of the Hutterite movement.[52]

The Hutterite colonies grew rapidly in Moravia, in towns like Austerlitz and Auspitz (now Hustopece, Czechoslovakia). The experiment of holding all things in common was not without its trials, however. In the early 1530s, the colonies were visited by Anabaptist Jacob Hutter, under whose leadership many of the wrinkles of communal living were worked

---

48. Boese, *Prussian-Polish Mennonites*, 93–100.
49. Dyck, *Mennonite History*, 49–51.
50. Dyck, *Mennonite History*, 52.
51. Dyck, *Mennonite History*, 53.
52. Dyck, *Mennonite History*, 54.

The Prehistory of the Agrarian Cultures That Came into the Land 59

out. It was Jacob Hutter (executed in 1536) who gave his name to this movement, which eventually became known as the Hutterian Brethren.[53]

After the Treaty of Augsburg in 1555, the Hutterite movement in Moravia entered its Golden Age, which lasted until 1595. There were as many as twenty thousand to thirty thousand Hutterites in some one hundred colonies during this period. They became known all over Europe as excellent craftsmen, noted especially for their fine china.[54] War with the Ottoman Turks (1593 to 1606), and then the Thirty Years' War (1618 to 1648), led to renewed persecution and pressure on Hutterite colonies in Moravia, and the colonies were caught in the middle of many battle fields as well.[55] In the early 1620s, remnants of the Hutterite colonies were forced to move southeast to Hungary and Rumania. One group relocated to Transylvania at Alvinz (near Hermannstadt, now Sibiu, Rumania).[56]

Remnants of the Hutterite colonies lived in Transylvania from the 1620s to the 1760s, but the colonies continued to suffer from both Hapsburg persecution and the depredations of warfare with the Ottoman Turks, who laid siege to Vienna in 1683.[57] Religious persecution at the hands of the strongly Catholic Hapsburg court reached its peak during the reign of Empress Maria Theresa (1740 to 1780). She charged the Jesuit priest Delphini to either convert the Hutterites or drive them from the land. The children of Hutterites were required to be baptized as infants and to attend Catholic schools.[58] Eventually, the Hutterites were offered some freedom if they submitted to a few Catholic practices—infant baptism and attendance at Catholic services. The Hutterites who accepted this compromise to become half-Catholic came to be known as Habaner.[59]

In 1755, the remaining true Hutterites in Transylvania were bolstered with the arrival of a group of Lutheran immigrants from Carinthia in southern Austria, who were actually more Anabaptist than Lutheran. Exiled to Transylvania by Maria Theresa, some of these Lutherans joined

---

53. Dyck, *Mennonite History*, 54–56.
54. Dyck, *Mennonite History*, 56–57; Smith, *Smith's Story*, 230–31.
55. Dyck, *Mennonite History*, 58–59.
56. Smith, *Smith's Story*, 239.
57. Smith, *Smith's Story*, 239.
58. Smith, *Smith's Story*, 241–42.
59. Smith, *Smith's Story*, 242–43.

the Hutterite colonies adding a coterie of new names to the roster of typical Hutterite names, including Hofer, Kleinsasser, Glanzer, and Waldner.[60]

Continuing to face persecution, a small band of faithful Hutterites, sixty-seven in all, left Alwinz and crossed the Carpathian Mountains into Walachia, where they settled near Bucharest, Rumania, in 1767. Escaping religious persecution, this Hutterite remnant found itself again caught in warfare, this time a conflict between Russia and Turkey.[61] At this time a Russian general, Semetin, arranged for these refugees to be resettled on the lands of Count Rumyantsov on the river Desna at Wischenka in the Ukraine, northeast of Kiev, near the city of Tchernigov, in 1770. There they were eventually joined by others of their brotherhood who came from Transylvania and Hungary to rejoin them.[62]

At Wischenka, the Hutterite colonies began to re-establish themselves, and they lived on the count's estate until his death around the year 1800. After his death, the count's son attempted to reduce the Hutterites to the status of serfs. After a court case which ruled in favor of the Hutterites being renters and not serfs, the new count threw the Hutterites off his lands, and in 1801, the Hutterite colony moved to nearby Raditschewa, where it received Russian crown land on the same terms that were given to German Mennonites at that time.[63] The Hutterite colony remained in Raditschewa until 1842. However, at Raditschewa the Hutterite group gave up communal living in 1819, after a tragic fire destroyed their settlement.[64]

The Hutterites made one final move within Ukraine before coming to America. In 1842, their community had outgrown their land base, and they were given the opportunity to move their colony to land near the Mennonite colony of Molotschna, near the Black Sea. They were assisted in settling in this area near Melitipol by Johann Cornies, the Mennonite educational and agricultural leader of the Molotschna colony. Eventually, the Hutterites established four colonies in southern Ukraine. Hutterthal, Johannnesruh, and Neu Hutterthal were not communal in their pattern of living. The communal history of holding all things in common was reestablished by some in the village of Hutterdorf, begun in 1859.[65]

60. Smith, *Smith's Story*, 243–44.
61. Smith, *Smith's Story*, 244–45.
62. Smith, *Smith's Story*, 245.
63. Smith, *Smith's Story*, 246.
64. Smith, *Smith's Story*, 247–48.
65. Smith, *Smith's Story*, 247–48. See Figure 4, Hutterite Migrations in Eastern Europe.

In all, 1,250 Hutterite people immigrated to Dakota Territory in the 1870s. About a third of them (450) chose communal ownership of property, establishing the three mother colonies from which all other Hutterite colonies in the United States and Canada have grown. These three colonies were Bon Home, west of Yankton on the Missouri River, and Wolf Creek and Elm Spring Colonies along the James River in Hutchinson County. The other two-thirds of Hutterite immigrants (eight hundred people) settled west and north of Freeman on private homesteads as the *Prairieleut* (Prairie People), and in the 1870s established three congregations—Hutterdorf, Neu Hutterthal, and Hutterthal.[66]

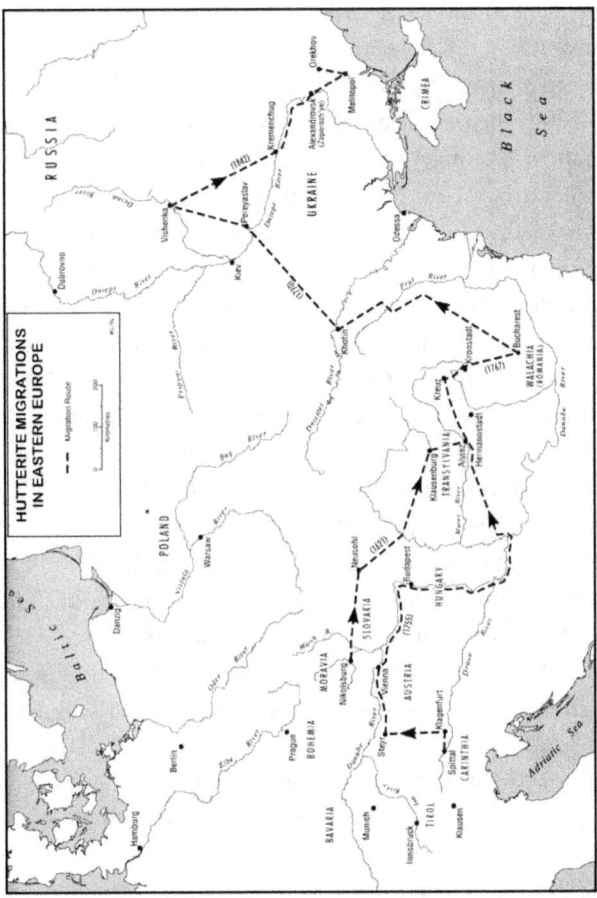

66. Norman Hofer, in Heritage Hall, *Three Groups, One Story*; Hofer, "Hutterite Colony."

Hutterite family names that go back to the original colonies in Moravia are: Gross, Mendel, Pullman, Stahl, Tschetter, Walter, Wipf, and Wollman. Family names of Lutherans from Austria who joined the Hutterites in Transylvania are: Glanzer, Hofer, Kleinsasser, Waldner, and Wurtz. In Russia a number of Low German names were added to the Hutterite roster of names: Decker, Entz, Fast, and Knels.[67]

The European Origin of Other Russian-Germans in the Freeman Area

Several other groups of Germans-from-Russia also came to this area of Dakota Territory in the 1870s. The first settlers from Russia in 1873 were from Johannestal in the Beresan settlement north of Cherson, who settled west of Freeman near the James River, and established the Johannestal Church. Most of the people at Johannestal were from Wuerttemberg and the Palatinate in Germany and entered Russia in the second decade of the nineteenth century.[68] Common family names in this group include Auch, Delzer, Holzwarth, Mutchelknaus, Schempp, and Schatz.[69]

In 1874, people from several villages in Crimea—Neusatz, Friedental, Zuerichtal, and Heilbronn—settled south and southwest of Freeman.[70] Most of these people had gone to Crimea from Wuerttemberg in Germany and the Alsace in France between 1804 and 1810, and some of these village names, like Heilbronn, reflect their German town of origin.[71] This group established the Trinity Lutheran Church southwest of Freeman. Common names in this group include Guenther, Huber, Hafner, Schamber, Schoppert, and Stern.[72]

Other settlers came from the villages of Glueckstal and Kassel in the Glueckstaler settlement along the Dniester River north of Odessa. These groups had their origin in Wuerttemberg and the Alsace and moved to Russia from 1804 to 1824. Here in Dakota Territory they settled mostly around Menno and in the area between Menno and Freeman.[73] Family

---

67. *Three Groups, One Story*; Hofer, "Hutterite Colony."
68. Stumpp, *German-Russians*, 13, 17; Rath, *Black Sea Germans*, 4, 93, 404.
69. Rath, *Black Sea Germans*, 404.
70. Rath, *Black Sea Germans*, 2, 93.
71. Stumpp, *German-Russians*, 18
72. Rath, *Black Sea Germans*, 404.
73. Rath, *Black Sea Germans*, 5, 92.

names in this group include Dewald, Dubs, Ellwein, Haar, Hafner, Mettler, Nuss, Pfeiffer, and Walz.[74] Still another group from Kassel came in 1879 and settled north of Freeman in what was called Klein Kassel. Family names in this group included Amman, Goering, Koerner, and Nuss.[75]

Most of these groups who moved from areas in Germany to the Black Sea in the early nineteenth century were recruited by the Russian Empire to settle the Black Sea area. Many of them were escaping the continual wars that plagued the French/German border areas in the early nineteenth century as a consequence of Napoleon's imperial adventures.[76] There were nearly 1.8 million Germans living in Russia in 1897, with the vast majority of those living in the Ukraine in colonies along the Black Sea.[77] As many as 350,000 to 400,000 people with Germans-from-Russia ancestry were living in the United States in 1940.[78]

MANY ORIGINS, MANY SOJOURNS

For the casual reader who does not share the heritage of the people involved, the previous sections of this chapter must be exceedingly tedious, replete as they are with dates and places and historical events that are now obscure and seemingly irrelevant. It was important for me to document in a succinct way the origin and many movements of the people among whom I live. Even a superficial reading of these sections drives home the complex and convoluted communal history of the people who settled in this part of Dakota Territory in the 1870s. These communities originated in and/or migrated to nearly every part of Europe, from the North Sea to the Black Sea, and from the Baltic Sea to the Alp Mountains.

In addition to their diverse origins and migrations, what I find most striking about this history is the way it was integrally related to what we refer to as world events, the larger history of the emerging nation-states of Europe in these centuries. As Anabaptist groups, we have long understood this relationship in its negative expression—the persecution Anabaptist communities experienced at the hands of civic and religious authorities that often drove them from the places of their origin

74. Rath, *Black Sea Germans*, 404.
75. Rath, *Black Sea Germans*, 92, 404.
76. Bosch, *German-Russians*, 46.
77. Stumpp, *German-Russians*, 20.
78. Stumpp, *German Russians*, 31.

or temporary sojourn. Indeed, we have often ascribed this persecution as the primary reason and motivation for the migration of Anabaptist groups from one place to another. It is characteristic of minority cultural groups to see themselves as victims in this way of the larger socio-economic/religious/political powers under which they lived. And there is of course some degree of truth in this way of seeing things.

What I don't think we have understood as well or appreciated is the way these groups were drawn into the dominant cultural movements by the many invitations to find refuge in the lands of one or another ruling power. It is what accounted for movements of Anabaptist groups to the Palatinate (invited by Karl Ludwig), the Alsace, Montbeliard (invited by Leopold Eberhard), Prussia, Galicia (invited by the Austro-Hungarian king Joseph II), Moravia (invited by Leonhard von Liechtenstein), Volhynia (invited by Polish princes), Russia (invited by Catherine the Great and others), and ultimately, the American Great Plains (invited by the United States). In many of these instances, these agrarian cultures became agents of colonization on behalf of these imperial powers, often dispossessing native inhabitants of these lands.

When we have observed this positive expression of our interactions with political rulers and states, we have tended to understand them as saviors destined by God to provide sanctuary for a people under duress and needing to find a new home. We have not, even in retrospect, reflected on our own culpability for our historical fate due to our own choices, the way in which we allowed ourselves to be drawn into a stream of historical events that brought oppression to others and ultimately bore ill-fruit also within our own cultural history and life in prejudicial attitudes and actions towards other groups and cultures among whom we came to live and sometimes dispossessed.

The point, in any case, is that however withdrawn from the world we perceived ourselves to be as minority cultural groups living within a largely hostile socio-economic/religious/political world, our story is indeed linked inextricably to that larger historical context of the powers and nation-states and their struggles with each other for dominance, land, resources, and control. It would have been wise for us to be more discerning about the implications for our involvement in this larger history. This is not to negate or criticize the choices our forebears made at any particular juncture of our history in this long sojourn. It is only to suggest that a more thoughtful and critical appraisal of the consequences of our own choices may have changed the way we related both to those powers themselves, but also to the many local and indigenous cultures with whom we interacted in all of these various settings.

THE AGRARIAN HERITAGE OF THE GERMANS FROM RUSSIA

It might be easy to suppose from the chronicle of the preceding section that the people involved were so spiritually intent in seeking to preserve their faith at such great costs that they must not have cared much for the actual earthly lands of their origin or their sojourn. That would be a mistake! It is often supposed in our urban world that lowly peasants are hardly capable of speech, much less tuned to the finer beauty of the natural world. Peasants are hardly credited with the ability to read and write, much less to engage in artistic endeavors or reflect on the interplay of their interactions with the natural world that sustained them. We assume it is only trained scientists who have the ability to deduce the effect of a certain course of action on the natural environment and the human community that is interacting with it. Yet agrarian cultures the world over contradict these painfully absurd assumptions about their capabilities.

Among the Swiss families who were exiled to the Palatinate in 1671 was a Krehbiel family, three sons of a Jost Krehbiel. They lived in the Palatinate for more than a century and prospered there. One might assume that they had the skills to do that anywhere, and that it didn't matter to them that they had to leave their homeland in Switzerland. But Peter, one of these Krehbiel brothers, has left us a ten-stanza poem expressing his sense of loss upon leaving his homeland in Switzerland. These few verses from that poem give us the flavor of his grief, but also his determination to persevere.

> Farewell you Alps, you beloved provinces,
> You homelike village in the still valley;
> You beloved fields, someone else will farm.
> O father-house, I will no longer see you,
> May God protect you! Farewell for the last time.
>
> Farewell you valleys with cliff walls,
> That stretch to the heavens, severe and bare,
> That send their streams from high above,
> That end in spray in the deep,
> Also to you, I say farewell for the last time.

> There on the Alpine meadows I see healthily running
> The well-nourished cattle in great numbers.
> Do you hear the Alpine horn sounding over there?
> Do you hear the cowherd lustily yodeling?
> Oh I hear you for the last time.
>
> And you who have persecuted me with rage and vengeance,
> Meanwhile, I commend you to the grace of the Lord,
> Do you believe that I will permit my cherished beliefs
> Of my Lord and Savior to be robbed?
> Also, fare all you well for the last time.[79]

The Swiss Brethren who fled to the Palatinate and Alsace in the 1670s, whether of Amish or Mennonite persuasion, took with them long generations of farming on the steep hillsides of the Alps. In common European practice they built house/barn combinations that enabled both humans and livestock to stay warm and minimized forage needs for the animals during the long winters. Having livestock enterprises for grazing by necessity, they had learned the art of fertilizing with animal manure and saw the interplay of field, livestock, and manure as essential to their farming operations. So, for instance, in the Palatinate, Swiss Brethren introduced crop rotations including clover for nitrogen fixation. They introduced the South American potato to the region in the eighteenth century and used beets and turnips for both cow feed and human tables. They also introduced lime as a mineral fertilizer for their clover fields.[80] A Graber family in Montbeliard is credited with developing a new breed of cattle.[81]

In Volhynia, the Swiss Brethren did not find life easy. With the exception of Waldheim and Kotosufka, the Swiss villages did not own their land, but rented it from noblemen of the area on a long-term twenty-four-year lease. Apparently, the lease was made to the community as a whole, which then distributed the land to the members of the community. Imagine the communal constraints (and opportunities) of such an arrangement! While nearly everyone engaged in subsistence food production, in typical agrarian village fashion there were blacksmiths, weavers, millers, carpenters—the whole range of crafts needed to make life sustainable

---

79. Emil J. Waltner, *Banished for Faith*, 145–46.
80. Waltner, *Banished for Faith*, 148–49.
81. Nolt, *History of the Amish*, 84.

The Prehistory of the Agrarian Cultures That Came into the Land   67

in a subsistence village economy.[82] But under these conditions, it is not surprising that the Swiss Volhynian villages left nearly en masse in 1874 for America. They had little to lose or leave behind in Volhynia, however used to their familiar life they had become, and so much to gain by the promise of land in America.

The Low German Mennonites, originating in Holland and the Low Countries, brought with them a different agricultural expertise on their sojourn east that eventually took them to the Ukraine. Driven by persecution eastward to Prussia beginning in the 1530s, these peasant farmers took with them their expertise in draining flooded lands which they had achieved in Holland. "Mennonites practiced agriculture for over four hundred years in West and East Prussia, most of their families being farmers throughout the entire period of their occupancy, 1534–1945 . . . The chief and extraordinary agricultural achievements of the Mennonite farmer lie in the field of land drainage."[83] It was this ability of land drainage that "secured the privilege of settlement in the Vistula delta for the Dutch Mennonite refugees of 1534 and later."[84] Having drained the land, Mennonite farmers established a rich and productive agriculture centered especially around dairying and its associated products.

After these Low German Mennonites moved to Russia at the beginning of the nineteenth century, they adapted their considerable agricultural knowledge to the steppes of the Ukraine—quite a different ecological setting than the swamps of Prussia. However, in the colonies of Chortitza and especially Molotschna, they were able to develop a rich and varied agricultural economy. Indeed, under the gifted leadership of Johann Cornies, who founded the Agricultural Association and developed a model farm on his estate, the Mennonite colonies succeeded in making the steppes a rich agricultural environment. "His estate became a model in all branches of agriculture and an experiment station. Excellent Dutch dairy cattle and high quality breeds of horses were raised here. In 1847 there were nearly 100,000 fruit and shade trees on his estates and a large nursery from which trees were shipped to distant places. His industries included cheese and brick factories and the production of tobacco, silk and other commodities."[85]

---

82. Emil J. Waltner, *Banished for Faith*, 182.
83. Driedger, "Farming Among the Mennonites," 16.
84. Driedger, "Farming Among the Mennonites," 16.
85. Krahn, "From the Steppes," in *From the Steppes*, 3.

The Hutterian Brethren who came to the Freeman community brought still other elements of agrarian culture and heritage with them. While living in communal, self-sustaining communities that produced everything needed to sustain their life together, the Hutterite colonies, beginning in their Golden Age late in the sixteenth century in Moravia, developed the production of high-quality pottery. Hutterite colonies were able to capitalize on their communal structures to produce china that rivaled Chinese or Italian imported pieces. The colonies became famous for their exquisite and delicate china, decorated with colorful naturalistic motifs, they sold to the noble houses of Europe. Many of these pieces, known as Habaner Fayence, are held in museums and estates throughout central Europe, where the Hutterite colonies lived. These traditions were carried forward throughout the sojourns of the Hutterite colonies, into Russia, and into the colonies' existence in America.[86] This Hutterite tradition of pottery-making reflects the rich culture of agrarian communities throughout the world.

All of these groups that came to the prairies of the Great Plains in the 1870s brought with them a rich and long and varied ethnic heritage and agrarian culture. Their centuries-long agrarian sojourn in the varied ecological settings of central and eastern Europe all contributed to the strength and vitality of cultural and communal life they brought with them to America, and enabled them to adapt their wisdom and experience to the unique ecology of the Great Plains. And fortunately, many of these groups arrived here as intentional communities of faith, used to looking to each other for support and to putting the needs of the community ahead of their own personal or selfish wishes.

---

86. Gary J. Waltner, "Hutterite Pottery."

PART II

A Rural Community's Life Cycle

4

The Community's Birth in Immigration and Displacement (1874)

SYNOPSIS

IN 1858 THE YANKTON Sioux Nation, which had used what was to become southeast South Dakota as their hunting grounds for some decades, signed a treaty with the United States government ceding their rights to approximately the southeast quarter of what would later be South Dakota in exchange for a reserve in Charles Mix County along the Missouri River. This opened the way for European pioneers to immigrate and settle in this area. Hutchinson and Turner Counties in southeast Dakota Territory were surveyed and laid out in townships in the 1860s, and beginning in the 1870s European settlers began to stake claims in this area based on the 1862 Homestead Act of the United States Congress. The United States government was eager to have farmers of European origin come to the Great Plains to colonize this land of the Louisiana Purchase recently acquired from various First Nations.

In 1870 Czar Alexander II revoked the special privileges granted to German colonists in Russia, requiring them to learn Russian, adopt Russian schools and institutions, and serve in the Russian military. This caused great consternation among all the German colonists in Russia. Among the Mennonite communities, delegations were sent to St. Petersburg to see if this policy might be revoked. When this appeared to be a vain hope, the Mennonites in 1873 gathered a delegation of twelve men representing the various Anabaptist constituencies in Russia to visit the

Great Plains of North America and explore possible destinations for immigration. From the area of Volhynia west of Kiev, Andreas Schrag was chosen to represent the isolated Swiss German communities of Amish background, and Tobias Unruh was chosen to represent the isolated Low German communities. Paul and Lorenz Tschetter were chosen to represent the Hutterite communities. Ironically, the communities these men represented all ended up settling in the larger Freeman community in 1874, though none of the 1873 delegation actually visited Dakota Territory.

The first Mennonite group to settle in Dakota Territory was the extended family and entourage of Daniel Unruh, a wealthy Mennonite from the Crimea who immigrated in 1873 and then came to Turner County in the spring of 1874 after wintering in Yankton, the territorial capital. It may have been his influence that led the delegates named above to Dakota Territory. In any case, several Swiss German villages immigrating from Russia settled in the area east and south of what would later be Freeman. Several Low German communities settled north and east of Freeman. Hutterite colonies were established along the James River, while the *Prairieleut* Hutterites, those who had abandoned communal living, settled west of Freeman.

Many of these immigrants from the Ukraine were nearly destitute. Established Mennonite communities in the eastern United States loaned money for travel fares and provided other assistance to these communities in Dakota Territory. There being no infrastructure in this vast prairie, the first years of pioneering were marked by economic hardships, and natural disasters severely tested these Mennonite immigrants. The prairie had to be broken for agricultural crops, and while the land was incredibly fertile, a harvest could not be guaranteed.

TWO SIMULTANEOUS DEVELOPMENTS GIVE RISE TO THE BIRTH OF THE FREEMAN COMMUNITY

The second chapter of this book described the imperial encroachment onto the Great Plains of North America and the subsequent disenfranchisement of the traditional Dakota First Nations living in the northern Great Plains in the eighteenth century. This was the first development that made possible the formation of the Freeman community as agrarian cultures with European ethnic roots. It is impossible to overstate the

The Community's Birth in Immigration and Displacement (1874)

importance of this development, however much it is simply assumed and taken for granted by most of us. If the United States had not purchased Louisiana from the French and then explored and opened up the Great Plains for settlement by European people through the disenfranchisement of the resident First Nations, the Freeman community and all the other communities like it on the Great Plains would not be here.

More specifically, we are here because through intimidation and coercion, some leaders of the Yankton Sioux Nation agreed to sign a treaty with the United States government in 1858, ceding their rights to most of the southeast quarter of South Dakota in exchange for a reservation in Charles Mix County along the Missouri River, along with some other promised benefits.[1] The European agrarian communities of the Great Plains all had their birth in the displacement of aboriginal cultures, whose displacement also involved the dismantling of their traditional culture.

A simultaneous but somewhat different development was occurring in the Russian Empire in the 1850s and 1860s. The autocratic rulers of Russia came to the realization that they would need to address the situation of the majority of their population—the serfs who lived as virtual slaves on the vast estates of the Russian nobility. Throughout this period the Russian ruling class was contemplating reforms that would set the peasant serfs free and grant them at least some of the land which provided their livelihood. This culminated in the proclamation of emancipation for the serfs in March 1861,[2] coincidentally nearly the same time that Abraham Lincoln proclaimed the Emancipation Proclamation for slaves in the United States in 1863. As it turned out, the emancipation of the serfs was too little, too late, to prevent the Bolshevik Revolution in 1917, but yet it was a most dramatic and sweeping socio-economic and political reform within the Russian Empire.

This proclamation to free the serfs was part of a larger Slavophile movement in Russia. For nearly two centuries Russia had been ruled by czars who were either from European royal houses themselves or were strongly influenced by European culture. In the second half of the nineteenth century, the movement toward Russian nationalism grew rapidly. So it is not surprising that the court of Alexander II should also cast its eyes at the privileged and wealthy German colonies that had come to Russia at the invitation of Catherine the Great and Alexander I, and had been granted

---

1. For treaty information, see Sansom-Flood and Bernie, *Remember Your Relatives*. See also Figure 1, Yankton Treaty Cession of 1858, in ch. 2.

2. Pares, *History of Russia*, 368.

special privileges allowing them to rule themselves, keep their German language and culture, and avoid Russian taxation and conscription. Too often, these German colonies, as agents of Russian imperial colonial expansion in the Ukraine, had themselves become agents of oppression toward the Slavic, Turkic, and Northern Caucasian people among whom they lived. This was true as well for the Mennonite colonies of southern Ukraine.

In 1870, Czar Alexander II, who ruled from 1855 to 1881, proclaimed an edict requiring Germans in Russia to become completely Russianized within ten years or to leave Russia. Germans in Russia were required to learn and use the Russian language, adapt to Russian educational systems, and forgo the self-rule they had enjoyed within their colonies.[3] In addition, the exemption from military service was suspended, which was particularly concerning to the non-resistant Anabaptist groups, although all German groups were likely loath to serve in the Russian army.

It was this movement toward Russian nationalism and its consequent restriction on German self-rule and culture that led to the migrations of Germans-from-Russia to America in the 1870s. In all, some eighteen thousand Mennonites came to the United States and Canada during that decade, about eight thousand to Manitoba, and the rest to the Great Plains states of the United States.[4] This was only a fraction of the total number of Germans-from-Russia who came to America.

Ironically, the edict affected scattered German villages in Volhynia, the source of several of the Anabaptist villages that formed the Freeman community, as well as large Mennonite colonies like Molotschna on the Black Sea. The villages in Volhynia had come to that area at the invitation of local Polish nobles rather than at the invitation of the Russian Empire, but had come under Russian rule through the third partition of Poland in 1795.[5]

The point to be made is that the Freeman community, like many others in the Great Plains, had its birth in the *push* and *pull* of the imperial powers of the world. In Russia, the *push* came to minority agrarian communities of Germanic ethnic identity from an increasingly Slavophile empire seeking to assert its national identity and to liberate its own oppressed people. In America, the *pull* came from a new American empire that had disenfranchised its native, aboriginal people and was seeking

---

3. Smith, *Smith's Story*, 284.
4. Dyck, *Mennonite History*, 154.
5. Pares, *History of Russia*, 282, 285.

European colonists to settle the vast lands of the Great Plains. The communities that immigrated to America in the 1870s had a strong heritage and agrarian culture, as we saw in the last chapter, but their existence and their movements followed the whims and edicts of imperial power. They were doing, perhaps, the best they could under difficult circumstances laid out for them by the imperial powers of the world.

The question is whether a community born out of the displacement of another people, in this case the Yankton Sioux Nation, can be sustained. When will the injustices of the past come home to roost, as they did for the Mennonites in Russia during the 1870s and in the decades that followed for those who stayed in Russia? But more to the point, might the rebirth of the Freeman community involve a righting of the wrong done to the Yankton Sioux Nation? Is it possible that the future of the Freeman community might involve and even depend on the building of a relationship with the people displaced by our coming a century and a half ago? In any case, the birth of the Freeman community is fraught with all the perils of small agrarian communities sojourning among the imperial powers of the world. We might wish to think of our communities as masters of our own destiny, but the reality is that we are shaped more than we know or acknowledge by the forces of imperial history.

TWELVE "SPIES": AN EXPLORATORY DELEGATION TO THE GREAT PLAINS IN 1873

As the various Anabaptist groups of German ethnicity began learning about Czar Alexander II's Russianization policies, there was significant consternation in these communities. The czar's edict gave German colonists in Russia ten years to comply with the 1870 edict, but it seems the royal court made little effort to even inform German colonists about the edict. The czar and his court, while hoping for compliance to the edict, were likely well aware that their actions could mean the exodus of a large and wealthy and industrious class of people from Russia.[6] Indeed, an envoy of the czar visited a number of Mennonite colonies as late as May 1874, with authority to mitigate the strongest requirements of the edict related to military service in an effort to keep the Mennonites from leaving Russia.[7]

6. Gering, *After Fifty Years*, 15.
7. Smith, *Smith's Story*, 291–92.

On the other hand, the royal court was not responsive to the series of Anabaptist delegations that visited St. Petersburg beginning in the winter of 1871 with appeals to have the policy repealed or changed.[8] While that first delegation was from the large Mennonite colonies near the Black Sea, the Swiss Volhynian Amish and scattered Low German Mennonite communities in Volhynia sent two of their leaders, Elders Jacob Stucky and Tobias Unruh, to St. Petersburg, but these men had even less success in learning about much less negotiating a reversal of the czar's edict.[9] All the Anabaptist groups in Russia met to assemble a group of representatives who could speak for all the Anabaptists in Russia, and this delegation arrived in St. Petersburg early in 1873, but also had no success in changing the czar's edict.[10] Eventually Mennonites who remained in Russia were granted the option of forestry and medical service as non-combatants in lieu of military service.[11]

The same all-Anabaptist meeting that sent a final delegation to St. Petersburg in 1873 also made the first serious overture toward emigration. Twelve *spies* were appointed to make an exploratory visit to the Great Plains of the United States and Canada in the summer of 1873. These twelve men represented all the Anabaptist groups living within the Russian Empire. Jakob Buller and Leonhard Sudermann represented the Molotschna Colony; Heinrich Wiebe, Jakob Peters, and Cornelius Buhr represented the Bergthal and Chortitza Colonies; Cornelius Toews and David Claassen represented the *Kleine Gemeinde*. The next four delegates in this contingent represented the three Anabaptist groups that eventually came to South Dakota, with Andreas Schrag representing the Swiss Volhynian Amish, and Tobias Unruh representing the scattered Low German Mennonite settlements in Volhynia (sometimes called the Prussian-Polish Mennonites). Paul and Lorenz Tschetter (nephew and uncle) represented the Hutterite colonies by then living at Johannesruh near the Mennonite Molotschna Colony. The final member of the delegation was Wilhelm Ewert, not from Russia at all, but representing the Mennonites still living in Prussia, the area from which most of the Mennonites in Russia had come.[12]

8. Smith, *Smith's Story*, 284–85.
9. Schrag, *European History*, 79.
10. Schrag, *European History*, 79.
11. Smith, *Smith's Story*, 285–86.
12. Smith, *Smith's Story*, 289.

The Community's Birth in Immigration and Displacement (1874)

After the twelve delegates for the 1873 exploratory trip to North America were chosen, the visit itself was arranged and overseen by an American Mennonite without whose help the visit would have been very difficult. John Funk lived in Elkhart, Indiana, where he was the publisher of a newspaper for Mennonites, *The Herald of Truth*, published in both German (*Der Herold der Wharheit*) and English. He was assisted by Cornelius Jansen, a Prussian Mennonite who had been consul for Prussia in Berdiansk, South Russia.[13] Already in 1872, Funk began publishing news about the plight of the Mennonites in Russia in his paper.

For their part, the Anabaptist groups in Russia realized that many of those wishing to emigrate were quite poor and would need help with the costs of travel and for settlement in America, and they began appealing to their American and Canadian co-believers for this assistance. Funk made contacts with the United States and Canadian governments and with railroad companies, who were eagerly seeking settlers to come to the Great Plains now open for settlement by European people. Also in 1872, four young Russian Mennonite men made a trip to the Great Plains, visiting Illinois, Missouri, Kansas, Nebraska, Colorado, Minnesota, and Dakota Territory.[14]

The Russian Mennonite delegation of 1873 came to America in several groups, all of whom made visits to Elkhart, Indiana, the base of John Funk's work. The first to arrive was the Bergthaler group of three who came in April and apparently went on to tour Kansas and Texas before joining the main delegation in Minnesota. The five delegates from the Molotschna colony, Volhynia, and Prussia arrived in late May and three of these men visited Mennonites in Ontario and Pennsylvania on their way west, prior to arriving in Elkhart on June 6. The last four delegates representing the Hutterites and the *Kleine Gemeinde* came to Elkhart on May 24 and traveled with John Funk.[15]

After several missteps all twelve delegates met at Fargo, North Dakota, on June 9.[16] In his diary of this trip, John Funk lists the twelve delegates and the others who completed this party. In addition to Funk and the twelve Russian delegates, present were H. M. Hiller and C. B. Powers, representing the Northern Pacific Railroad and the guides who brought the party of five

---

13. Schnell, "John F. Funk," in Krahn, *From the Steppes*, 69.
14. Schnell, "John F. Funk," in Krahn, *From the Steppes*, 70.
15. Schnell, "John F. Funk," in Krahn, *From the Steppes*, 73.
16. Schnell, "John F. Funk," in Krahn, *From the Steppes*, 74.

to Minnesota; Jacob Schantz of Waterloo, Ontario, who guided those who had gone to Canada; and Isaac Leatherman of Elkhart, Indiana.[17]

From Fargo, the group had a rail tour into Dakota Territory, viewing the James, Red, and Cheyenne River valleys for several days. On June 12, the group was met by William Hespeler, a representative of the Canadian government, who invited the group to visit Manitoba. The group boarded a boat on the Red River and proceeded to Winnipeg, arriving there on June 17. After a foray into southern Manitoba, several of the delegates, those from Prussia, Volhynia, and the Hutterites, decided by June 21 against settling in Canada and were led by John Funk back up the Red River to Dakota Territory, where they explored the Pembina Valley. They were greatly impressed with this area as a possible destination for their people. For another week or more, these delegates explored the Red River Valley around Fargo and Moorhead.[18]

On July 6, all twelve delegates were reunited in Fargo and after exploring the area around Breckenridge, they traveled by rail back to the Twin Cities, arriving there on July 12. On July 14, the group left the Twin Cities and traveled to Mountain Lake, Minnesota, which became a destination for a number of immigrants later that year and in 1874. The group proceeded to Worthington, Minnesota, and then down to Sioux City, Iowa, and finally Omaha, Nebraska. The group explored the areas around the Platte, Little Blue, and Republican Rivers. By July 23, the group found itself back in Lincoln, Nebraska.[19]

At Lincoln, the twelve delegates parted ways. Several, including Ewert and Unruh, visited Kansas and Texas. Several others, including Suderman and Schrag, made a speaking/visitation itineration among the Mennonite settlements in Ontario and Pennsylvania, speaking about the needs the Anabaptist immigrants from Russia would have and beginning the process of raising contributions for the eventual migration.[20] By mid- to-late August, delegates were beginning to return to Russia. For instance, Andreas Schrag boarded a ship in New York on August 21.[21]

---

17. Hiebert, *Brothers in Deed*, 76.

18. Gary J. Waltner, "Andreas Schrag Diary," 15; Schnell, "John F. Funk," in Krahn, *From the Steppes*, 74. See also Swiss-German Centennial Committee, *Swiss Germans*, 11.

19. Schnell, "John F. Funk," in Krahn, *From the Steppes*, 75.

20. Waltner, "Andreas Schrag Diary," 16–17.

21. Waltner, "Andreas Schrag Diary," 25.

Several extant journals and accounts of this delegation to America have been preserved. Heritage Hall Museum and Archives has journals or copies of journals made by Andreas Schrag, Tobias Unruh, and Paul Tschetter, representing the three groups who eventually came to Dakota Territory.[22] The scrapbook, *Brothers in Deed to Brothers in Need*, has reprinted the entire account of this journey written by John F. Funk in *The Herald of Truth*.[23] While there are inevitable inconsistencies and contradictions in these accounts, they all present valuable and important information about the significance of this historic journey.

Along the way, but particularly in Philadelphia and New York in the weeks prior to their return to Russia, members of the delegation were in negotiations with the railroads and authorities of Canada and the United States regarding the terms under which they could immigrate.[24] One of the most significant of these negotiations occurred on August 8 when Tobias Unruh and Paul and Lorenz Tschetter had an audience with President Ulysses S. Grant in New York City. At this audience, the three men presented a petition to the president seeking assurances that they would not be subject to military service in the United States nor required to pay for substitute soldiers for a period of fifty years. They also sought some measure of self-rule, education in German, exemption from serving as judges and jurors, and the option of non-participation in civic affairs such as voting. Of course, President Grant was unable to grant this petition, but assured them that it was unlikely that they would be subject to "involuntary military service."[25] Later in April 1874, similar petitions were debated in the US Congress.[26]

As it turned out, of the various groups represented in the 1873 delegation, the Bergthaler and the *Kleine Gemeinde* immigrated to Canada, some eight thousand in total. Almost all the Hutterite and Swiss Volhynian groups came to Dakota Territory and Kansas, along with some of the scattered Prussian-Polish Mennonite communities from Volhynia. Other Mennonites from the colonies in the Ukraine came mainly to Kansas but

22. See Waltner, "Andreas Schrag Diary"; Abe J. Unruh and Verney Unruh, *Tobias A. Unruh*. The Diary of Paul Tschetter is reprinted in Hutterite Centennial Steering Committee, *History of the Hutterite Mennonites*, 29–47.

23. Hiebert, *Brothers in Deed*, which has a reprinting of Funk's account of the journey in *Herald of Truth*, beginning on 57 and continuing on intermittent grey pages.

24. Waltner, "Andreas Schrag Diary," 24–25.

25. Hiebert, *Brothers in Deed*, 65.

26. Hiebert, *Brothers in Deed*, 123–46.

with significant communities also in Nebraska, South Dakota, and Minnesota. In all, about ten thousand Anabaptists came to the United States in 1874 and subsequent years of the 1870s.[27]

I have undertaken a fairly extensive description of the 1873 delegation to North America because of what it tells us about the nature and character of the various parties involved. I am struck, first of all, by the solidarity of faith exhibited by the various Anabaptist groups in question. While the various groups shared a Germanic ethnic and cultural identity, it was their Anabaptist faith that bound these groups together. That was true first of all in Russia itself, where all the Anabaptist groups cooperated in responding to the Russian edict of 1870, first in making appeals to the czar and then by organizing the 1873 delegation to explore emigration to North America. But the solidarity extended beyond that to include the Mennonites in North America who were captivated by the plight of the Anabaptist groups in Russia and rallied to support their cause with moral and financial support. It was this solidarity that was responsible in no small measure for the transplantation and then the formation in North America of the agrarian communities under discussion.

Secondly, I am struck by the amount of interest and assistance given to these Anabaptist groups by the various secular agencies involved, including the governments of Canada and the United States, and the railroad companies who were so instrumental in arranging for the transplantation and early settling of these Anabaptist communities in North America. To be sure, much of this was self-interest on the part of these secular powers. They were quite eager to have the vast lands of the Great Plains, so recently taken from First Nations, to be settled by industrious, frugal, and resourceful peasants of European ethnic heritage. But no small attention was paid to the unique character of this minority sect of Christian faith, particularly in the newspaper accounts describing the arrival of these immigrants from Russia. The *Brothers in Deed to Brothers in Need* scrapbook is replete with newspaper clippings describing these prospective or new settlers and their strange non-resistant faith.[28]

Thirdly, I'm fascinated by what this delegation of 1873 suggests about the motives of these would-be immigrants. While freedom to practice their non-resistant Christian faith was clearly paramount in their search

---

27. Dyck, *Mennonite History*, 154–55.

28. Representative clippings can be found in Hiebert, *Brothers in Deed*, in secular newspapers from New York, 60; Topeka, 66; Yankton, 152, 153; Manitoba, 153; and Topeka, 163.

for a new homeland, these Anabaptist groups were also clearly seeking a *promised land*. They had been living on the margins of European imperial powers for several centuries, often as little more than serfs beholden to the nobility that put up with their strange faith in order to gain from their agrarian proclivity and productivity. While living as second-class citizens was their preference, without the obligations of citizenship which involved conscription and taxation for war, it is wearisome to live at the margins of civilization. The promise of land to make their own along with religious freedom was in no small measure the lure that brought these Anabaptist immigrants to the New World.

All this brings us back to the title of this section—twelve *spies*. While I have found no references to confirm that the Anabaptist groups were trying to emulate the experience of the children of Israel in the wilderness, sending out twelve spies to reconnoiter the promised land in Num 13 and 14, I hardly think it was accidental that a delegation of twelve men representing all the Anabaptist groups in Russia was chosen. Those preparing to leave Russia for the New World were on their way to their promised land, after centuries of wandering in the wilderness of European empires. This sense of a new destiny in promised land had both positive and negative implications for the agrarian communities that came to be planted on the prairies of the Great Plains in the 1870s, a subject to which we shall return.

EMIGRATION PREPARATIONS

It would be fascinating to be able to sit in on the reports the twelve delegates to North America made to their respective constituencies in September 1873, after their long trip. A good portion of Andreas Schrag's diary is devoted to a description of the fearsome storm he and some others traveling back at that time experienced on the Atlantic crossing back to England.[29] I am not aware, however, of primary descriptions of the delegates' reporting to their communities. Undoubtedly, however, their positive report regarding the land of the Great Plains, the support of their North American Mennonite brothers and sisters, and the generous terms offered to them by the governments of Canada and the United States, sealed the incipient conviction that they must emigrate.

29. Gary J. Waltner, "Andreas Schrag Diary," 27–29; Gering, *After Fifty Years*, 21.

Nevertheless, this was not a decision made without many doubts and fears as well. One early historian of the Swiss Amish group, P. R. Kaufman, says that he had a book at his home in Russia describing North America as a "land of poison snakes, lions, tigers, and dangerous Indians."[30] Indeed, it was likely the stories about the Indians that would have most fed the fears of these would-be immigrants, as they were often portrayed as violent savages.

Plans for emigration began on both sides of the Atlantic Ocean throughout the fall and winter of 1873. In the villages of Volhynia, this involved the process of acquiring passports and visas allowing them to leave the Russian Empire. Among the Swiss Amish communities, a committee composed of Jacob Wedel, Andreas Gering, and a sympathetic Lutheran who knew Russian well, Mr. Foss, was appointed for this task. When it became evident that legal help would be needed, the committee engaged a Russian lawyer, Iliasiwicz, to assist them. There was much paperwork to fill out and eventually the cost of the passports (one per family) came to nearly fifty dollars each, but by March 1874, most of the families in these villages had their passports. Families were also provided with official birth and marriage certificates by their congregations, as the church records were the primary source of this information in these closed and isolated villages.[31]

The other major task of these soon-to-be emigrants was the disposal of whatever properties they had in Russia, arrangements for financing the voyage, and packing what could be taken along. Among the Swiss Amish villages, only some of those in Waldheim and Kotosufka owned their land. In most of the villages land was rented or leased from local noblemen, sometimes on long-term contracts. The leases were held by the community and the land divided among the village residents.[32] Several members of the community were appointed to seek buyers for the property of the families, and these men traveled as far as Warsaw seeking prospective buyers. In spite of this, many sold what little they had at a loss, since there was a glut on the market with entire villages selling their goods.[33]

30. Schrag, *European History*, 81.
31. Schrag, *European History*, 81.
32. Schrag, *European History*, 75.
33. Schrag, *European History*, 81.

The Community's Birth in Immigration and Displacement (1874)

Leaders of the Swiss Amish and Low German (Prussian-Polish) Mennonites in Volhynia were keenly aware that many of their members would need financial assistance for the trip to America. Leaders of the Swiss villages sent a letter to American Mennonites seeking financial assistance for those of their brethren who had no resources for the trip.[34] Similar overtures were made to American Mennonites on behalf of the Low German Volhynian villages like Karlswalde, despite their own efforts to raise funds among themselves in the months prior to emigration.[35] Seven Low German villages eventually received around $40,000 from the American Mennonites for the voyage. All the fares for the trip from point of origin to United States destinations averaged about forty dollars per person, with children under fifteen going for one-half fare.[36] Needless to say, these figures represent no small sum in today's dollars.

While these preparations were being made among the Anabaptist groups in Russia, a similar urgent set of plans was being put into place in North America. Primarily through the publications and efforts of John Funk, American Mennonites had been made aware of the plight of their Russian Anabaptist brothers and sisters, beginning in 1872 and continuing through the delegation visit of 1873. In December 1873, representatives of two committees representing two regional Mennonite associations, the Western District Conference and the Indiana Mennonite Conference, met in Summerfield, Illinois. These two committees merged to form the Board of Guardians to oversee both the solicitation of funds from Mennonite congregations and the administration of these funds to the Anabaptist groups in Russia. Officers of this committee were Christian Krehbiel, David Goerz, John Funk, and Bernhard Warkentin.[37]

In addition to the Board of Guardians, a similar committee with the name Canadian Aid Committee was established under the leadership of Jacob Y. Schantz in Ontario in 1873.[38] Early in 1874, still another committee, the Mennonite Executive Aid Committee, was established in Pennsylvania under the leadership of John Shenk, Gabriel Baer, Herman Godshall, and Casper Hett.[39] Funk wished to combine these three committees as one,

34. Schrag, *European History*, 80–81.

35. Boese, *Prussian-Polish*, 65–68.

36. Abe J. Unruh, *Helpless Poles*, 98; Schnell, "John F. Funk," in Krahn, *From the Steppes*, 82.

37. Schnell, "John F. Funk," in Krahn, *From the Steppes*, 78.

38. Schnell, "John F. Funk," in Krahn, *From the Steppes*, 79.

39. Schnell, "John F. Funk," in Krahn, *From the Steppes*, 80.

but there were differences regarding which rail line to use to transport immigrants from the East Coast to the Great Plains. There was nonetheless significant cooperation between these three committees in the aid and assistance they offered to the Anabaptists in Russia, both in fundraising and later in assisting the immigrants upon their arrival in North America in 1874 and following years. Both the Canadian Aid Committee and the Board of Guardians raised more than $40,000 to assist the Russian Anabaptists, and it is believed the Pennsylvania Mennonite Aid Committee may have raised even more, but the records were apparently lost in a fire.[40]

It was no small thing to contemplate a move and journey of this magnitude. Jacob Stucky, an elder of the Swiss Volhynian villages who led his village of Kotosufka to Kansas in 1874, wrote *Ein Auswanderungs Lied* (An Immigration Hymn) which apparently was sung by many of the Anabaptist groups in Russia as they embarked on their journey to America. The simple verses relay some of the hopes and fears of these people on the eve of their generation's great adventure.

> The time and hour is now at hand,
>   We're moving to a foreign land;
> Where souls by thousands prosper well,
>   Dauntless with tears, we say farewell.
>
> The time and hour is now at hand,
>   We're moving to a foreign land;
> Our wagons loaded stand in row
>   With wives and children we shall go.
>
> The time and hour is now at hand,
>   We're moving to a foreign land;
> Our horses hitched, to wagons stand,
>   We're leaving for an unknown land.
>
> To our beloved ones and our kin,
>   We say farewell and sigh within;
> Weep not so hard that we must part,
>   It grieves our weary saddened heart.
>
> Be manly and renew your strength,
>   As time goes on we'll meet at length;
> We still remain upon this sphere,
>   Where God's protection will be near.

40. Schnell, "John F. Funk," in Krahn, *From the Steppes*, 88–89.

When we embark the ship at sea
    We'll join in songs of jubilee;
We fear no water and no waves,
    For God is there and His love saves.

When we'll arrive on yonder shore,
    God's holy name we will adore;
We'll shout when we step on the strand,
    America, thou blessed land!

Welcome, thou fatherland, afar
    Where favored gates stand wide ajar;
We now our land of birth disown,
    We've chose a home in lands unknown.

Farewell, farewell, my fatherland,
    Farewell again, my kindred band;
Some day we'll meet on heaven's shore,
    'Neath peaceful Palms forever more.[41]

THE JOURNEY TO AMERICA

For most of the immigrants under discussion, the trip to America was a complex and difficult journey. It involved first of all taking their families and possessions by carts or wagons from their villages to railroad stations nearby. Then came a long several-day rail journey across eastern and northern Europe to ports in Germany or Belgium or England. Then came the trip across the Atlantic by steam ship to ports in America, generally New York but sometimes also Philadelphia. Upon arrival in America, the bulk of immigrants again traveled by rail to the Great Plains, though some stayed in the East for a time to work off their debts and earn money for settlement. Those coming to Dakota Territory came by rail to Yankton, the capital of Dakota Territory on the Missouri River. From Yankton they again traveled by wagon or oxcart or on foot the thirty some miles to the eventual site of their homesteads around what became the Freeman community.

    Few of these people had ever traveled by rail, much less by steam ship. Under good conditions, the whole journey might be concluded in just over a month, as in the case of the first Swiss emigration under the

---

41. Translation by Abe J. Unruh of Montezuma, Kansas, in Tschetter, *Benjamin G. Boese*, xxix, with original German in side-by-side columns. Another translation by P. J. Albrecht can be found in Stoddard, *Turner County*, 40–41.

leadership of Andreas Schrag. This group left their homes on April 10 and arrived in Yankton on May 27, 1874.[42] On the other hand, those on the ill-fated SS Abbotsford spent two months on the Trans-Atlantic voyage alone, waiting for repairs and backtracking after storms at sea.[43]

It is possible for many descendants of these immigrants to identify the specifics of the journey made by their ancestors through ship lists and informal family histories.[44] On the other hand, it is much more difficult to provide a comprehensive and accurate account of the number of immigrants who arrived in the Freeman area in the 1870s.

We know, for instance, that virtually all the people in the four Swiss Volhynian Amish villages (about a thousand people in all) emigrated en mass to America in four groups, beginning with arrivals in New York on May 18, and continuing through August 31, 1874. This latter group, from the village of Kotosufka, nearly all settled in Kansas; all the rest came to Dakota Territory. All told, some eighty-five to one hundred families with perhaps a population of about five hundred people came to Dakota Territory, with an additional eighty or more families going to Kansas. Those coming to Dakota Territory all took homesteads in the area east and south of the current location of Freeman.[45]

A similar emigration occurred among the scattered Low German Mennonite (Prussian-Polish) villages in Volhynia. However, these villages emigrated a little later, mostly in the fall and early winter of 1874. The first group to emigrate from Volhynia was the village of Heinrichsdorf, located southwest of Kiev, near Berdichev. This village left for America in the summer of 1874, arriving in New York on September 2, on the SS Colina, After wintering along the Missouri River near Yankton, this group of over twenty families (about 150 people) settled south of what would later be the town of Avon, South Dakota, about sixty miles southwest of the Freeman community. However, in the early years in particular, this

---

42. Gering, *After Fifty Years*, 23.

43. Boese, *Prussian-Polish*, 68–70, story told below.

44. For instance, my father's grandfather Christian came on the SS Chester from Liverpool to New York, arriving August 24, 1874, and my mother's father, Abraham Boese, came on the SS Colina from Antwerp to New York, arriving on September 2, 1874; Hiebert, *Brothers in Deed*, 167, 175.

45. Ship lists for the Swiss Volhynian people can be found in Hiebert, *Brothers in Deed*, 152, 162, 167–68, 172–73. See also Figure 2, Migrations of the Swiss Volhynian Mennonites.

community maintained close relationships with the Anabaptist groups around Freeman.[46]

The village of Michalin near Berdichev was the first Prussian-Polish village in Volhynia, established in 1791. Thirty-two families from this village arrived in Philadelphia on November 27, 1874. About a half dozen of these families eventually came to the area around Marion, South Dakota, while others settled in Kansas.[47]

The largest and leading village of Prussian-Polish Mennonites in Volhynia was Karlswalde. The spiritual leader of the Prussian-Polish Mennonites was Tobias Unruh, one of the 1873 delegates to America, who died soon after coming to Dakota Territory in 1875 and is buried at the Schartner Cemetery northeast of Freeman. People from Karlswalde and associated villages emigrated in three groups. The first two arrived in New York on November 18 and Philadelphia on November 27, 1874.[48] The third group left Antwerp on November 13 but had the most difficult journey. Their ship, SS Abbotsford, collided with another ship in the English Channel and limped into London for repairs, where small pox broke out leading to a number of the group being quarantined in London on a ship. The rest of the group continued on the SS Abbotsford after repairs, but the ill-fated ship broke down in a storm and nearly sank. After being pulled back to Queenstown, Ireland, the passengers were taken back to Liverpool to board the SS Kennilsworth, finally arriving in Philadelphia on January 9, 1875. The quarantined group of thirty-five families in London finally arrived in Philadelphia on January 29, 1875.[49]

The majority of people in this group wintered in Kansas, where some stayed and homesteaded. Others of this group moved to Dakota Territory in the early spring of 1875, settling in the area just east of Silver Lake north of Freeman. They purchased a building built the previous year by the Hutterite Wolf Creek Colony that then settled along the James River. The Karlswalders used the building as a settlement house for new settlers coming to the area.[50]

---

46. Boese, *Loretta's Settlement*, 9–10, 96,
47. Abe J. Unruh, *Helpless Poles*, 112–13.
48. Unruh, *Helpless Poles*, 111–12.
49. This story is chronicled in multiple sources that do not always agree on details, including Boese, *Prussian-Polish*, 68–70; and Unruh, *Helpless Poles*, 118–24. A fictionalized story of this voyage is found in Jones, *Land of Their Own*, 155–61, 167–79.
50. Boese, *Prussian-Polish*, 75–77.

The largest group of Prussian-Polish Mennonites, those from the Antanofka villages, arrived at Philadelphia on Christmas Day 1874, after a long twenty-one-day journey across the Atlantic hindered by storms and breakdowns of their ship, SS Vaterland. The bulk of this group of 682 people settled in Kansas, and many eventually joined the Church of God in Christ, Holdeman, denomination.[51] Many of these Prussian-Polish Mennonites were quite poor (hence the title of Abe Unruh's book, *The Helpless Poles*). Arriving as they did in the middle of winter and somewhat unexpectedly, the ability of the American Mennonites to cope with their needs was challenged. While most of the Prussian-Polish Mennonites emigrated, there were those who stayed behind. Some of them did emigrate later. These groups also were more likely to be separated in the United States, with some staying with Mennonite families in various places to work off their travel debts and earn money for homesteading.

In addition to the Low German Mennonite (Prussian-Polish) settlement from the Karlswalde villages that settled east of Silver Lake, another Low German Mennonite group also came to settle in the area between Freeman and Marion. This was actually the first larger Mennonite group to come to America, arriving in Dakota Territory in September 1874. They were a part of a larger group of immigrants from the Molotschna Colony in southern Ukraine that settled in Henderson, Nebraska, and Mountain Lake, Minnesota, as well as Dakota Territory. The Dakota group eventually formed the core of the Bethesda Mennonite Church.[52]

The third Anabaptist group that begin emigrating from the Ukraine to America in 1874 was the Hutterite community. Nearly all the people of Hutterite background (about 1,250 in all) came to America between 1874 and 1879. The first large group of 382 arrived in New York on June 17, 1874. This group got stranded west of Lincoln, Nebraska, where thirty-six of their children died, before coming to Dakota Territory in the summer of 1874. Here they established the Bon Homme Colony along the Missouri River west of Yankton, and the colony that settled east of Silver Lake north of Freeman. This latter group sold their building the next year to the Karlswalde Low German Mennonites in 1875 and moved to Wolf Creek along the James River nine miles west of Freeman, becoming the Wolf Creek Colony. Others in this group, the *Prairieleut*, settled on

---

51. Abe J. Unruh, *Helpless Poles*, 115–17, 179.
52. Bethesda Mennonite Church, 125th Celebration, 18.

private prairie homesteads just west of where Freeman would be established, where they eventually formed the Hutterdorf Church.[53]

One other Hutterite *Prairieleut* group arrived in New York late in 1874, November 6. After wintering in Elkhart, Indiana, with Mennonite hosts there, they came to Dakota Territory in the spring of 1875, settling between Freeman and Bridgewater on individual homesteads to form the Neu Hutterthal Church. This group was led by Paul Tschetter, who had been one of the twelve delegates to America in 1873. Another larger group of Hutterites arrived in 1877 and formed the Old Elm Spring Colony west of Bridgewater. Two further groups of *Prairieleut* people that came in 1878 and 1879 settled just northwest of Freeman on individual homesteads where they established the Hutterthal Church.[54]

In all, about eight hundred of the Hutterites settled on individual homesteads west and northwest of Freeman to become the *Prairieleut*, the Prairie People of the Hutterites. The other 450 Hutterites established the three original Hutterite colonies on the Missouri and James Rivers, and from these three mother colonies all the other Hutterites colonies in the United States and Canada have descended.[55]

During these same years, 1873 to 1879, Dakota Territory became the home for the Reformed and Lutheran communities that settled south and west and north of Freeman, as described in chapter 3. In some cases, we can determine to some degree the number of households that made homestead claims. Heritage Hall Museum and Archives has maps of the Swiss Volhynian, Low German, and Hutterite homesteads in the area.[56] While all these Germans from Russia found a few homesteaders already making claims in the area, families often had the opportunity to make claims near each other on the prairie. This virgin land that before had witnessed only a passing band of aboriginal Americans now found itself encroached upon and populated, often with three or four families per square mile, each with a 160-acre homestead. One estimate is that about two thousand people of Anabaptist origin came to Dakota Territory in the 1870s.[57]

---

53. Hofer, "Hutterite Colony."
54. Hofer, "Hutterite Colony."
55. Hofer, "Hutterite Colony."
56. See Figure 5, Settlements of the Germans from Russia in the Freeman Area, for the location of these various 1870s immigrant groups.
57. John D. Unruh and John D. Unruh Jr., "Daniel Unruh," 203.

The story of the journey to America highlights again the fact that all these people, whether Anabaptist or Reformed or Lutheran, tended to come to America not as individuals or even as families, but as villages that also were and understood themselves to be worshipping congregations. These people understood their journey not as an individual or family adventure but as a community endeavor. This communal solidarity was the hallmark of their identity both as individuals and as a community, and was perhaps a key factor in both their survival and their success as they came to this virgin prairie.

Settlements of the Germans from Russia in the Freeman Area

HOW DID THEY COME TO DAKOTA TERRITORY?

Earlier in this chapter when I wrote about the 1873 delegation to America, I indicated that the Volhynian delegates, Andreas Schrag and Tobias Unruh, as well as the Hutterite delegates, had been quite taken with the Red River Valley in what is now North Dakota and planned to recommend that as the destination for their communities. None of the group of delegates in 1873 visited southeast Dakota Territory, where Freeman is now located, although they did visit Minnesota and Nebraska. Yet when the Swiss Volhynian, Prussian-Polish Low German Mennonite, and Hutterian communities arrived in America, they all seemed to make a beeline for southeast Dakota Territory. How are we to explain this uniform change of plans that led to the formation of the rural community of Freeman, South Dakota?

It is likely due to the first Mennonite settler to come to Dakota Territory—Daniel Unruh, who came to America on August 15, 1873, along with a party of nearly a hundred Mennonites from Crimea. Daniel Unruh was a wealthy Mennonite, originally from the Molotschna Colony in Russia, who moved to Crimea in the late 1850s. He and his party were early arrivals in America, arriving about the time the twelve Anabaptist delegates were returning to Russia with their report. This group of Mennonites traveled to Elkhart where the bulk of the group found temporary work while Daniel Unruh and several others explored the West in search of a place to settle. He apparently made one trip from the end of August to the end of September, exploring Kansas, Minnesota, and northern Dakota Territory, as well as portions of Iowa and Wisconsin. The group was strongly courted by William Seeger of the Minnesota Immigration Board and eventually a few of this group did settle in Mountain Lake, Minnesota.[58]

After returning to Chicago, Daniel Unruh was approached by James S. Foster, Commissioner of Immigration for Dakota Territory, who convinced him to explore southeast Dakota Territory, which he did in early October 1873. By mid-October, Daniel Unruh had made up his mind. He would take his group to southeast Dakota Territory. On October 16, his group of seventy-seven people left Elkhart by train and traveled to Yankton, then capital of Dakota Territory. After wintering in Yankton, the group made its way to the area along Turkey Ridge Creek about fifteen miles southeast of Freeman where they established their homes.[59]

Daniel Unruh was something of an anomaly among the Anabaptist immigrants to Dakota Territory. He purchased land from previous homesteaders or the government rather than claiming land under the Homestead Act, buying one section (four quarters) of land in 1874 and several additional tracts of land through 1879. He also initially established homes for himself and his family on the European village pattern, with seven houses in a row, though this pattern was abandoned a few years later. Unruh could do this because he bought the land, and he and

---

58. John D. Unruh and John D. Unruh Jr., "Daniel Unruh," 206–8.

59. Unruh and Unruh Jr., "Daniel Unruh," 208–9. See Figure 5 for the location of Unruh's settlement.

his family didn't have to reside on the land in order to prove their claim. Unruh and his seven children and their families established a large farm with sheep, cattle, and horses in addition to field grains.[60]

It is fairly clear that Daniel Unruh's decision to bring his family to Dakota Territory in 1873 is the seed that sprouted the growth of three Anabaptist communities around Freeman. However, the exact contacts that brought these groups to join Daniel Unruh in Dakota Territory remain a mystery. It was long assumed that there had been a meeting in New York City between Daniel Unruh, just arriving in New York, and Andreas Schrag, just embarking on his return trip to Russia as part of the 1873 delegation. Indeed, Schrag himself in his diary recounts a meeting with "Mennonites from the Russian Crimea" who were disembarking as he was embarking on the same ship.[61] John J. Gering, in *After Fifty Years*, assumed that this was a meeting between Schrag and Unruh which later led to Schrag taking his first Swiss Volhynian group to Dakota Territory in 1874.[62]

John D. Unruh and his son, John D. Jr., in their *Mennonite Quarterly Review* article on their ancestor Daniel Unruh, describe in a footnote how this was impossible.[63] Unruh and his party left for Elkhart by train on August 18, and Schrag did not embark on his return voyage to Russia until August 21.[64] Schrag must have met a different group of Crimean Mennonites also making an early arrival in America. However, we do know that Jacob Buller, another of the twelve delegates who traveled with Andreas Schrag and Tobias Unruh, was an old friend of Daniel Unruh, so perhaps through their correspondence Schrag and Unruh learned of Unruh's settlement in Dakota Territory. It should also be noted that the Dakota immigration commissioner was quite active in recruiting immigrants to Dakota Territory, so perhaps that is a channel by which later Anabaptist immigrants were led to learn about Daniel Unruh's settlement in Dakota Territory. John Funk himself might be the most obvious link in these mysterious chains of information, since he was acquainted with both Daniel Unruh and the twelve delegates. In any case, it turns out that some Anabaptist immigrants arriving in America in 1874 and thereafter ended

---

60. John D. Unruh and John D. Unruh Jr., "Daniel Unruh," 209–10.
61. Gary J. Waltner, "Andreas Schrag Diary," 26.
62. Gering, *After Fifty Years*, 20.
63. Unruh and Unruh Jr., "Daniel Unruh," 212–13.
64. Waltner, "Andreas Schrag Diary," 26.

The Community's Birth in Immigration and Displacement (1874) 93

up coming to Dakota Territory close to Daniel Unruh's settlement, including half the Swiss Volhynian group, a good number of the Prussian-Polish Mennonites from Volhynia, the Hutterite groups, and Low Germans from the Molotschna Colony as well.

THE FIRST WINTER, 1874 TO 1875

Arriving as they did on virgin prairie and most of them in mid-to-late summer 1874, the first immigrant communities in Dakota Territory faced the daunting prospect of establishing their lives in this harsh environment. They first had to build shelters for themselves and their families—initially sod houses constructed with slabs of prairie sod cut from the prairie grasses they were also breaking for the crops they hoped to plant. But in 1874, they could scarcely expect to plant and harvest more than some vegetables and perhaps a few small patches of grain.

It's difficult for any of us to imagine what the virgin prairie of this community looked like when these immigrant communities arrived here in the 1870s. The land had only recently been surveyed and laid out in sections (640 acres) and quarters (160 acres), a work completed in 1866 and 1867.[65] Turner County was officially established by the Territorial Legislature on January 13, 1871, by taking eight townships from Hutchinson County to the west and ten townships from Lincoln County to the east, both previously established counties.[66] The county was named for John W. Turner, a settler and educator from the area and a member of the Territorial Legislature. The first white settlement in Turner County was made in 1869,[67] and a settlement at Swan Lake was the first county seat.[68]

There were no roads in 1874, only the markers in the sod marking out the quarter sections, as described by Rölvaag in his novel of the Norwegian settlers north of Sioux Falls.[69] The lines between these markers later laid out the township section-line gravel roads that grid the community so uniformly into square miles north and south and east and west. But there were apparently some wagon trails meandering across the prairie. I know this because the remnants of one such trail crossed the

---

65. Stoddard, *Turner County*, 13.
66. Stoddard, *Turner County*, 13–14.
67. Stoddard, *Turner County*, 20.
68. Stoddard, *Turner County*, 169.
69. Rölvaag, *Giants in the Earth*, 109–13.

yard of the farm I grew up on about six miles east of Freeman, crossing in front of our barn. Remnants of that trail can still be seen in that yard, which we were told was a wagon trail from Marion to Yankton. Had it been previously a trail laid out by Native American bands crossing the broad prairie?

The first shelters of these pioneers were simple structures. Based on interviews with then-living members of the pioneer generation, Gary Waltner describes the construction this way.

Author's photo from Sod House on the Prairie at Sanborn, Minnesota

> The sod houses were built of sod that had been broken with a "sod breaker" that each farmer had purchased in Yankton. The plow was pulled by a team and sometimes by two teams, because the grass roots were very tough. As the farmer turned the sod with his plow, someone would cut it into "bricks" of two-foot lengths. Then the "bricks" of sod were laid much in the same order as bricks. The walls were about a foot and a half thick, which kept the heat inside during the winter and the heat outside during the summer . . . The sod house roofs were made of long grass. Long poles needed for the roofs and other parts were cut at the James River or other streams and hauled to the

settlement on the running gear of a wagon. Roofs were shaped like an inverted V or sloped down to one side only.[70]

Small stoves were purchased in Yankton to heat these sod houses and for cooking, though a few larger homes built *Russian ovens*, structures five or six feet high of mud or clay (or later, bricks) in the interior of the house, which was an efficient way to heat houses that had more than one room. Twisted bundles of prairie grasses and buffalo and cow chips (dried manure) were used as fuel as there were no trees on the prairie except along the creeks and rivers.[71]

These new settlers were granted no reprieve! John Gering in his booklet, *After Fifty Years*, notes how the community already experienced prairie fires during their first fall on the prairie.[72] This is his description of their first winter on the prairie.

> It not only came sooner than they were ready for it but was much more severe than they had expected it would be.... Crowded in their small, hastily constructed sod houses with poorly fitting doors and windows, without heaters and only the tall grass twists to burn, with a poor supply of clothes and bedding, they were exposed to untold suffering from the cold. Snow fell for days and the genuine old-time Dakota blizzards, like howling lions, swept over the bare prairies laying siege to the little sheltering places of the settlers as if bent on annihilating them. Some could not leave their shanties for days on account of the immense drifts of snow blockading their openings. Food supplies became scarce and some families were compelled to live on corn bread and water. Entire families remained in their beds most of the time to keep from freezing and the only water obtainable was by melting snow.[73]

New born infants are quite helpless, and we expect that they need the help of adults, usually their parents, to survive and to grow. We should not be surprised that infant communities are much the same. Had it not been for the help and generosity of established Mennonite communities in the eastern United States, this newly-born community on the prairie might have been decimated, and might not have survived at all. In September 1874, a delegation of four men from the Mennonite Executive

70. Gary J. Waltner, "Economic Conditions," 2. See also Figure 6, Sod House.
71. Waltner, "Economic Conditions," 3.
72. Gering, *After Fifty Years*, 30–31.
73. Gering, *After Fifty Years*, 33.

Aid Committee of Pennsylvania visited the newly established Anabaptist communities in Dakota Territory. They brought with them one thousand sacks of flour which were left to be divided among all the Anabaptist groups in the area by a local committee composed of Andreas Schrag, Dirk Tieszen, and Daniel Unruh.[74]

Also in 1874, about $400 was received from the Mennonite Board of Guardians in Elkhart in response to an appeal by Andreas Schrag in June 1874, and a church in Johnson County, Iowa, provided a loan of $657.[75] These are amounts reported by the Swiss Volhynian Amish group, and perhaps similar help was received by the Low German and Hutterite communities. John Gering speaks about two thousand sacks of flour purchased in spring, 1875, through a donation made by a Mr. Yoder and a Mr. Nafziger, which was then distributed by the same local committee that distributed the first one thousand sacks of flour.[76] Perhaps this flour was purchased with the $300 Waltner and Unruh note was given in 1875 by a Butler County, Ohio, church,[77] or perhaps Gering is speaking in error about the earlier one-thousand-sack donation of flour in the fall of 1874. Amazingly, these pioneer communities survived their first winter on the Dakota prairie with relatively few losses, due to the significant help they received from Mennonites in the East and undoubtedly also the sharing done within the community itself, as neighboring families looked out for each other.

The arrival of the pioneer immigrants in 1874 marked the birth of the Freeman community. It was a tenuous and fragile community, in many ways as helpless as an infant, as indeed it was. All of the groups that came to this area were so small! How from these few pioneer families and immigrant villages could a thriving and healthy and sustainable community grow? That is the question we will explore in the next chapters of this book.

---

74. Gary J. Waltner, "Economic Conditions," 7.
75. John D. Unruh and Gary J. Waltner, *Andreas Schrag Document*, 4.
76. Gering, *After Fifty Years*, 34.
77. Unruh and Waltner, *Andreas Schrag Document*, 4.

5

The Community's Growth to Maturity (1875 to 1925)

SYNOPSIS

THE MENNONITE GROUPS THAT came to America in 1874 arrived as villages that had lived and worshipped together in the Ukraine. Though they had known and related to one another in the Ukraine, their daily life was limited to the isolated villages where they lived which were also their congregations (parishes). Given the constraints of settlement options, living in village settings was not possible here in Dakota Territory, as isolated homesteads needed to be claimed. On the other hand, all three groups under discussion (Swiss German, Low German, and Hutterian) were living in closer proximity to each other than they ever had in the Ukraine. While this presented opportunities for greater cooperation between them, it also presented them with the challenge of living and worshipping and working with others who while so similar to themselves were still known primarily by their village or ethnic origin. This often led to conflicts, particularly in the establishment of churches. Swiss and Low German churches were separate from each other, but even within these groups, conflict often erupted as congregations were established within each of these groups based on their village identities in the Ukraine.

Despite the fractious history, congregations were the first institution beyond the family to be established on the prairie. Church buildings began to be built by 1879, and church leadership began to transition to a new generation. These church leaders functioned as pastors and often also as social, political, and educational leaders. Despite the village and ethnic loyalties and identities, the character of these early congregations also took shape, with these congregations reaching out both to one another and to the other Mennonite immigrant communities as well as the earlier Mennonite settlements in the eastern United States. Congregations in the Freeman area were at the founding of an area conference and joined and hosted a national Mennonite assembly.

Indicative of the growing cooperative spirit among the immigrant communities around Freeman was the establishment of South Dakota Mennonite College in 1900 at the instigation of a far-sighted leader, F. C. Ortman. These pioneers recognized the need for an educational institution that would preserve the German language and train teachers for the rural country schools, all within the context of religious instruction. While two world wars with Germany effectively killed the German language of these communities, Freeman Junior College was soon training teachers, preparing them to teach in the rural schools. The college not only broke down the ethnic barriers between the sponsoring groups, but also brought to this rural community a spirit of inquiry and openness to the world.

These early decades also saw the establishment of towns and villages to serve as commercial centers for the scattered rural population. The railroad came through in 1879, and the city of Freeman was incorporated in 1893, along with other towns and villages along the rail line. The railroad became a key link for rural communities like Freeman with the rest of the world, bringing to the community needed commodities and materials and providing a market for the agricultural produce of the community. Cooperatives of various kinds were established for marketing and communication, often in partnership with other surrounding communities of Germans-from-Russia who also came to the Midwest at the same time.

HOMESTEADING ON THE GREAT PLAINS IN THE LATE NINETEENTH CENTURY

Despite being purchased by the United States from France in 1803 as the Louisiana Territory, the vast area of the Great Plains, stretching west from the Mississippi River to the Rocky Mountains, had hardly any American residents through the first half of the nineteenth century.

Louisiana became a state in 1812, Missouri in 1821, and Arkansas in 1836,[1] but it wasn't until the 1840s that there was significant settlement west of the Mississippi River beyond these states.[2] In the first half of the nineteenth century, the frontier for United States settlement was still in the states west of the Appalachian Mountains and east of the Mississippi River—Tennessee, Kentucky, Ohio, Indiana, and Illinois. United States expansion in those years was primarily in the south and southwest, with Texas becoming a state in 1845 and the war with Mexico in 1846 to 1847 conquering the Southwest.

The frontier began to expand seriously across the Mississippi River in the 1840s, with Iowa statehood in 1846, Wisconsin in 1848, and Minnesota in 1858. By 1850, the Missouri and Big Sioux Rivers were the frontier. But it was also the eastern boundary of what was still thought of as the *Great American Desert*. American imperial ambitions had shifted to the West Coast in the 1840s, and the territories of California and Oregon. California became a state in 1850, and Oregon in 1859. American interests had leapfrogged across the Great Plains to the West Coast. The Great American Desert was simply the obstacle to cross on the way to the West Coast, but not a place to live.[3]

Crossing the Great Plains was accomplished by pioneers along the Mormon, Oregon, and California Trails of the 1840s, particularly following the Mormon trek of 1846 and the California Gold Rush of 1849. The Pony Express crossed the Great Plains in the early 1860s until the Transcontinental Railroad was built from Omaha, Nebraska, to the West Coast and completed in 1869.[4] The first treaty of the United States with First Nations of the Great Plains, the 1868 Treaty of Laramie, was designed to protect the railroad and the pioneers on their trek west.

From the first purchase of Louisiana Territory from France in 1803, the imperial designs of the young United States of America on the entire American continent was evident. The Lewis and Clark Expedition of 1803 to 1806, commissioned by President Thomas Jefferson, had the initial aim of finding a transcontinental, mostly river route to the Pacific Ocean. The first resource coveted and exploited by the United States was the fur trade of the Great Plains and Rocky Mountains previously managed by the French,

1. Hicks et al., *Federal Union*, 307, 392, 481.
2. Lavin et al., *Atlas*, 81–85.
3. Hicks et al., *Federal Union*, 568.
4. Hicks et al., *Federal Union*, 541, 717.

the Spanish, and the British, using Native American First Nations as trading partners. However, Jefferson himself recognized the finite nature of the fur trade, and foresaw the day when there would be an influx of American settler expansion onto the Great Plains both through the westward migration of American citizens and through immigration from abroad.[5]

Confronting both of these movements onto the Great Plains were the Indian nations inhabiting the continent. Jefferson envisioned the civilization of Indians east of the Mississippi, and the expulsion of those who resisted being Europeanized across the Mississippi into Louisiana Territory. Stephen Ambrose recognizes the hypocrisy of Jeffersonian policy toward the Indian nations. "Join us or get out of the way, the Americans said to the Indians, but in fact the Indians could do neither. By pushing them ever west, the Americans made it impossible for the Indians to become civilized as they meant the term, and it turned out there was almost no place where the Indians would be out of the way of the onrushing pioneers."[6] American settlement of the Great Plains would come at the cost of the destruction of the cultures and peoples of the Indian nations.

Iowa was largely settled by 1850, and much of Minnesota was opened for white settlement in the Treaty of Traverse des Sioux in 1851. The American frontier was now the Missouri, the Big Sioux, and the Red Rivers on the western borders of Iowa and Minnesota. Though settlement was slowed by both the Civil War and the so-called Indian War of 1862 in Minnesota, the end of the Civil War in 1865 opened the way for further expansion of settlers onto the Great Plains. Indeed, provisions were made in the Homestead Act of 1862 for the preferential treatment of Civil War veterans in settling the Great Plains.[7] Steven Kinsella in *900 Miles From Nowhere*, describes the settlement of the Great Plains in these terms: "It mattered not who you were, what language you spoke, your religion or ethnic background, or the social status of your family; all you had to do was find your way to the Great Plains, where a promising future awaited you. Union Civil War veterans, adventurers, seekers of wealth and status, college graduates, freed slaves, newlyweds, Europe's economically and socially downtrodden, speculators, extended families,

---

5. Ambrose, *Undaunted Courage*, 346–47.
6. Ambrose, *Undaunted Courage*, 348.
7. Kinsella, *900 Miles from Nowhere*, 7.

The Community's Growth to Maturity (1875 to 1925)

and single women all seized on the opportunity to share in the wealth and bounty of America's land."[8]

This was the background of the huge migration to the Great Plains in which our forebears who came to the United States in the 1870s participated. Again quoting Kinsella, "In the second half of the nineteenth century, the world was still largely an agriculture-based society, and land ownership signified prosperity and social status. Free or cheap land under the Homestead and Preemption acts opened doors of promise for Europeans, including Russians, who had endured generations of poverty, and Scandinavians, who lived under a system in which only oldest sons could inherit land. Millions of Norwegians, Swedes, Finns, Irish, English, Scots, Germans (including ethnic Germans residing in Russia), Dutch, Czechs, and religious minorities such as Mennonites and Hutterites flowed onto the prairies in search of economic opportunities."[9]

It is doubtful that our forebears who came to settle around Freeman understood very well the implications of this wave of migration onto the Great Plains in which they were participating. They were willy-nilly engaged in an enterprise of nation/empire building that would forever impact the unique ethnic and religious heritage they brought with them so assiduously from their previous homeland in the Ukraine. The question was how long they could maintain their unique identity before being swallowed up by the energy and vitality of American imperial ambitions for the vast region of the Great Plains. Did our forebears really know what they were getting into when they decided to settle in America? Just as the people of Israel's choice to have a king in 1 Sam 8 set the course for Israel's development of a national identity at the expense of their local, agrarian culture, so our choice to become landed in the United States set the course for the loss of our cultural/ethnic identity and our acculturation into the dominant American society.[10]

THE FIRST FORMATIVE YEARS

The first years of these neighboring Russian-German cultures were formative in the same way that a child's infancy and childhood is formative. These communities were susceptible to all kinds of influences present

---

8. Kinsella, *900 Miles from Nowhere*, 7.
9. Kinsella, *900 Miles from Nowhere*, 7.
10. See Kaufman, *Healing*, ch. 8, for a fuller discussion of these themes.

on the American frontier and within the dominant culture of American society. They were dependent for their communal life and even their physical existence on the North American Mennonites who had already assisted them on their journey to America. These Mennonite communities from the eastern United States functioned in many ways as surrogate parents for these recently arrived settlers on the Great Plains.

We have already noted the aid and loans made to all the immigrant Mennonite groups by the three aid committees set up among the established Mennonite communities in Ontario, Pennsylvania, and Indiana. These aid committees also assisted the Anabaptist groups around Freeman with flour during their first winter in Dakota Territory. A grasshopper invasion that devastated at least half the crop of 1876 precipitated another crisis in the Schweitzer community.[11] Two leaders, Andreas Schrag and Joseph Graber, went to Pennsylvania in January 1877, to appeal for additional aid from the Amish and Mennonite churches of Lancaster County. In addition to a gift of over $1,000, the two men came back with $7,400 given as loans from specific farmers in Pennsylvania, to be distributed to the various members of the community in Dakota Territory.[12]

Records kept by Andreas Schrag are available for fifty-four of these notes—some for $50, the majority for $100, and a few for up to $300—made as loans to specific farmers in the Schweitzer community. Schrag acted as the middle man in this process, collecting the loan payments from local farmers and forwarding the payments to leaders in Pennsylvania, who repaid the original lenders. In addition to the individual notes, the Schweitzer community also drafted and signed (sixty-eight signatures) a document committing the whole community to repayment in the event that individual loans were defaulted on. After Andreas Schrag's death in 1899, his brother-in-law, Rev. Christian Mueller, continued the record keeping. The last loans were repaid in 1905, twenty-eight years after the loans were first made.[13] While to us these may seem like paltry loans, in the economy of the 1870s a $100 loan represented the potential for a considerable investment in livestock, field equipment, and building supplies, allowing a farmer to become established on the Great Plains.

Despite the assistance they received, the resilience of these pioneer communities of the Great Plains cannot be overstated. This is surely due

---

11. Gary J. Waltner, "Economic Conditions," 12.
12. John D. Unruh and Gary J. Waltner, *Andreas Schrag Document*, 7.
13. Unruh and Waltner, *Andreas Schrag Document*, 7–12.

to their long history of informal communal living in subsistence village economies. The Germans-from-Russia who came to Dakota Territory in the 1870s had lived for decades, in some cases centuries, as self-sustaining agrarian villages. Frequently they did not own the land they lived and worked on in Europe, but lived as second-class citizens improving the lands of the noblemen or rulers who invited them. As agrarian villages, these enterprising agriculturalists had within their village the whole range of skills required for a subsistence economy. There were blacksmiths, wood and leather craftsmen, wagon-makers, wheelwrights, brick-makers, millers, basket-weavers, and other crafts people. Women engaged in spinning and weaving cloth. Even without canning and freezing foodstuffs, people had learned to preserve food by drying vegetables, smoking and salting meat, making yogurt and cheeses from dairy products, and storing produce and fruits and dairy products in cellars or well houses. Taken together, these various skills of daily living enabled agrarian villages to develop a comfortable if yet simple lifestyle utilizing the gifts the land provided in each place to which they sojourned.[14]

These subsistence economies created the vast majority of the tools the people needed to sustain their lives. It was no matter to them that towns and cities were thirty or more miles away. One or two visits to the city in a year enabled them to purchase the few supplies like coffee and sugar and salt and cloth they needed or desired. And in any case, they had no ready source of income with which to pay for anything beyond these bare essentials. In the first years on the prairie especially, they were fortunate just to have the land produce what the family could survive on through the winter. The point is that these peasant, agrarian people who came to the Great Plains were skillful and resourceful people who together could create a sustainable life from the land.

If there was a handicap these pioneers faced here on the Great Plains, it was that the pattern of land tenure given to them didn't allow them to live in villages. Instead, they needed to homestead and live on the land they claimed when they arrived. That disrupted the village economy to which they were accustomed. It is much easier for a subsistence economy to function when all the skills and crafts necessary for life are in proximity to each other. The isolation of individual homesteads was particularly hard for women, who were often confined to the homestead

---

14. Many of the artifacts at Heritage Hall Museum and Archives bear witness to the persistence of these skills in the Freeman community well into the twentieth century.

by the demands of the household and had little opportunity to foster relationships with neighbors and peers.[15]

Early Pioneer Homestead. Painting of the Miller Homestead by George J. Kaufman, Freeman artist.

It is interesting to ponder how the geography of a place might mitigate some of the challenges of living on isolated farms. I grew up on the edge of the Turkey Ridge Valley, looking down into the valley and onto Turkey Ridge itself beyond the creek from my home place. It was easy for me to grow up with a sense of who our neighbors were and where they lived, as the contours of the valley exposed the various farmsteads in the neighborhood.

THE FORMATION OF PIONEER CONGREGATIONS

While these small, agrarian cultures around Freeman received financial and physical support from other more established Mennonite communities in America, they also received spiritual help and guidance. These small communities had related to other groups of their faith in Russia, but the transition and settling here in North America was disorienting for

15. See Figure 7, Early Pioneer Homestead, a painting by a local artist, George J. Kaufman, of the farm of Jacob Miller. Courtesy of Heritage Hall Museum and Archives.

these infant communities. While they shared the socio-economic challenges of pioneer life on the prairie with their *English*, non-Anabaptist neighbors, there was a language barrier, and the theological and cultural beliefs and practices of these neighbors proved challenging, at least for these small Anabaptist-related groups.

Swiss Volhynian Churches

The Swiss Volhynian group of Amish background I know best was perhaps particularly challenged in this way. Not only did they confront zealous missionaries like Seventh Day Adventists who proselytized in their community,[16] but they were still trying to figure out their own identity as well. While parts of three different Swiss Volhynian villages settled east of Freeman, two groups dominated—the Waldheimers and the Horodischers. As early as 1876 these two groups had organized into separate congregations.[17]

The Horodisch group's elder, Peter Kaufman, suffered a stroke in 1878 and was unable to provide strong leadership for this part of the community. Meanwhile, the Waldheim elder, Johann Schrag, cultivated relationships with the Amish communities in the eastern United States, attending Amish bishops' meetings in Illinois and Ohio in 1875, 1876, and 1878, when this series of meetings ended.[18] Schrag's Amish leanings apparently disqualified him from being considered for leadership by the Horodisch contingent.[19] Clearly, the Swiss Volhynians suffered both a leadership and an identity crisis.

The community dealt with the leadership crisis by choosing and appointing new leaders. In April 1878, the Horodisch group invited Elder Jacob Stucky from the Kotosufka village that had settled at Moundridge, Kansas, to come to South Dakota and assist in the selection of new leaders. Potential ministers were nominated during a communion service on May 6, after Elder Stucky had led services for several days. The following Sunday, May 12, lots were drawn to choose leaders from among those nominated. The lot fell to Christian Mueller, the brother-in-law of one of the community's leaders, Andreas Schrag, and Christian Kaufman, who

---

16. John D. Unruh, *Century of Mennonites*, 52.
17. Swiss-German Centennial Committee, *Swiss-Germans*, 50.
18. Nolt, *History of the Amish*, 290.
19. John D. Unruh and Gary J. Waltner, *Andreas Schrag Document*, 23.

happened to be a half-brother of Stucky's wife. That afternoon these two men were ordained by Elder Stucky as *predigers* (preachers), and they were to give leadership to the Horodisch group for the next generation. The following year (1879), Elder Stucky returned from Kansas and Christian Kaufman was chosen and ordained to be the elder (bishop) of this group.[20] Meanwhile, the Waldheim group also chose new leaders in 1879. Jacob R. Schrag, son of the Amish-leaning Johann Schrag, and Joseph Kaufman, son of Elder Peter Kaufman, were chosen and ordained by Elder Johann Schrag.[21]

The original Salem Church (1880)   The Zion Church (1881)

In this Swiss Volhynian community two congregations were formed: the Zion church two miles east and two miles south of Freeman (Turner County, Childstown Township, Section 7, SE quarter), and the Salem church four miles east of Freeman (Turner County, Rosefield Township, Section 34, NW quarter; 27844 443rd Avenue). The Zion church was led by Elder Johann Schrag, and the Salem church by the two leaders chosen in 1878—Christian Mueller and Christian Kaufman. Both congregations built meeting houses at the sites noted above, the Salem Church in 1880

---

20. John D. Unruh and Gary J. Waltner, *Andreas Schrag Document*, 24.
21. Salem-Zion Mennonite Church, *Looking Back 100 Years*, 91.

and the Zion Church in 1881.²² The Zion Church was referred to locally as the *Schpitzige Kirche* for the steeple that adorned the church. In 1888 a good number of the Zion Church, including their pastor, John R. Schrag, left to re-settle in Oregon. The remainder of the Zion congregation decided in 1894 to join the Salem congregation, forming the Salem-Zion congregation. Services were held at both locations until 1902, when a storm destroyed the Zion church building, and it was never re-built.²³

While the Waldheim and Horodisch village loyalties were resolved with the merger of the Zion and Salem congregations in 1894, these village loyalties may have been operative again when a new Salem congregation left the Salem-Zion church in 1908. This was for the most part a friendly split occasioned by the growth of the Salem-Zion congregation, which by 1908 had well over 350 members. The new Salem congregation established itself and built a meeting house (Turner County, Childstown Township, Section 16, NE quarter; 28103 443rd Avenue), two and a half miles south of the Salem-Zion congregation on the *Church Road*, so the two churches came to be known as the *North* and the *South* churches. The logic of the location on the edge of the Turkey Ridge Valley was to make the meeting place more accessible by horse and buggy to those who lived in the valley. It is a dramatic and scenic location on the edge of the valley, as I can attest, having lived in the parsonage on that location for eleven years as the church's pastor!

The fact is, however, that by 1908, the Salem-Zion congregation was again in the midst of another leadership crisis. The congregation's first elder, Christian Kaufman, died in 1906 on a mission trip to Alsen, North Dakota, where he had helped establish a small congregation of Swiss Volhynians who had moved there.²⁴ As the pastor of the Salem Mennonite Church in 2008, its centennial year, I had a series of sermons on the church's heritage. I posited that the leadership issue was one of the reasons for the withdrawal of Salem from Salem-Zion. The Salem church, composed of many Horodischers, were advocating for seeking pastoral leadership from the larger Mennonite world, while the predominantly Waldheimers who remained at Salem-Zion retained the older Amish pattern of calling leadership from within the congregation until well into the 1930s. While the Salem-Zion pastor, Christian Mueller, withdrew and

22. Salem-Zion Mennonite Church, *Looking Back 100 Years*, 48, 91. See Figure 8, Salem and Zion churches.

23. Salem-Zion Mennonite Church, *Looking Back 100 Years*, 91.

24. Salem-Zion Mennonite Church, *Looking Back 100 Years*, 66–67.

provided leadership for the new Salem congregation in 1908, by 1911 the Salem congregation had called Christian Hege, a trained pastor from the eastern United States, to be their pastor.[25]

In addition to these internal leadership questions, the Swiss Volhynian community also had to resolve the question of its identity. Were they *Amish* or *Mennonite*? Already in Volhynia, this group had learned to know and work together with the other Mennonites in Russia, and both Mennonites and Amish in the eastern United States had assisted them in their immigration from Russia and their settlement on the Great Plains. We've already noted above that the Waldheim elder, Johann Schrag, clearly wanted to maintain the Amish identity, attending Amish bishops' meetings in the eastern United States in the mid-1870s.

Meanwhile, the community was also being visited and courted by Mennonites. Already in 1877, the Anabaptist groups around Freeman were visited by Samuel S. Haury, a missionary representing the General Conference Mennonite Church, organized in 1860 with the intention of bringing together all the Anabaptist groups in North America.[26] Samuel F. Sprunger, pastor of a Mennonite congregation in Berne, Indiana, who had come to America directly from Switzerland, visited the Freeman community three times, in 1877, 1879, and in June 1880, for the dedication of the first Salem church building.[27] Sprunger was the *Reiseprediger* (traveling preacher) for the General Conference, but the common Swiss heritage of Sprunger and the Schweitzers was likely a bond between them. Both of these Mennonite leaders expressed concern for the spiritual well-being of these isolated Anabaptist groups out on the Great Plains, saw their vulnerability to other Christian proselytizers, and invited them to affiliate with the General Conference.

In a letter to Sprunger in September 1879, Salem-Zion pastor Christian Mueller wrote that the "conference question" was unresolved, but that he personally was advocating for conference affiliation.[28] The Salem-Zion church did join the General Conference already in 1881, sending delegates to the ninth General Conference meetings at Halstead, Kansas, held November 14 to 21, 1881.[29] Indeed, only nine years later, the Salem-

---

25. Kaufman, Centennial Sermons and Talks, tenth sermon on "Leadership Changes"; also John D. Unruh, *Century of Mennonites*, 57.

26. John D. Unruh, *Century of Mennonites*, 49.

27. John D. Unruh and Gary J. Waltner, *Andreas Schrag Document*, 24–27.

28. Unruh and Waltner, *Andreas Schrag Document*, 25.

29. Krehbiel, *History of the General Conference*, 378.

Zion congregation hosted the twelfth national session of the General Conference, held October 16 to 22, 1890. This source identifies the location of the church as "Childstown (Ourtown)."[30] The town of Freeman was barely on the map in 1890! A year later, the Salem-Zion pastors were instrumental in the formation of the Northern District Conference in Mt. Lake Minnesota, an area conference of the General Conference Mennonite Church.[31]

The die was cast! The Swiss Volhynian congregations of South Dakota would be Mennonite, not Amish, though elements of Amish practice and culture continued to characterize the community. It was, nonetheless, a monumental communal choice that shaped the subsequent agrarian character of the community significantly.

Low German Churches

The Low German groups settling northeast of Freeman came from the villages associated with Karlswalde in Volhynia, along with a group from the Molotschna colony in the Ukraine, some families from Michalin (province of Kiev), as well as Crimea. Bound together by a common language and ethnic heritage, these groups initially sought to form one large congregation of Low German people.[32] The large group from the Molotschna colony came to the area without a resident minister,[33] while the Karlswalde community had several ministers. One of these was Elder Tobias Unruh, who had been one of the 1873 delegates to America, but he unfortunately died only a few months after he arrived in the area early in 1875.[34]

The death of Elder Tobias Unruh in July 1875, precipitated a leadership crisis within the Low German community in Dakota Territory. The community had two ministers, Peter P. Unruh Sr. and Peter T. Unruh, but they had not been ordained as elders and could not meet the demands of leadership for the large number of immigrant families. Late in 1875, the Low German communities in the area, including those settled northeast of Parker, chose four new ministers: Dietrich Neufeld, Seibert Goertz,

---

30. Krehbiel, *History of the General Conference*, 384–88.
31. Schmidt, *Northern District Conference*, 1–2.
32. Boese, *Prussian-Polish*, 82–83.
33. Bethesda Mennonite Church, 125th Celebration, 13.
34. Boese, *Prussian-Polish*, 82–83.

Peter Becker, and Friedrich Schartner. These men were ordained as ministers, and Peter Becker as an elder, early in 1876, at the home of Daniel Unruh in Childstown Township (the first Mennonite to settle in the area) by none other than Johann Schrag, the Amish-leaning Schweitzer elder.[35] Efforts were made to have worship services in homes, but in the spring of

The Derk P. Tieszen House/Barn

Die Grosse Kirche (1879)

35. Boese, *Prussian-Polish*, 87.

1878 the group began to meet in the large earthenware house/barn structure built by "Bonesetter" Dirk Tieszen three miles west of Marion.[36]

The new elder chosen in 1876, Peter F. Becker, did not resolve the leadership crisis. Becker, from the Karlswalde group, left the main group of Low Germans with some followers already later that year, once again leaving the community without an elder of their own. In 1879 another group of leaders were chosen and ordained, including Abraham Williams, Karl Schartner, and (another) Tobias Unruh, again ordained by Johann Schrag. Also in 1879, another of the ministers chosen in 1875, Friedrich Schartner, was chosen and ordained as elder by Johann Schrag.[37] That year, 1879, the Low German group also built the meeting house five miles west and one-half mile north of Marion, called the *Grosse Kirche* (Big Church), the first meeting house built by the Anabaptist groups that came to America from Russia.[38]

Things now seemed more stable in the Low German community until 1883, when Elder Friedrich Schartner precipitated another split in the *Grosse Kirche*. Two groups in the church vied for control of the church and there were even threats to saw the church in two! Elder Schartner withdrew and later joined with Elder Peter Becker to form the Schartner church six miles west and a mile north of Marion. Meanwhile those left in the former *Grosse Kirche*, mostly those from the Molotschna colony, built their own church later in 1883, the Bethesda church, four miles west of Marion. This church continued to struggle for stable leadership until Dirk P. Tieszen was ordained as elder in 1894.[39]

In this Low German community, it turned out that socio-economic factors and village loyalties prevented the dream of having one unified Low German church from becoming a reality. Perhaps those from the Molotschna Colony were wealthier and more organized, since the Mennonite colonies in Russia had governed themselves for many years. Perhaps the Karlswalde villagers who were quite poor resented their neighbors, but hid their envy behind theological and religious objections about their neighbors being too worldly.[40] Perhaps it was a matter of

36. Boese, *Prussian-Polish*, 88. See Figure 9, Tieszen House/Barn; *Grosse Kirche*.

37. Boese, *Prussian-Polish*, 88–89.

38. Bethesda Mennonite Church, 125th Celebration, 20. See Figure 9, *Grosse Kirche*.

39. Bethesda Mennonite Church, 125th Celebration, 20–21; Boese, *Prussian-Polish*, 89.

40. Engbrecht in *Three Groups, One Story*.

leadership struggles and the desire to exercise power and control in the community. Perhaps it was a lack of clear identity that made these groups vulnerable to outside influences. There is evidence of many, especially in the Parker community, leaving the Mennonites to join the Seventh Day Adventist church.[41]

It is not necessarily a bad thing that smaller, localized communities emerge from within a larger social grouping, as happened within this large Low German community. Effective communal endeavors depend on face-to-face, daily relationships that support and inspire and discipline all the members of the community to contribute their gifts to the work of the community. Smaller, more localized groupings can often be more effective in developing productive communal life, so long as cordial and cooperative and hospitable relationships with neighboring communities exist to facilitate cross-fertilization and prevent in-breeding. Where the history of the Low German community around Freeman went wrong is that the fracturing of the community was too often hostile and divisive, based on power struggles that built walls between the different groups instead of providing for avenues of cooperation and hospitality. While many evidences of a common heritage and history persisted between these Low German communities, the divisive religious fracturing of communal harmony probably weakened the long-term viability of these people as agrarian cultures.

In any case, the centennial historical marker for the Low German community at the Schartner Cemetery six miles north and two miles east of Freeman identifies seven congregations that emerged in the history of the community with significant original Low German immigrant membership since its founding in 1874.

1. There was the first Union Congregation in Bonesetter Tieszen's large house/barn and later in the *Grosse Kirche* (Turner County, Dolton Township, Section 33, NW quarter).

2. There was the *Karlswalde Deutsche Alt Mennoniten Gemenide* (Karlswalde German Old Mennonite Congregation), formed by Elders Peter Becker and later Friedrich Schartner after they withdrew from the Union Church, and which persisted as an independent Mennonite congregation until 1940 (Turner County, Dolton Township, Section 32, NW quarter).

---

41. Boese, *Prussian-Polish*, 101.

3. There is the Bethesda Mennonite Church formed from the other main group of the Union Congregation, a congregation that joined the General Conference Mennonite denomination but then in the mid-1990s withdrew to become an independent Mennonite church (Turner County, Dolton Township, Section 34, SE quarter; 44354 273rd Street).

4. There was the Brothersfield Mennonite Brethren congregation northeast of Parker (Turner County, Brothersfield Township, Section 25, SW quarter), which later became a Methodist church and whose building still stands at this location. Some members of this church later joined the fifth congregation.

5. Silver Lake Mennonite Brethren Church (Hutchinson County, Silver Lake Township, Section 26, SE quarter) was a Mennonite Brethren church just west of Silver Lake that closed its doors in 2003.

6. There was the Bethel Mennonite Church which existed east of Dolton for a hundred years—1892 to 1992, as a General Conference Mennonite Church, until closing its doors (Turner County, Dolton Township, Section 10, NW quarter).[42]

7. There is the Evangelical Mennonite Brethren church, formed in 1893 through a revival movement as part of that denomination (Turner County, Dolton Township, Section 28, SW quarter; 27196 442nd Avenue).[43]

Only two of these seven congregations still exist, the Evangelical Mennonite Brethren Church and Bethesda Mennonite Church, both of them aging, struggling country churches about two miles apart.

Hutterian (*Prairieleut*) Churches

As previously noted in chapter 4, of the Hutterian group of 1,250 immigrants, about a third, roughly 450, formed the three communal colonies from which the historic Hutterite colonies of the Great Plains in the United States and Canada have descended. These were the Bon Homme Colony (1874) on the Missouri River west of Yankton, the Wolf Creek

---

42. The Bethel Mennonite Church building was moved to the grounds of Heritage Hall Museum and Archives in Freeman, where it is preserved and on display.

43. Picture of this Low German marker at the Schartner Cemetery is in Bethesda Mennonite Church, 125th Celebration, 74.

Colony (1874) that settled originally at Silver Lake and then moved to the junction of Wolf Creek with the James River, and the Old Elm Spring Colony (1877), that settled on the James River west of Bridgewater, South Dakota. In Hutterite communal pattern, each of these colonies were also worshipping congregations.[44]

The other two-thirds of the people of Hutterite ethnicity and faith, about eight hundred people in all, came to be called *Prairieleut* (Prairie People), or locally, *Hutters*, because of their unique dialect and ethnicity. These people settled on individual homesteads mostly west and north of Freeman, between Freeman and the James River and the town of Bridgewater to the north. Eventually, these people formed three congregations.

The first group that arrived in 1874 settled mostly immediately west of what was later Freeman, and by 1880 established the Hutterdorf congregation, after the name of their village in the Ukraine (Hutchinson County, Grandview Township, Section 32, SE quarter). This congregation met in the school house built in 1880 in the neighborhood, and built a meeting house in 1901, which served the congregation until it disbanded in 1961.[45]

A second Hutter church which also took the name of its Ukrainian village, Neu Hutterthal, began in 1875 under the leadership of Paul Tschetter, the Hutterite delegate in the 1873 exploration delegation. This group came to America late in 1874 and wintered in Elkhart, Indiana, before coming to Dakota Territory in the spring of 1875. They settled northwest of Freeman toward Bridgewater and also met in a local school until 1888 when a meeting house was built (Hutchinson County, Pleasant Township, Section 27, SE Quarter; 27165 432nd Avenue). This congregation, though small, continues to meet regularly at its original location near Wolf Creek.[46] Until 2017 it was part Central Plains Mennonite Conference, when it withdrew to become an independent Mennonite congregation.

A small group of families from Neu Hutterthal living further north around Bridgewater began meeting together and in 1920 bought a former Methodist church near Bridgewater and established the Zion Mennonite Church in 1940. This congregation also belonged to the General

---

44. Hofer, "Hutterite Colony."
45. Hutterite Centennial Steering Committee, *History of the Hutterite*, 134.
46. Hutterite Centennial Steering Committee, *History of the Hutterite*, 133.

Conference Mennonite Church before withdrawing to become an independent congregation.[47]

Other Hutter groups arrived in 1877, 1878, and 1879, and settled northwest of Freeman.[48] In 1882, this group under the leadership of John Waldner and John L. Wipf built a meeting house about four miles northwest of Freeman. This is the Hutterthal Mennonite Church. It had its origins as a congregation formed in the Ukraine in 1877. The original meeting house built in 1882 was replaced by a larger structure in 1889, and in 1952 the present brick church was erected (Hutchinson County, Grandview Township, Section 9, SE quarter; 27473 437th Avenue).[49] It remained an independent congregation until 1941, when it joined the General Conference Mennonite Church (Northern District Conference).[50] It remains today a strong and vital rural congregation affiliated with Central Plains Mennonite Conference.

As with the other Anabaptist groups we have discussed, the Hutter *Prairieleut* were susceptible to many influences in this new vast setting of the Great Plains. It was a struggle to remain spiritually vital and with a clear Christian identity. In the 1880s, evangelistic meetings led by Mennonite Brethren brought a revival among Hutter families belonging to the Neu Hutterthal church. Led by John Tschetter, a brother of Neu Hutterthal's founding pastor Paul, a new congregation emerged in 1886 and affiliated with the Krimmer (Crimean) Mennonite Brethren Church.[51] It was the Salem KMB Church until the Krimmer group merged with the larger Mennonite Brethren denomination in 1961.[52] Today the Salem Mennonite Brethren Church remains a strong congregation of the Mennonite Brethren, with a building dating to 1974 just a mile south of the Neu Hutterthal Mennonite Church (Hutchinson County, Pleasant Township, Section 34, NE quarter; 43173 272nd Street).

Still one more Anabaptist-related congregation emerged in the 1890s in the City of Freeman, under the leadership of both Swiss Volhynian and

---

47. Hutterite Centennial Steering Committee, *History of the Hutterite*, 133; Schmidt, *Northern District Conference*, 154–55.

48. Hofer, "Hutterite Colony."

49. Hutterite Centennial Steering Committee, *History of the Hutterite*, 134; John D. Unruh, *Century of Mennonites*, 59.

50. Schmidt, *Northern District Conference*, 152.

51. Unruh, *Century of Mennonites*, 62–63; Hutterite Centennial Steering Committee, *History of the Hutterite*, 135.

52. Unruh, *Century of Mennonites*, 63.

Hutterian leadership—Bethany Mennonite Church. Leaders from these groups led services for Mennonites living in Freeman, beginning in the late 1890s.[53] In 1902 a teacher serving the new South Dakota Mennonite College, H. A. Bachman, took over leadership of the congregation, which officially organized in 1905.[54] The current building at 509 South Juniper Street in Freeman was built in 1950. It remains a vital congregation with a diverse Anabaptist-related membership and an affiliation with Central Plains Mennonite Conference.

Reformed and Lutheran Churches in the Freeman Community

While the focus of this book is on the Anabaptist groups around Freeman, it should be noted that Reformed and Lutheran churches were also being formed in other Russian-German immigrant groups who settled in what became the Freeman community. These groups arrived in the same mid-1870s that brought the Anabaptist groups to Dakota Territory. The pattern of their immigration seems very similar to that of the Anabaptist groups, coming as villages or partial villages from colonies in the Black Sea region. In the Ukraine, they were Reformed by faith, and perhaps there was not always a clear separation between Lutheran and Reformed denominations. At least among the immigrant communities, there was a willingness to share worship space as Lutheran and Reformed people.[55] Opinionated leaders often had other ideas.

The Johannestal group was the earliest to arrive in 1873, from a settlement of the same name in Russia, settling about eight miles west of Freeman near the James River (Hutchinson County, Wolf Creek Township, Section 34, NE quarter). Originally Lutheran, the church was organized as a Reformed congregation by several early Reformed pastors in the area including Joseph Orth. Originally reluctant to preach to this group, he finally relented and using the text from 1 Kgs 18, asked "How long hold ye between two opinions." That sealed the Reformed identity of Johannestal. When later a Missouri Synod Lutheran pastor showed up, he wouldn't even enter the church when he heard that Reformed pastors had preached there![56] The Johannestal church built its first building in

---

53. Hutterite Centennial Steering Committee, *History of the Hutterite*, 135–36.
54. John D. Unruh, *Century of Mennonites*, 63.
55. Rath, *Black Sea Germans*, 167.
56. Rath, *Black Sea Germans*, 173.

1877, which was replaced in 1902 by the building now on display at the Heritage Hall Museum and Archives campus. The building was moved to Freeman after the church closed its doors in 1967. Most of Johannestal's members joined the Zion Reformed Church in Menno, as they had shared pastoral leadership with that congregation.[57]

A sister congregation to Johannestal was the Zion-Kassel Reformed Church. This congregation really belongs to the Menno community, originally located just two miles north and a mile east of Menno (Hutchinson County, Kassel Township, Section 34, NE quarter). But being between Menno and Freeman and having many connections with the Freeman community, it is fair to include this congregation in a discussion of Freeman community congregations. The Kassel congregation was formed in 1874 by Joseph Orth. It is said to be the oldest Reformed parish in South Dakota. A meeting house was built in 1879, and in 1958 a new church was built on the east edge of Menno.[58]

A pioneer Reformed congregation whose history has almost been lost is that of the Klein Kassel group who settled north of Freeman. The Klein Kassel community was established by settlers who arrived in 1879.[59] In 1891, the German Reformed Bethany Church was formed and a meeting house was built (Hutchinson County, Grandview Township, Section 5, NE quarter). The congregation dissolved in 1959, with most of its members joining the Johannestal Church, where their pastor (William Korn) was serving. The church had a cemetery a half mile north of the meeting house.[60]

Another Reformed congregation of Germans from Russia, Bethlehem Reformed Church, was established in Freeman in 1892 by Henry Teichrieb. A church with a tall steeple was built in 1892, and replaced by the present structure at 300 South Relanto Street in 1964.[61] This church has had a complicated history of relationships with Reformed denominations. In 1939 the church affiliated with the Zion-Kassel congregation.[62] Today the congregation is affiliated with the Orthodox Presbyterian Church.

---

57. West Freeman Reformed/Lutheran Tour.
58. City of Menno, *Menno: The First 100 Years*, 281–85.
59. Rath, *Black Sea Germans*, 404.
60. West Freeman Reformed/Lutheran Tour.
61. Freeman Centennial Steering Committee, *Freeman Facts*, 63–69.
62. Mendel, *History of Freeman*, 64.

In addition to these Reformed congregations, two Lutheran congregations emerged, both organized by the same Missouri Synod minister. Trinity Lutheran Church was formed by 1874 immigrants from Heilbronn in the Crimea in an area about six miles southwest of Freeman (Hutchinson County, Valley Township, Section 7, SE quarter). In 1875, John F. Droescher preached in this community, and in 1876 organized the church. In 1877, a brick meeting house was built, which was replaced by a wood frame building in 1924.[63] After this country church merged in 1958 with the parish formed in Freeman, the building was moved to Hurley, where it is now the Zion Lutheran Church.[64] There is a marker in memory of Trinity Lutheran Church at its country site. Trinity was the first Lutheran church established in Hutchinson County.[65]

John F. Droescher also organized St. Paul Lutheran Church, Missouri Synod, in Freeman in 1882, the first church established in the new town of Freeman.[66] The first building was completed in 1886, and was replaced by a larger church in 1899. A third, large brick church was built in 1963, at 615 East 7th Street in Freeman. This parish also sponsored a parochial school for elementary students beginning in 1888, which continued into the 1960s.[67]

I have taken pains to outline the formation of the historic Russian-German congregations because I believe that the formation of these churches was integral to the formation and success of the Freeman community. These churches were the first social institutions established by these immigrant communities. Most of them reflect the agrarian cultures and villages that settled close to each other here on the Great Plains. These congregations bear witness to the deep faith of these pioneers, and also to the strength of the cultural heritage they brought with them to America. Many of the pioneers who came to the Great Plains from the eastern United States to take advantage of the promise of free land in the Homestead Act did not have the advantage of this cultural heritage, and the West is full of their failed homesteads.

---

63. Mendel, *History of Freeman*, 70–71.
64. West Freeman Reformed/Lutheran Tour.
65. Mendel, *History of Freeman*, 71.
66. Mendel, *History of Freeman*, 63.
67. Freeman Centennial Steering Committee, *Freeman Facts*, 74–83. Models of each of these church buildings, schools, and parsonages, are in Heritage Hall Museum and Archives.

This chronicle of congregational life in pioneer days is filled with stories of conflicts and separations both social and doctrinal, as well as efforts toward establishing a broader cultural and religious foundation for the community. While we may deplore the divisiveness among these pioneers, as well as the poor spiritual state many of them exhibited, the churches provided nonetheless a solid basis on which to build the fabric of a sustainable rural community.

THE FORMATION OF EDUCATIONAL INSTITUTIONS

After breaking the prairie and establishing their homesteads on a subsistence economy and organizing their religious life as congregations, the pioneer cultures of the Freeman community formed educational opportunities for their children. This is in some ways surprising. The large Mennonite colonies in southern Ukraine had indeed developed a fairly sophisticated educational system, including some higher educational opportunities. But many of the immigrants to the Freeman community came from scattered villages of western Ukraine where anything beyond minimal elementary education was rare. These would seem to have been quite simple peasant people, perhaps literate in their German language, but scarcely more than that. What led them so quickly to seek educational opportunities for their children?

One factor was surely that the United States saw public schools to be a part of the settlement of the West. An early county superintendent of schools, Louis N. Alberty, who served from 1879 to 1884, describes early school history in Turner County. Dakota Territorial laws made provision for both a poll and a property tax to form and support public elementary schools in each township of every county. A county superintendent of schools had the authority to divide the county into districts and subdistricts as need arose and settlements expanded.[68] The first county superintendent in Turner County was James A. Childs (for whom my home township of Childstown is named) in 1872, and he organized six districts for the county.

Successive superintendents in subsequent years kept organizing more districts. At the end of Alberty's term of service in 1883 and 1884, more districts were organized for the western Turner County townships of Dolton, Rosefield, Childstown, and Salem, where many of the

---

68. Stoddard, *Turner County*, 213–28.

Mennonite settlers lived.[69] This development is also noted in essays included in the *Turner County Pioneer History*. An eighth-grade student, Harry J. Kaufman (my father), describes how four schoolhouses were built in 1885 in Childstown Township, after the districts were organized, and that by 1917 there were seven districts in the township.[70]

John C. Mueller, who in 1917 was chair of the local Childstown school board, writes that a school was opened at the home of James A. Childs in 1874, and then was moved to the home of Christian Kaufman (Salem-Zion elder) across the road, and that other schools met in other homes. He confirms that four districts were established in 1884, and writes that in 1912 the township was further divided into seven local school districts, 92 to 98 inclusive.[71] Hillside District #92 was the school I attended from 1950 to 1958. I assume similar local school districts were formed in other townships at roughly the same time throughout the larger Freeman community among these German-speaking immigrants.

Of course, these being American public schools, instruction was in English, and many early students, including my older siblings in the 1930s, knew hardly any or no English when they began school, speaking only their Schweitzer dialect and understanding only German. On the other hand, the advantage of these local school districts was that they were governed by local school boards, neighbors in approximately a four- to eight-section area of each township. These neighbors governed their own schools locally and hired their own teachers, under the guidance and direction of the county superintendent.

Still, it should be observed that as a matter of public national policy, the introduction of public schools was seen by the government of the United States as a primary vehicle to promote the acculturation of the disparate cultural groups that were settling the Great Plains. This was a way to guarantee that English would be the spoken and written language of these immigrants, and as well, a way to teach the civic duties, rights, and obligations of being an American citizen. We have only to remember the important role Boarding Schools had in the intention of *civilizing* Native American nations, weaning them from their land, their culture,

---

69. Stoddard, *Turner County*, 225.
70. Stoddard, *Turner County*, 109–12.
71. Stoddard, *Turner County*, 117–19.

their language, and their distinctive way of life. The intention was to "kill the Indian in him and save the man."[72]

In this regard, I find it fascinating to read the lists of teachers who taught in these early schools of the Swiss Volhynian community. There is nary a single German surname! The teachers of these schools in John Mueller's account were all what Amish people call *Englishers*—all non-German people![73] If these immigrants had reservations about having *English* Americans as the teachers of their children, it did not seem to dampen their commitment to register their children in these country schools. Additionally, about half of the teachers listed were female.

On the other hand, the fact that these immigrants were conscious of how these public schools could compromise their ethnic and cultural heritage is clear from the way they sought to regain more control over the instruction of their children. This happened, as already seen, in the formation of parochial schools like the one established in Freeman in 1888 by St. Paul Lutheran Church.[74] The first public school in Freeman was built in 1882 where the Lion's Park is today, after Freeman School District #41 was organized in 1880.[75] German-speaking Missouri Synod Lutherans did not lose much time before they reasserted ecclesiastical and cultural control over the education of their children!

The concern can also be seen in the formation of Freeman Jr. College, or South Dakota Mennonite College, as it was first called. This school originated with the vision of Friedrich C. Ortman in the 1890s. Ortman was a second-generation descendant of four brothers of Lutheran origin who immigrated to America with the Volhynian Anabaptist groups in 1874, some of whom affiliated with the Anabaptist groups. Ortman married a Low German woman and affiliated with the Low Germans living east of Dolton. In the 1890s he visited Kansas Mennonites and formed a vision for "providing teachers' training facilities which would help to supply rural district schools with Mennonite teachers capable of teaching both the required English subjects and the German religious classes."[76]

In 1899, he took his idea to Elder Christian Kaufman, the leader of the Swiss Volhynian group east of Freeman. Together they envisioned the

72. Graber, *Gods of Indian Country*, 139–42, quote on 140.
73. Stoddard, *Turner County*, 118.
74. Mendel, *History of Freeman*, 63.
75. Freeman Centennial Steering Committee, *Freeman Facts*, 99.
76. Waldner and Ortman Hofer, *Many Hands*, 1.

building of a school in Freeman to accomplish this purpose, involving all the Anabaptist-related churches and ethnic groups of the emerging Freeman community.[77] After a second meeting with Kaufman in February, 1900, a public meeting was planned and an invitation given to all the Anabaptist churches for March 11, 1900. After a second meeting in Freeman, a third meeting was held on June 17 to settle the location of the school, with several towns including Marion offering their facilities. At a fourth meeting on July 8, Freeman was chosen as the location for the school, and a committee was established to draw up Articles of Incorporation and bylaws. On December 10, 1900, South Dakota Mennonite College was organized and a Board of Directors was chosen. Then came the interlude during which funds were raised and plans made for the building of the school. In 1903, the building was erected, and with the hiring of H. A. Bachman as principal, classes were offered in September 1903.[78]

South Dakota Mennonite College (1903)

Initially, classes were offered for both elementary and secondary students of both genders. One hundred nine students enrolled in the 1903/1904 school year, and 130 the next school year, more than any comparable Mennonite school in the Midwest.[79] The 1905 school year offered

77. Waldner and Ortman Hofer, *Many Hands*, 2.

78. Waldner and Ortman Hofer, *Many Hands*, 2–5. See Figure 10, South Dakota Mennonite College.

79. Waldner and Ortman Hofer, *Many Hands*, 7–8.

courses in four areas: "a two year preparatory course, a three-year academic course, a three-year normal course [to train elementary teachers], and a four year Bible course."[80] Four students graduated that school year, in the spring of 1906.[81] The following year there were eight graduates, four of whom graduated from the normal course, presumably to become teachers in local elementary schools. Elementary grades were discontinued in 1910.[82] In 1918, the first college courses were offered.[83] A gymnasium was built in 1923 and the large instructional building, Memorial Hall (or the Ad Building as it is known to students), was built in 1926.[84]

In 1923, the name of the school was changed to Freeman Jr. College, and in 1927 the school was accredited by the state as a junior college. In 1930, the school was accredited as a two-year teacher training facility.[85] Thus the school was fulfilling the vision of its founders to provide a teacher training facility to provide teachers for the public elementary students in the country schools of the community. This continued until school consolidation began occurring in the 1960s along with the state mandate that all elementary school teachers needed to have a BA degree in elementary education.[86] For more than three decades, Freeman Jr. College churned out a supply of elementary school teachers. Women in particular, who had limited career choices in this conservative community, would get their two-year teacher training degree and teach in local schools for several years, perhaps until they were married. Two of my older sisters followed this pattern.

Until World War I, classes were taught in both English and German. Bible courses were part of the curriculum, and throughout the 1930s winter Bible courses were held for anyone interested in furthering their knowledge of the Bible. After World War I, most courses were taught in English, and German was only offered as a modern language class. Beginning in 1945, the school offered the degree of Associate in Arts for students planning to continue their studies at four-year colleges and universities.[87] Since 1921, the secondary school associated with the college,

80. Waldner and Ortman Hofer, *Many Hands*, 9.
81. Waldner and Ortman Hofer, *Many Hands*, 9.
82. Waldner and Ortman Hofer, *Many Hands*, 10.
83. Waldner and Ortman Hofer, *Many Hands*, 14.
84. Waldner and Ortman Hofer, *Many Hands*, 15.
85. Waldner and Ortman Hofer, *Many Hands*, 16–17.
86. Waldner and Ortman Hofer, *Many Hands*, 160.
87. Waldner and Ortman Hofer, *Many Hands*, 39–40.

Freeman Academy, has been an accredited four-year high school.[88] From then until 1986, the school offered six years of high school and college courses. In 1986, the college closed.[89] Currently Freeman Academy offers classes for grades 1 to 12 as a Mennonite alternative to public schools.

Throughout its history, the core constituency of Freeman Jr. College and Academy has been the Anabaptist groups of the Freeman community. It is evident that the original board of directors had members from all three Anabaptist communities—the Hutter, Low German, and Swiss German groups surrounding Freeman.[90] In all, thirteen congregations are identified as the school's constituents. Nine of these were General Conference Mennonite congregations, and the other four represented Mennonite Brethren, Evangelical Mennonite Brethren, Krimmer Mennonite Brethren, and United Missionary denominations.[91] In addition to these local Anabaptist congregations, from the 1940s to the 1970s the school also received much support and many students from the Mennonite communities of Mt. Lake, Minnesota, and Henderson, Nebraska, each about 150 miles from Freeman, where the churches shared these denominational identities. The school had less success in attracting support and students from the non-Mennonite Russian-German segments of the community and from the town of Freeman. But there was nonetheless always a trickle of students from the larger community who came to receive their teacher training certificates, despite its parochial Mennonite identity.

On the other hand, the school did much to unify and provide a coherent identity for the three Anabaptist groups that were its core constituency. These three groups lived with a keen awareness of each other, and owned their common faith and identity as Anabaptists. Still, their ethnic dialects and customs and cultures frequently created barriers and prejudices that often threatened the harmony and perhaps also the progress of the community's development. So having the school as a common project and a meeting ground did much to break down these ethnic identities and create a common bond between these groups.

The school also brought to the community the influence of other Mennonite communities across the United States through the administration and faculty members it recruited. These more highly educated

---

88. Waldner and Ortman Hofer, *Many Hands*, 14.
89. Waldner and Ortman Hofer, *Many Hands*, 103.
90. Waldner and Ortman Hofer, *Many Hands*, 3.
91. Waldner and Ortman Hofer, *Many Hands*, 51.

members of the community did much to enrich the cultural life of the community. They brought with them new ideas and new perspectives that broke down the narrow ethnocentrism that too often had taken root in these Anabaptist groups, both through their administrative and teaching roles, but also in their participation in the churches of the area.

While these outside influences were by and large positive and progressive for the life of the community, there were at times less helpful influences. The college did not escape the fundamentalist/modernist theological controversies of the 1930s. A president in 1929 to 1930, P. R. Schroeder, a pastor from Berne, Indiana, who then also assumed a pastorate at the Salem Mennonite Church from 1930 to 1940, was an ardent fundamentalist, though he also maintained a strong Mennonite identity and affiliation.[92] While leaders like Schroeder did much to bring a stronger biblical and theological awareness to the community, their influence was also sometimes divisive and probably weakened the traditional agrarian Anabaptist cultures of the community, a point that will be elaborated in chapter 7.

Overall, the school did succeed in fulfilling much of the vision of its founders. Seeing their children taught by *English* teachers with little understanding of the culture and heritage of their students made the community aware of the rapidity of their acculturation to general American society, or what we might call the dominant culture of America. The school enabled them, at least until the convulsions World War I brought to this German pacifist community, to preserve their German language and unique culture. In the school, they were able throughout their history and until today to provide religious instruction for their youth through Bible classes, chapel services, and other Christian influences. And, as noted above, the school did enable them to train their own public-school teachers, so that their students in the rural country school districts would have teachers who understood and reinforced the cultural values and heritage that the immigrants brought with them to America.

---

92. Salem Mennonite Church, A Moment, 48; see also Waldner and Ortman Hofer, *Many Hands*, 17.

THE COMING OF THE RAILROAD
AND THE BIRTH OF FREEMAN IN 1879

The fortunes of the pioneer community on the prairie changed dramatically with the coming of the railroad in 1879. The Chicago, Milwaukee, and St. Paul Railroad extended its rail line from Hull, Iowa, to Running Water on the Missouri River that year. The branch line running southwest from Marion to Running Water is the line on which the towns of Freeman and Menno were established on the normal ten-to-twelve-mile interval between stations.[93] This particular line served the Freeman community until it was abandoned in 1974.[94]

The importance of the coming of the railroad in 1879 to the development of the Freeman community cannot be overstated. Previous to this, the nearest source of supplies or markets of any kind for these Russian-Germans was the city of Yankton on the Missouri River. With a local railroad, farmers in the area had a ready market for the produce of their farms. And they had local sources for groceries for their homes and supplies for their farms, whether that meant coal to heat their homes, building supplies for their buildings, seeds and fertilizers for their fields, or feed for their animals.

The names for the stations of Freeman and Menno have been the subject of some controversy. The most plausible explanation is that the towns were named for the individuals from whom the railroad bought land for the stations—Fred Reiser at Menno and Fred Waldner at Freeman. Reiser worked as a miller at nearby Hutterite (Mennonite) colonies, hence the name Menno. Freeman was a corruption of the name Fred (Waldner). Another version of Freeman's name also involves the name of the original landowner, Fred Waldner. When he was paid by the railroad for his land he supposedly said in German, "Now I am a free man." And so the name of Freeman emerged.[95] But the most popular and enduring, though probably false, explanation for the name is that the rail-workers got the signs for these stations mixed up, so that the Menno name was given to Menno, where there were no Mennonites, while the Freeman name was to have belonged to Menno.[96]

---

93. Mendel, *History of Freeman*, 1.
94. Freeman Centennial Steering Committee, *Freeman Facts*, 8.
95. Freeman Centennial Steering Committee, *Freeman Facts*, 9.
96. Freeman Centennial Steering Committee, *Freeman Facts*, 6–9.

Christ Buechler (1843 to 1904) is credited as being the "Father of Freeman," opening a general store at the corner of what became Third and Main Street in 1879. An 1873 German immigrant and teacher from Odessa, Russia, Buechler and his family settled in Yankton and opened a store there. When the railroad was built and a station established at *Freeman*, Buechler moved his store here (literally, on a hayrack) from Yankton. Two years later he sold his store to the Schamber Brothers and continued to open commercial and banking enterprises which he then sold to various partners.[97] It is said that in 1887, "he purchased the town site and subdivided it."[98] Properties purchased for the building of Freeman belonged to Fred Waldner, Mike Tschetter, and David Kleinsasser, three Hutter men who had homesteaded in Section 35 of Grandview Township, Hutchinson County, where the city of Freeman is primarily located.[99]

While some form of informal organization existed in the 1880s, the earliest minutes of city meetings are dated December 19, 1891, conducted and recorded in German, with Christ Buechler as chair of the council. The city of Freeman was legally incorporated on January 26, 1893.[100] The names of early City Council members confirm that the early leaders of Freeman were indeed nearly all Germans from Russia. While there are Hutter names, it is notable that fewer people from the Anabaptist groups were involved in the early civic life of the community. Perhaps this reflects the sectarian identity of Anabaptists, who always tended to be wary of civic engagement throughout their history.

The first public school was built in Freeman in 1882 at the site of the current Lion's City Park. A hardware and implement store was established in 1882, the latter by Fred Haar and Christoph Guenthner, that later became the John Deere dealership in Freeman. A drug store was established in 1885. St. Paul Lutheran church was built in 1886, the first church in town.[101] Other early enterprises were blacksmith and barbershops, a hotel (1883), a harness shop, and a livery barn. The first grain elevator in Freeman was erected in the 1880s, to facilitate the sale of local farmers' grain and move it out along the railroad.[102] Two local banks, Merchant's State Bank and First National Bank, were established by local

97. Mendel, *History of Freeman*, 1–2.
98. Freeman Centennial Steering Committee, *Freeman Facts*, 10.
99. Freeman Centennial Steering Committee, *Freeman Facts*, 6.
100. Freeman Centennial Steering Committee, *Freeman Facts*, 19.
101. Freeman Centennial Steering Committee, *Freeman Facts*, 16–17.
102. Mendel, *History of Freeman*, 4–6.

entrepreneurs in 1899 and 1902.[103] A local creamery was established in the 1890s. Initially rural farmers would bring their whole milk to town for the cream to be drawn off. Then the skim milk was hauled back home by the farmer for home and livestock use. When cream separators made on-farm separation of cream possible, cream would be collected from the farms and brought to town to be made into butter and dairy products that could be sold elsewhere.[104]

The town of Freeman had a symbiotic, reciprocal relationship with the rural farmers in the area around the city. On the one hand, the city offered farmers goods and services, both for their family and home life and for their farms—feeds and seeds for their animals and fields, lumber and hardware for buildings, and machinery to work the fields. On the other hand, farmers provided the city and its merchants and business people with the products of the land for sale—grain, poultry, livestock, eggs, cream, milk, and other products of the land.[105]

As time passed early in the twentieth century, towns like Freeman offered still more goods and services for both its own residents and the rural population around it. The *Freeman Courier* began to be published in 1901, and was published by J. J. Mendel from 1902 to 1960. In 1960, Pine Hill Printery moved into Freeman from the countryside and Glenn Gering bought the *Freeman Courier* from Mendel.[106] Pine Hill Printery was originally founded by Swiss Volhynian immigrant John C. Gering on a farm two miles east and four miles south of Freeman in the first decade of the twentieth century. His brother Henry meanwhile established a jewelry store in Freeman.[107]

The first medical doctor to practice in Freeman was A. A. Wipf in 1894, with J. P. Isaac opening his practice in 1905.[108] Ernest Hofer, nephew of Wipf, began his lifelong medical practice in Freeman in 1932.[109] Irvin Kaufman opened a practice in 1948, joined by his brother Leroy in 1952, and this grew to be Rural Medical Clinics.[110] In the later 1940s, a number of medical personnel and community members began planning

103. Mendel, *History of Freeman*, 5.
104. Mendel, *History of Freeman*, 8.
105. Freeman Centennial Steering Committee, *Freeman Facts*, 50–53.
106. Freeman Centennial Steering Committee, *Freeman Facts*, 243–47.
107. Freeman Centennial Steering Committee, *Freeman Facts*, 299.
108. Freeman Centennial Steering Committee, *Freeman Facts*, 348–50.
109. Freeman Centennial Steering Committee, *Freeman Facts*, 336.
110. Freeman Centennial Steering Committee, *Freeman Facts*, 346.

for a community hospital. The hospital opened in 1952, with the addition of a nursing home in 1979.[111] Mennonites in the community opening the Salem Home for the Aged in 1949 as a residential home for the elderly.[112] All of these initiatives and others made Freeman a regional health hub.

By fortuitous chance, the city of Freeman was established rather neatly in the middle between the various Russian-German pioneer communities that had been established in the 1870s. There does not seem to be anything deliberate about this. It was an accident of the rail-line being established between Marion and Running Water. It probably led to the success of the town, as it had a large but relatively cohesive rural clientele in every direction from which to grow. There were the Reformed and Lutheran settlements mostly west and south and north of Freeman, the Hutter settlements west and north of town, the Low German settlements north and east of town, and the Swiss Volhynian settlement south and east of town.[113]

I have also found it interesting that the town of Freeman was built at the top of three watersheds that define the geographical setting of the Freeman community. Indeed, the town of Freeman is directly on the boundary between the James and Vermillion River watersheds. The west half of Freeman drains into the James River valley, while the east half drains north into Silver Lake and then eventually into the West Vermillion River northeast of Freeman. And just up the hill to the south of Freeman a mile and a half, the view opens to the southeast toward the Turkey Ridge Creek valley. Indeed, one can stand on that hill south of Freeman on 438th Avenue and see spread out in every direction the vast expanses of these three watersheds merely by turning around 360 degrees! Sometimes chance turns out to be more fortuitous than planning! Here geography in the form of watersheds confirms the centrality of Freeman for these Russian-German immigrants who came to the Great Plains.

---

111. Freeman Centennial Steering Committee, *Freeman Facts*, 336–39.

112. Freeman Centennial Steering Committee, *Freeman Facts*, 302.

113. See Figure 5. Settlements of the Germans from Russia in the Freeman Area, in ch. 4.

6

The Community in Its Maturity (1925 to 1975)

SYNOPSIS

BY THE 1920S THE larger Mennonite community around Freeman had come into its maturity. Churches and schools had been established and taken root. The infrastructure for a viable and sustainable agricultural life had been laid. There was room for the Mennonite community to expand its boundaries and the transportation technologies to make that feasible. Land tenure practices made it possible for many young people to remain in the community and to engage in farming. Additional institutions for health and elder care were being built. Original structures built as houses of worship had been or soon would be rebuilt and enlarged.

By this time the community had acculturated both to the larger American society and to the unique agricultural possibilities and challenges of the land to which their parents and grandparents had come some fifty years earlier. Acculturation to American society took the shape of abandoning the German language, accepting the social and educational mores and practices of American society, and becoming full-fledged citizens of the United States who exercised the privilege of voting and paying taxes and sought the legal recourse of alternative service in lieu of the draft into military service. This acculturation was not without its risks, for it meant the dilution of many of the religious and theological convictions that had brought their forbears to these shores. It was nevertheless

The Community in Its Maturity (1925 to 1975)

a necessary process in order for this community of Mennonites to engage the larger society and dominant culture of America.

The community's acculturation to the unique agricultural possibilities and challenges of the land was a far more important and significant development, marking the emergence of a mature agrarian culture. Agricultural practices known to their forebears in the Ukraine and earlier had to be adapted to reflect the land and climate of the prairie with all its rich possibilities as well as its frequent and harsh constraints of limited rainfall and drought, bitter winters, hailstorms and other natural calamities. The prairie landscape was altered by the planting of shelterbelts and homestead wood lots, and over the years the native prairie nearly all disappeared in favor of crop and pastureland.

What emerged was an odd mix of a fruitful and sustainable agrarian culture that could also function within the dynamic, expanding culture of American society. The solution seemed to be small, nearly self-sufficient farms of limited size oriented toward producing the goods required for a family's sustenance with enough spare production to market and provide for what could not be produced on the farm. There was a strong component of human labor on these farms, along with the use of draft animals and later small tractors. Crop rotations were used, and every farm had animal husbandry to complement the produce of the fields—usually small dairies, chicken flocks, and herds of pigs. Cooperation in extended families and/or neighborhoods augmented the use of relatively modest and non-intrusive technologies. To a large degree the community retained control over the land and its use despite the claims of private ownership imposed upon it by the state. People looked out for one another and sought the welfare of the community at large.

UNITED STATES LAND TENURE POLICY ON THE GREAT PLAINS

The Freeman community was born in the implementation of one of the most radical land tenure policies in history! This sounds like a radical statement. However, apart from the overwhelming fact that the land was in effect stolen from the Yankton Sioux Nation, the 1862 Homestead Act of the United States that enabled ordinary citizens to claim 160 acres of land for themselves was indeed a land tenure policy that is perhaps without precedent in the annals of history. In other words, having taken the land from Native American nations, the United States was in effect giving the land back to its own citizens and thousands of immigrants like the Russian-Germans who came to America in the 1870s.

The 1862 Homestead Act and other similar acts of the United States government were intentional land tenure policies of a growing empire. Having *bought* the Great Plains from France in the Louisiana Purchase of 1803, and then in the next decades successfully disenfranchised and/or destroyed the Native American cultures that lived on the Great Plains, the United States was colonizing the Great Plains with a white, European, Christian population of its preference. The Homestead Act was the primary instrument of this colonization.

Unjust and racist and imperialist as it was at its root, the land tenure policy reflected in the Homestead Act was nonetheless a powerful and historic instrument for putting a vast geographic area of the North American continent into the hands of private property owners, something nearly unprecedented in the annals of history. It enabled the settlement of the land and the creation of countless rural communities like that of Freeman. The residents of these communities became private land owners with a great deal of freedom to utilize their land as they saw fit, either to its and their detriment or to its and their success as farmers and rural communities.

In this book, I intend to be clear about my skepticism regarding private property as the best land tenure policy for sustainable rural communities. It is at its root a misnomer. For all their touted freedom, land owners in the United States were not really free agents. They were beholden to the laws of the land which ultimately assert that the land belongs not to these individuals but to the state (empire), which gave the land to them. In itself, that is not a bad thing, for successful societies need to be governed by laws and legal systems and governmental bureaucracies. But whether intentionally or by design or not, this also enabled the state to exercise control over how landowners use the land. When such controls enable the conservation of the land and its resources, that is a great and needed thing, and something many agricultural policies of the United States achieve. When it dictates that farmers use the land for the interests of the state and the increase of its wealth and power, it can destroy the land, its owners, and their communities. Subsequent chapters will argue that the state through the fiction of private property forced farmers to become beholden to it and the corporations that serve and sometimes control the state.

Still, the fact remains that the Homestead Act is what enabled the birth and maturation and success of the Freeman community. Here every settler, however well- or ill-suited to the agricultural enterprise, was given the opportunity to claim a quarter section to experiment on, to see whether they could succeed, first of all, in surviving on it, and then make a living and grow a community from it. Apart from its racist and imperialist underpinnings, the land tenure policy reflected in the Homestead Act was a radically egalitarian proposal. In addition, those who settled near each other as interrelated ethnic agrarian cultures had the advantage of corporate solidarity and mutual aid to succeed, something many of the prairie homesteaders did not have.

LAND TENURE PRACTICES OF THE FREEMAN COMMUNITY

How did this land tenure policy of the United States take shape in the land tenure practices of the agrarian cultures that made up the Freeman, South Dakota, community? I cannot vouch for how typical the experience of my extended family is, but it is the story I know best.

My pioneer great-grandfather, Christian Kaufman, homesteaded on a quarter section of land in Childstown Township (Section 23, SW quarter), Turner County. Turkey Ridge Creek runs through the southwest corner of this quarter, making the quarter a coveted homestead with access to a perennial stream. Most homesteads in the community had to rely on hand dug wells for their water supply, and sometimes water was hard to find. Until public rural water systems came into the community in the 1970s and 1980s, rural farmers all relied on private wells dug or drilled at or near their homesteads.

Christian Kaufman was in his mid-thirties when he and his family came to America. He and his wife Anna had five children, two sons and three daughters, when they immigrated from Volhynia, and a final son, my grandfather, John C. Kaufman, was born in 1879 here in Dakota Territory. Soon after coming to America, in 1878 and 1879, Christian was called to be a pastor and elder of the Swiss Volhynian community, so soon found himself immersed in pastoral duties. That left his wife Anna and the children to manage the farm. By then his oldest son, Tobias, was a teenager and capable of a man's work.

Christian succeeded in providing a quarter section of land for each of his three sons. The middle son, Jacob, inherited the original homestead. Tobias, the eldest, got a quarter section of land adjoining this homestead (Section 23, SE quarter). John C., the youngest, gained a quarter section two miles north (Section 15, NE quarter). Christian's three daughters married farmers in the local community. It seemed relatively easy for second generation settlers in Dakota Territory to keep access to the land and thus grow the community.

The next generation, my father's generation, began to have difficulty. John C. Kaufman had six sons and one daughter. One son inherited John's farm, and four other sons including my father began life as farmers. The eldest gave up farming to become a blacksmith in Freeman, and the youngest followed various occupations in the community. John C. likely helped three of his sons, including my father, to find land, but they also likely found farms through the inheritance of the women they married. My father and mother bought eighty acres when they married in 1925, on the cusp of the Great Depression, and by frugal living and the grace of their bankers and by being able to rent an adjacent quarter section of land, held on to this farm through the Dirty Thirties, raising six children on it and earning a quiet and fulfilling retirement on the farm.

In my generation, the community's land base became even more fractured. My five siblings and I all went to our church school, Freeman Academy, and four of us went on to achieve college degrees. Two sisters married farmers in the community. One brother inherited a farm from his wife's grandfather and had a successful farm and dairy until his untimely death in 1992. The other brother became a university professor before returning to the land as an organic farmer in Michigan. Of the farms alluded to in the previous paragraphs, many are either abandoned or only rural residences rather than functional farming units.

My maternal grandmother, Helena Buller Boese, came to the Freeman community a little later. Her village of Karlswalde left late in 1874 and because of the series of mishaps detailed in chapter 4, did not arrive in America until January 9, 1875. Her parents, Heinrich and Helena Buller and the younger family members wintered in Newton, Kansas, living in dugouts along Sand Creek. In the spring in 1875 they traveled to southeast Iowa where they worked for their sponsor, Benjamin Eicher, a local Mennonite leader at Wayland, for four growing seasons.[1]

---

1. Boese, Life Story, 12.

Presumably during these years they worked off the debt incurred for their travel and perhaps laid aside some funds to begin a homestead. Late in 1878, Heinrich and Helena along with their five younger children, came to Dolton, South Dakota, where some of the other Karlswalde villagers had settled earlier, including several of Heinrich and Helena's older married children.

My great-grandfather Heinrich Buller bought a quarter section (Hutchinson County, Silver Lake Township, Section 13, SE quarter) between the village of Dolton and Silver Lake to the south. According to my uncle John Boese, Heinrich paid $1.25 an acre for this quarter section ($200.00), so it may have been a pre-emption claim, or he might have bought it from someone else who had homesteaded on it.[2] This homestead was between the homesteads of a son and a son-in-law, so again there was an effort to establish an extended family community. In addition to purchasing his land, Heinrich also mortgaged his land to borrow $1,250 to make improvements on the land. He lost his wife in 1885, and by 1888 he was unable to make payments on his debt. He sold his homestead to a new son-in-law and moved onto another son-in-law and daughter's farm just south of his claim to live out his days.[3] None of these farms are owned by the original families and several are abandoned and no longer in evidence at all.

It is of course difficult and perhaps dangerous to try to draw too many conclusions from these two anecdotal family stories. Not being aware of more substantial land tenure studies for Turner and Hutchinson Counties, however, and having looked at land tenure patterns in the sixteen sections surrounding Salem Mennonite Church during four prayer walks in 2009, I would risk drawing several conclusions.[4]

First, it would seem that pioneer families made some effort to settle on land near each other as extended families. Sometimes that was impossible due to previous land claims in the neighborhood. Not being able to sustain the village life of the *old country*, the pioneers around Freeman did the next best thing. They tried to make claims near each other in order to give support and help to each other on their farms. As transport was limited to foot or horse and buggy, this entailed a considerable sacrifice. Though holding land privately, these first immigrants clearly wanted

---

2. Boese, Life Story, 14.
3. Boese, Life Story, 15.
4. See chapter 7, and Kaufman, "Anatomy" for a review of these prayer walks.

and intended to exercise a measure of communal access to the land on which they lived.

Second, it would seem that second-generation immigrants, coming of age from 1890 to 1910, were able to maintain and sustain their agrarian community and land-holdings quite easily. Despite the early difficult start the pioneer farms had, they began to thrive in the 1880s and 1890s, and with land still being relatively available, farms were often found for each son in the family without compromising the territorial integrity of the community. While there was an exodus of community members in this generation to the West Coast and other communities in the Great Plains, the community grew rapidly. A plat map of Turner County in 1908 still shows quite a number of non-Mennonites living in the community, but the mutual aid and solidarity of the Mennonite community drove out more and more of these non-Mennonites as Mennonite farmers were able to buy them out.[5] In this generation, few community members chose vocations other than farming, though a few early professionals began emerging—teachers and doctors primarily.

Third, in the third generation of immigrant families coming of age in the 1920s, the community began to expand beyond its original, historic boundaries, having saturated these original boundaries. With the arrival of the internal combustion engine, the community could maintain its identity and cohesion over a broader area. So, for instance, the Swiss Volhynian community of East Freeman historically lay between Freeman and Marion on the north, the Marion Road directly south of Marion on the east, and US Highways 18 on the south and 81 on the west. Now the Swiss Volhynian community began expanding beyond these boundaries, particularly east of the Marion Road. This led to the growth of the community numerically, leading to its largest population in the mid-decades of the twentieth century. In this period, it was typical to find three or four farms in each section of land, indicating that the land was being utilized fairly intensively. I suspect similar dynamics occurred in the other agrarian cultures of the Freeman community.

Fourth, the Great Depression had a significant impact on the land tenure practices of the Freeman community in this third generation. The 1920s were boom years in farming, and many farmers, including my father who bought his farm for $200 an acre in 1925, bought land at then high prices. In the Dirty Thirties, many of these farmers abandoned

---

5. See plat map of Turner County for 1908, on the wall at Heritage Hall Museum and Archives, to see a portrait of land holdings at that time.

their impossibly high indebtedness to buy land which in the 1930s was *dirt cheap*. The exchanges of land in the community during the 1930s disrupted the land tenure practices of the community and hastened the trend toward individualized land holdings.

Fifth, in my generation, the fourth of the immigrant settlers, the community began to outgrow its land base. In this generation coming of age in the 1950s and 1960s, young people were encouraged to get an education and move out into the world in the vocations and professions of their choice. Fewer stayed in the community to farm. At the same time, farm size began to increase, due to the mechanization of agriculture. This put farmers in competition with one another for land. Farmers no longer saw one another as partners in the agricultural enterprise, but as competitors for land. Additionally, there was the pressure of a burgeoning population during the community's golden years.

Sixth, in this generation there was simply not enough land to support the agrarian cultures that gave birth to the community. Groups like the Amish confronting this dynamic spawn off new communities near and far, as we see in the spread of Amish communities throughout North America. The fact is that few agrarian cultures have learned how to sustain themselves generationally on their land base for the long haul, and the Freeman community was no exception.

Seventh, the land tenure policy of the United States gave a kick-start to the immigrant agrarian cultures of the Freeman community. Being able to settle on the land without the indebtedness of a major land purchase was an immense boon to local farmers. But it also contributed to the community's decline when the communal social structures of the agrarian cultures began to break down and farmers saw each other as competitors for scarce and increasingly expensive land as farms grew ever larger.

It was of course not foreordained that these cultures needed to acquiesce to the privatization of land ownership and abandon the communal social structures of their agrarian heritage. That was the fateful choice of nearly all the members of the community. In other words, the land tenure practices of the agrarian cultures of the Freeman community gradually transitioned from seeing the land as a communal, familial inheritance to accepting the dominant culture's fiction of land as private property to be used and held by the owner for his or her own wealth and privilege.

ASSIMILATION TO AMERICAN SOCIETY

Every agrarian culture exists as a minority within the larger dominant culture of a society. This has been the case ever since the simultaneous synergistic development of agriculture and urbanization more than six thousand years ago. Agrarian cultures have always had to learn how to navigate within the intricacies of a cooperative but often hostile dominant culture that depends on its agrarian cultures but at the same time frequently exploits them for its own purposes and benefit. And all the while, the agrarian cultures need somehow to preserve their own unique identity, folkways, and land base within that powerful, urban, dominant culture and society.

This process of acculturation or assimilation is something every immigrant population faces in coming to a new land. It is something every local culture encounters when it comes under the hegemony of a dominant or imperial power. Even cultures that resist acculturation, like the Amish or the Hutterites, have to make some accommodations to the dominant culture in order to make economic transactions and legalize their status in society. The most successful agrarian cultures find ways of accommodating their communities to the dominant cultures while maintaining the distinctiveness and locality of their heritage. It is always a process fraught with pain and discord and uncertainty, for it requires the agrarian culture to weigh every adaptation and change and to discern whether cooperation or subversion will be the most fruitful form of interaction with the dominant culture.[6]

Like most immigrant populations to a new land, the Russian-Germans who came to America in the 1870s had no intention of assimilating into American society! Bolstered by their strong ethnic and faith heritage and their communal identity, they saw themselves coming to America to preserve, not lose, their cultural identity. They saw America as a land and society where they could establish their communal identity as a bulwark against religious persecution and economic (land) privation. Here they were promised land and religious freedom, and in their minds, those were the necessary requirements to preserve their cultural identity and faith.

The Anabaptist groups that came to the Freeman community had sojourned for several generations in France, Germany, Prussia, the Austro-Hungarian Empire, Poland, and Russia as landless peasants. They

---

6. See Kaufman, *Healing God's Earth*, ch. 10, for a discussion of the ways agrarian cultures adapt to living within dominant societies.

were in effect aliens in these lands, or at best second-class citizens, living in agrarian villages at the largess of local nobility who could use their agricultural expertise to manage their extensive land holdings. In those circumstances, it was relatively easy to maintain their distinctive cultural, ethnic, and faith identity as a minority, dependent community living in a *foreign* land, as resident aliens without responsibilities of citizenship.

Therefore, these groups were perhaps ill-prepared for the way becoming a landed community in America would erode their cultural and faith identity. Suddenly they were in a situation where they had to come to terms with the economic, political, social, legal, and religious milieu of the dominant culture in which they had come to settle. As a newly landed people, they were suddenly *in the world*, confronting all kinds of choices and questions about how they would live in and adapt to the larger American society around them.

We already saw in the last chapter that all these Russian-German groups almost immediately adapted to and participated in the public-school system the government offered as a way to assimilate the diverse populations settling on the Great Plains. Only tardily did the Anabaptist groups realize that these schools would quickly erode not only their German dialects and language, but also their cultural heritage and their faith. So, perhaps belatedly, South Dakota Mennonite College was established to preserve the language, culture, and faith of the Anabaptist groups, but also to train their own youth as teachers who could in turn teach their children in the public schools.

The German language, in any case, was preserved in nearly all the Russian-German immigrant communities as their mother tongue and primary language, especially for worship, until the First World War. Newspapers like the *Dakota Freie Presse*, which began to be published in 1874 in Yankton, South Dakota, soon became a regional German newspaper and was a major source of news for Russian-German immigrant communities.[7] Of course, denominational religious publications and all religious instruction and worship were printed and conducted in High German, regardless of the German dialect—Hutterisch, Schweitzer, or Low German—spoken in the home. Interestingly, J. J. Mendel, the early and long-time editor of the *Freeman Courier* from 1902 to 1960, resisted the pressure of subscribers to publish the local paper in German, despite his own Hutterish heritage and roots.[8]

---

7. Wikipedia, "Dakota Freie Presse."
8. See Mendel display at Heritage Hall Museum and Archives.

The First World War spelled the beginning of the death knell for German as a public language in America. The German ethnicity of these Russian-German immigrants made them suspect by their *English* neighbors in the war with Germany. When they were also pacifists like the Anabaptist groups, they were doubly suspect as German sympathizers or partisans for their refusal to support the war effort against the Germans. German continued to be used as the worship language of most of these groups until the Second World War, and the dialects were spoken in the homes. But during and after the Second World War, German was used less and less, perhaps only once a month in worship services, before English became the only language used publicly. Today the local dialects are very nearly dead. Only a few people are left who speak Schweitzer or Low German or Hutterish. German is no longer studied even as a second language in the community. The American insistence on learning and using English if you wish to be an American had prevailed.

There is little evidence that the Russian-German immigrants resisted citizenship. Many immigrants became American citizens, and of course, children born to them in America were automatically United States citizens. Evidence is primarily anecdotal, but many in the Anabaptist groups in particular may have resisted civic duties like voting and jury duty, feeling uncomfortable with such participation in the political realm. However, there were from early years exceptions to this reluctance, Mennonites who served on township boards or as county commissioners and city mayors and even the occasional state representative, as well as Mennonites who became lawyers.

For Anabaptist groups, adherence to pacifism or non-resistance to war within American society reflects one way in which these groups navigated their acculturation into American society. Originally, they came with some assurance from governmental officials, including President Grant, that their convictions would be respected here in America. The First World War tested those assurances. No provisions were made in World War I for conscientious objectors to war. That and their German ethnicity combined to create an extremely dangerous situation for these Russian-German immigrants. Mennonites drafted into the military were court martialed for their refusal to bear arms or wear uniforms. Two Hutterite young men from the colonies along the James River died in detention.[9] Some Mennonites refusing to buy war bonds

---

9. This story is told by Stoltzfus, *Pacifists in Chains*, and was reprinted in the *Freeman Courier* in four issues, beginning November 15, 2018, the one hundredth

to support the war effort were tarred and feathered and threatened with more dire consequences.[10]

After World War I, the Anabaptist groups in America worked together in approaching the government and making arrangements for alternative service programs for conscientious objectors. Thus, by World War II, Civilian Public Service camps were organized for conscientious objectors in lieu of military service. In the years following World War II, conscientious objectors could apply for I-W status in the Selective Service System and fulfill their obligations to the state in a variety of humanitarian programs.[11]

The point is that these immigrant, agrarian cultures with a pacifist faith accommodated themselves to the dominant culture in order to make arrangements for the legal recognition of their rights as conscientious objectors to war and violence. In this case they joined forces as Anabaptist groups to engage civic authorities in a respectful but forceful expression of their minority cultural and faith identity, and were able to effect wider societal change that recognized the rights of minority cultures like their own. Since conscientious objection to war was at the heart of their identity as a minority culture, this was a highly significant step in their acculturation to American society.[12]

The irony is that while Mennonites as a whole were managing to retain and even gain legal status for their conscientious objection to war, many Mennonites were rapidly losing this key element of Mennonite identity. For instance, despite having Civilian Public Service camps as a legal alternative, a 1942 study revealed that 30 percent of Mennonite men in the study who were drafted entered the military.[13] While many factors may be involved in this loss of a key Anabaptist practice, the move toward individualism and loss of a communal identity as Mennonites acculturated surely played a role. In addition, having come to their *promised land* and claimed and inherited it, Mennonites increasingly felt that they needed to participate in defending and protecting it from their nation's enemies. Whereas in the villages of the Ukraine they were second class citizens with little to lose, they now had much to lose!

anniversary of their deaths.
- 10. Juhnke, *Vision, Doctrine, War*, 218–29.
- 11. Toews, *Mennonites in American Society*, 129–42
- 12. Toews, *Mennonites in American Society*, 123–28.
- 13. Toews, *Mennonites in American Society*, 149.

This leads to what I as a pastor and theologian consider to be the most crucial Mennonite acculturation to American society—their theological stance. Coming to America as simple agrarian people, the Mennonites struggled to know where they fit within the larger religious scene in American society. We already saw in the previous chapter their struggle to own their identity as Anabaptists. Would they be Amish or Mennonite, independent congregations or part of a Mennonite denomination? They were also easy targets for proselytizers active in the area, and according to some observers, lacked a deep spiritual life.

As Mennonites began engaging more broadly with American society in the first decades of the twentieth century, they were caught up in the controversies of fundamentalism and modernism that were raging in the American religious scene. Once again, Mennonites were challenged to define where they fit. While there were a good number of Mennonite leaders who were drawn to modernism with its emphasis on social justice, they were strongly challenged by more conservative Mennonite leaders who were drawn to fundamentalism. Being for the most part biblicists, Christians who took the Bible seriously and literally, the modernist skepticism regarding some key Christian doctrines were seen as a threat to the conservatives. Later, in the 1940s, Mennonite scholars like Harold S. Bender began to define Anabaptism as a third way, neither fundamentalist nor modernist. But in the 1920s and 1930s, this option had not been envisioned.[14]

Bringing this discussion home to the Freeman community, my home congregation, Salem Mennonite Church, called P. R. Schroeder as their pastor in 1930, and he served until 1940. Coming from a pastorate in Berne, Indiana, Schroeder was a staunch advocate of fundamentalism, and gave leadership to that perspective within the General Conference Mennonite Church. In 1934, he prepared catechetical materials with a distinctive fundamentalist flavor to use in preparing young people for church membership.[15] My grandfather, John C. Kaufman, took correspondence courses from Moody Bible Institute in Chicago, and sent two of his sons, including my father, to take a winter course at Moody. He served as a traveling evangelist for the Northern District Conference in the 1920s.

---

14. Toews, *Mennonites in American Society*, 82–83.
15. The author has a copy of the 1937 revised edition of this *Catechism*.

In these and many other ways, fundamentalist approaches to Christian faith were introduced into the churches of the community. This often led to a revitalization of the spiritual life of the congregations, but it also introduced theological controversies into congregational life. The history of many Mennonite congregations reveals that they were torn between more conservative pastors who were educated at Grace College of the Bible in Omaha, Nebraska (a fundamentalist-oriented school started by Mennonites),[16] and pastors who were educated in liberal arts Mennonite colleges like Bethel College in North Newton, Kansas, and Bluffton College in Bluffton, Ohio.

To be fair, Mennonite fundamentalists typically did not lose their Anabaptist/Mennonite heritage. They continued to espouse and advocate for non-resistance to war and to hold many of the values of historic Anabaptism. But fundamentalism did undermine some of the communitarian and discipleship emphases of Anabaptism. By asserting doctrinal adherence to particular Christian doctrines, they made Christian faith a matter of intellectual assent to propositional doctrines and minimized the historic Anabaptist emphasis on discipleship, following Jesus on a journey of faith. In addition, personal salvation and the assurance of eternal life took precedence over the Anabaptist way of seeing salvation as important for our communal life together here on Earth, how we follow Jesus together in our congregations.

How did this affect the agrarian cultures of the Freeman community? Traditional Anabaptism did not articulate a theology of creation care until recent decades. However, the traditional agrarian cultures of Anabaptism saw their faith as integral to the way they farmed and cared for the land and its life. They knew that creation was the gift of God to the human family, and that they were a part of a redeemed community called to care for God's Earth. The influences of fundamentalism divorced Christian faith from their daily life as agrarian people and undermined the communitarian aspects of their agrarian culture.

While it is understandable that conservative Mennonites early in the twentieth century saw fundamentalism as a more fitting theological perspective to their faith than modernism, the consequences of this theological acculturation to the American religious scene had profound and, in my mind, mostly negative implications for the rural cultures that they served. Agrarian cultures of the Mennonite Church are only in recent

---

16. Toews, *Mennonites in American Society*, 79.

decades beginning to articulate a theological perspective to undergird their agrarian life, and now they are often being taught this perspective by urban Mennonites who are formulating a theology of creation care. Meanwhile, earlier Mennonite accommodation to conservative, fundamentalist perspectives has only hastened the decline and disintegration of Mennonite agrarian cultures.

ADAPTING TO LIFE ON THE PRAIRIES OF THE GREAT PLAINS

The most crucial accommodation of the immigrant agrarian cultures who came to the Great Plains in the 1870s was their ability to adapt to this environment. We have already seen how these immigrants used to living in villages adapted to the pattern of living on individual homesteads. While this meant the loss of a truly self-sustaining subsistence village economy, it was mitigated by the networks of extended family and faith community settlements established by these agrarian cultures as they found homesteads close to their biological and spiritual kin.

Still, this homestead pattern meant that every member of the community had to become a farmer, even those who in their Volhynian villages practiced other trades. For instance, my great-grandfather Heinrich Buller was in Volhynia a drayman, hauling goods for Jewish merchants,[17] and I have to wonder if that is why he struggled to succeed as a homesteader, despite several seasons of working on a southeast Iowa farm to pay off his travel debts. On the other hand, many homesteader farmers persisted in the crafts and skills like carpentry and blacksmithing and masonry they had practiced in the old country, offering their skills to the neighbors who settled near them.

The agrarian cultures who settled on the Great Plains began by raising small grains and the vegetable gardens and orchards they needed for staple foods. In addition, they brought with them their skills in animal husbandry and soon had flocks of chickens, pigs, and cattle. Together, the agricultural endeavors provided the basis for a subsistence economy, providing most of their basic needs as well as some saleable products that could be turned into cash to build houses and barns and to buy the draft machinery needed to farm on the larger scale of the quarter section most of them had.

17. Boese, Life Story, 6.

In his book *Ecological Imperialism*, Alfred Crosby reminds us that European settlers to the New World always brought with them the flora and fauna and germs they had been accustomed to, all of which thrived in the New World and enabled the successful conquest of the Americas.[18] In the case of the agrarian cultures we are discussing, their expertise in animal husbandry and small grains and the suitability of these agricultural enterprises in the environment of the Great Plains greatly enhanced the ability of these settlers to thrive in their new setting.

A case in point for the introduction of European flora into North America is the Mennonite introduction of Turkey Red Hard Winter Wheat into the prairies of Kansas. Developed by a Mennonite miller in Russia, Bernhard Warkentin, this variety of wheat was brought over, a few pounds per family, in the 1874 immigration, and excelled on the Kansas prairie as a hard winter wheat excellent for baking bread.[19] Unfortunately, winter wheat was much more marginal in the harsher climate of South Dakota, so farmers in the Freeman area planted a local variety of wheat.[20]

Sources confirm that the immigrants brought many seeds with them in addition to Turkey Red Wheat. "The Russian Mennonites of 1874 brought their own seeds of wheat, rye, oats, and barley. In addition, they brought garden seeds, flower seeds, and fruit tree seeds. The kind and quantity of seeds brought varied from family to family according to its interests, needs, and economic capabilities."[21] Family tradition indicates that my grandfather, Abraham Boese of Avon, South Dakota, planted a large orchard of apples, plums, cherries, peaches, and mulberries, and there were also native crab apples, plums, and chokecherries, as well as other native berries.[22] I remember on my own parent's farm there was an old orchard of cherries and apples, supplemented in later years by a new large orchard my father planted in the 1960s.

Nearly all homesteaders planted a grove of trees around their homesteads to protect them from the harsh winter winds. In addition, some made timber claims, where an additional quarter section of land could be claimed by planting ten acres of timber. This radically changed the landscape of the treeless prairie to which these settlers came. In addition,

---

18. Crosby, *Ecological Imperialism*, chs. 7–9, 281–93.
19. Stucky, *Century of Russian Mennonite History*, 27–32.
20. John D. Unruh, *Century of Mennonites*, 30.
21. Stucky, *Century of Russian Mennonite History*, 27.
22. Bose, *Johnny Schmidt*, 40–43.

within several decades, these woodlots began providing fuel to heat houses with wood and coal burning furnaces. While coal was purchased to bank fires for the long winter nights, the bulk of the household heating and cooking was supplied by the wood from the wood lots. Early hand saws were supplemented by belt-driven buck saws in the mid-twentieth century, before chain saws eventually made the harvest of timber so much easier.

While most of the crops raised on local farms were familiar to the settlers and had been raised by them in the old country, that was not true of corn—a New World crop. Settlers soon began to plant corn. By the turn of the century, the horse-drawn corn planter was in common use. At first even these planters required a "trigger man" to release the seed at the right time, but when check wires were introduced, corn could be planted in a grid of squares so that cross cultivation could be done to control weeds.[23] While there were some early horse-drawn, ground-driven corn pickers, most corn in the community was picked by hand nearly until the middle of the twentieth century, when tractor-mounted corn pickers became more common.[24]

The harvesting of small grains made a rapid transformation in the first decades of the community. In the first years, grain was harvested by hand with scythes equipped with cradles to catch the grain as it was cut. The grain was then gathered into bundles that were tied by one handful of grain twisted to hold the larger bundle of grain. Originally, grain was threshed with flails and winnowed by hand on threshing floors, as has been done from time immemorial.[25] The reaper/binder was invented in 1872 in Janesville, Wisconsin, by Charles Baxter Withington. The earlier reaper invented by Cyrus McCormick in 1834 simply cut and dropped cut grain to the ground or to a platform where it was bundled by hand.[26] Binders mechanized the tying of the bundles, so that those who shocked the grain only had to gather the bundles to make shocks in which the grain was dried. Shocks were then gathered and brought to the farmstead and laid in stacks until the threshing machine arrived.[27] The first threshing machines were powered by a horse-power driven by several teams

23. Swiss-German Centennial Committee, *Swiss-Germans*, 113–15.

24. Bose, *Johnny Schmidt*, 141–42, gives an account of corn picking.

25. Boese, *Loretta's Settlement*, 117–18; Swiss-German Centennial Committee, *Swiss Germans*, 115.

26. Wikipedia, "Reaper," and "Reaper-Binder."

27. Boese, *Loretta's Settlement*, 118–19.

of horses circling the horse-power.[28] The entire harvest procedure was highly labor intensive and a communal endeavor involving neighbors working together.

There are quite a number of anecdotal stories about the early years of the community and the developments of agricultural technology, but many of them fail to put a date on the inception of these technologies in the local community. My uncle Ben Bose (1882 to 1965) wrote a series of short essays or stories about growing up on my mother's farm near Avon, South Dakota. Writing under the pseudonym Johnny Schmidt, he wrote *Son of a Dakota Pioneer*, where he chronicles many of the innovations that entered my grandfather Abraham Boese's farm. He writes that the family purchased an on-farm cream separator in 1902, a mounted plow in 1899, a telephone in 1904. The first automobiles began appearing shortly after 1900.[29] Each of these innovations radically changed the agrarian cultures and the life of the farm and reflect the development of an agricultural economy.

In *A Century of Mennonites in Dakota*, John D. Unruh's third chapter is devoted to "Social Economy of the Dakota Mennonites." The first section of this chapter is devoted to the agricultural economy from the 1870s to the 1920s. Based on a number of personal interviews, Unruh notes that Mennonite farmers logged a significant number of blue-ribbon showings of livestock at the South Dakota State Fair in the 1920s. Unruh notes that farmers of this era thrived in raising pure-bred livestock. He also notes two significant agricultural support industries that started in the 1920s—Park Lane Feeds started east of Freeman in 1925 by A. T. Kaufman and later moved to Freeman, and Gross Hatchery started in 1929 by Jacob T. Gross in Freeman.[30]

After World War II, electricity came to the rural homes and farms of the community through the REA, Rural Electric Administration. Earlier, telephone wires had followed the township roads, bringing the telephone to rural homes through township telephone companies. Now another set of poles and wires carried electricity to rural homes, and another new era began in the community. At the same time, each of these new technologies held the potential of reinforcing the independence of every farm home from its neighbors. These cultural adaptations to life on the Great

---

28. Bose, *Johnny Schmidt*, 143–46, gives an account of a threshing crew.
29. Bose, *Johnny Schmidt*, 65, 135, 159, 154.
30. John D. Unruh, *Century of Mennonites*, 33–35.

Plains made life easier and wealthier, but also made each home more and more dependent on the money economy of the dominant culture.

These rather random descriptions of agricultural life in the Freeman community in the early twentieth century confirm that the immigrants of the 1870s did indeed succeed and thrive on the prairie. They did this while contending with the harsh and unpredictable climate and environment of the Great Plains. There were tornadoes and hailstorms, prairie fires and floods, harsh winters and blizzards, grasshoppers and dust storms, the latter especially in the 1930s.

Gradually, and yet historically almost in a moment, the vast untamed wilderness of prairie grass took on the bucolic aspect of an agrarian settlement. Windbreaks, timber claims, and homestead groves broke the vast vista of the prairies, and farms grew to include wood frame houses and large barns for livestock with haylofts, and smaller barns for chickens and pigs. Section line roads were filled in, first for county roads and then also for township roads. Farmers fenced in the land on their property for use as pastures and livestock grazing. Whereas the prairie had presented a vast and overwhelming vista, a veritable sea of grass, the seasons now presented the variegated colors and shapes of an agricultural landscape—verdant green springs, sultry hazy summers, crisp golden autumns, and cold clear winters, all punctuated by the daily sunrises and sunsets so vividly displayed in the flat, open prairie land.

But while the pioneers altered the landscape of the prairie, the constraints of the prairie landscape also shaped the human community that came to it. Eastern South Dakota is on the western edge of what is called the Corn Belt, with twenty to twenty-five inches of precipitation annually.[31] At least until the advent of drought resistance corn hybrids in recent decades, local farmers always planted corn much more sparingly than their neighbors in states to the east.

More profoundly, the prairies have shaped the spirituality and character of those who endeavored to live on it. As Kathleen Norris reminds us, "Dakota is a painful reminder of human limits, just as cities and shopping malls are attempts to deny them."[32] "The Plains are not forgiving. Anything that is shallow—that easy optimism of a homesteader, the false

---

31. Lavin et al., *Atlas*, 41.
32. Norris, *Dakota*, 2.

hope that denies geography, climate, history; the tree whose roots don't reach ground water—will dry up and blow away."[33]

A PORTRAIT OF THE FREEMAN COMMUNITY IN THE 1950S

This chapter brings us to the *Golden Age* of the Freeman community—the middle decades of the twentieth century. Here we see the community in its maturity, vibrant and strong. Having myself grown up as a child in the 1950s, this attempt to describe the Freeman community in its maturity may well be seen as an exercise of nostalgia—a longing for the community to be as it was in the idyllic years of my own youth. While I cannot deny that there is some truth in this accusation, I hope that my description of this community in the decade of the 1950s will also be based on more defensible criteria. In particular, economic viability, ecological sustainability, and community cohesion and stability would be the measures I use in the following description of the community.

In this book I am defining the Freeman community as the eastern third of Hutchinson County, and the western three-quarters of Turner County. These two counties are 814 and 618 square miles in size, respectively. The townships in the areas defined here have about 276 square miles in Hutchinson County and 444 square miles in Turner County for a total of around 720 square miles. The populations of both counties peaked in 1930, at 13,904 and 14,891, respectively. In 2010, their populations were 7,343 and 8,347, respectively. Each of these counties has shrunk nearly by half from their largest to their current population. In 1950, the beginning of the decade I am looking at, Hutchinson County had a population of 11,423, and Turner County a population of 12,100, still relatively close to the peak population of twenty years earlier, despite losses during the Great Depression.[34]

---

33. Norris, *Dakota*, 38.

34. Wikipedia, "Hutchinson County," and "Turner County." See Figure 11, Hutchinson County, and Figure 12, Turner County; townships of the larger Freeman community are highlighted.

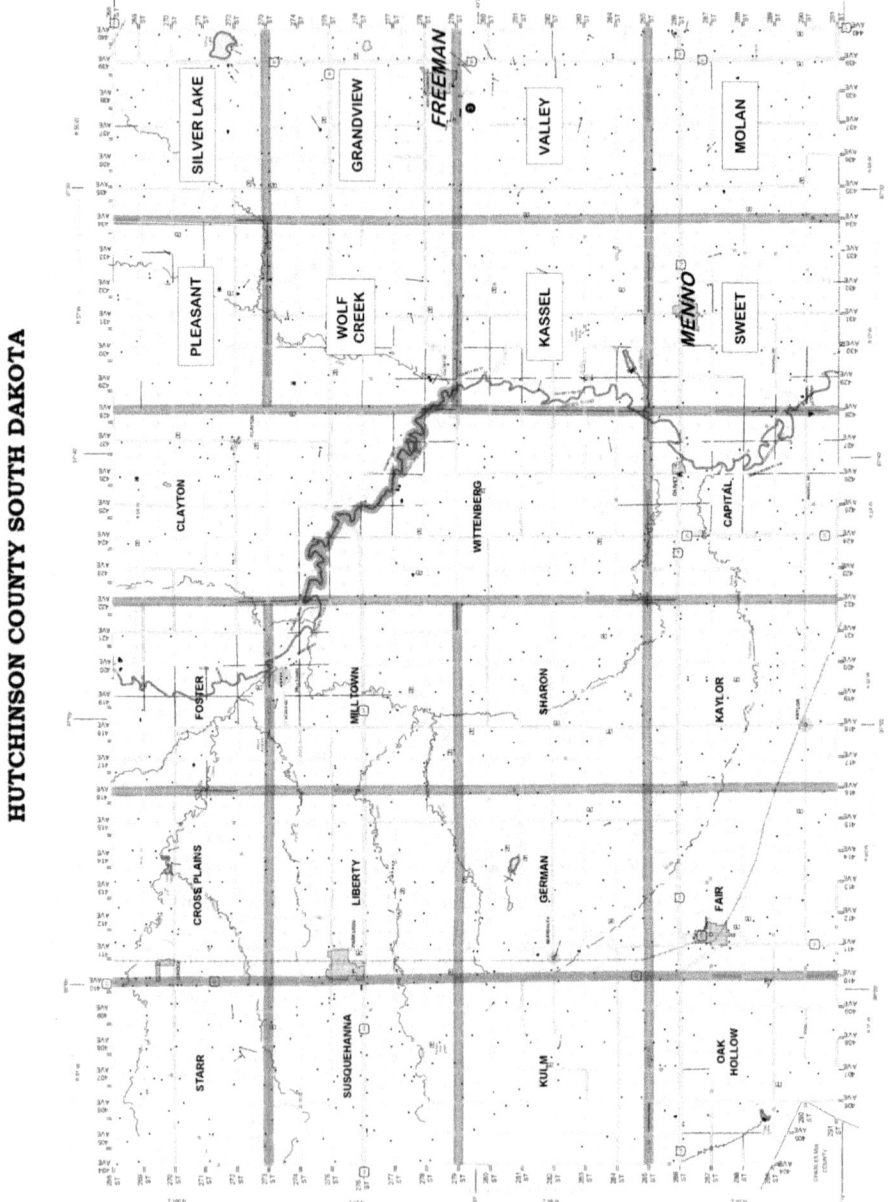

The Community in Its Maturity (1925 to 1975)

TURNER COUNTY SOUTH DAKOTA

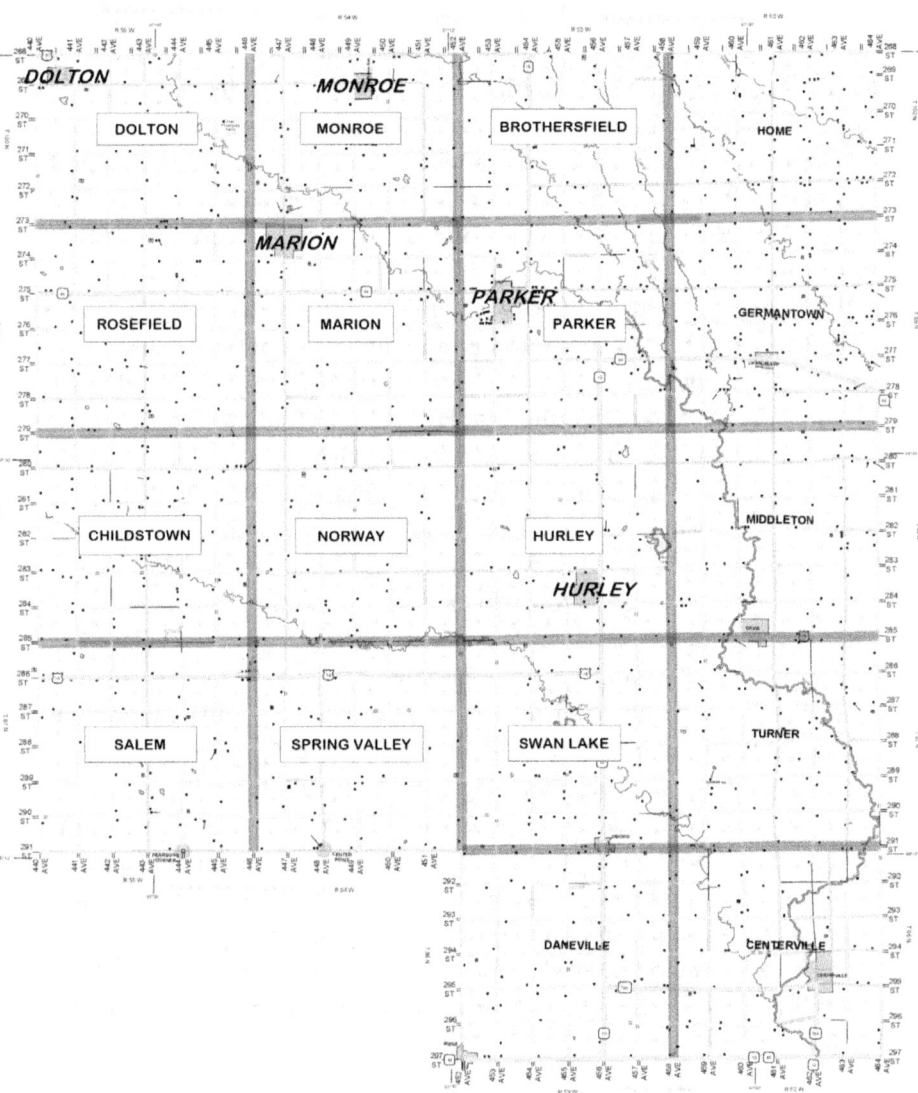

In his study of Mennonites in Dakota, John D. Unruh estimated that a total of 1,700 immigrants of Anabaptist faith came to Dakota Territory in 1874. The 1880 US census lists 1,861 residents of Mennonite faith, reflecting the births and arrivals since 1874.[35] A demographic note in Unruh's book indicates that in 1945 there were 1,517 Mennonites in Turner County and 1,393 in Hutchinson County, a total of 2,910, a little over 12 percent of the population of both counties.[36] These population percentages would be much higher in the townships defined above as the Freeman community. The *Atlas of the Great Plains* identifies both counties as having a Mennonite population of between 10 percent and 25 percent in 2000.[37] The ethnic origin of the population in 2010 was 67.7 percent German in Hutchinson County, and 47.7 percent German in Turner County.[38]

The town of Freeman lies pretty much at the center of the community we are examining, but the community radiates out in all directions as far as the towns of Bridgewater to the northwest, Marion and Monroe to the northeast, Parker to the east, Hurley and Viborg to the southeast, and Menno and Olivet to the southwest. By virtue of population (about 1,300), main street businesses, health facilities, and educational opportunities, Freeman tends to be considerably stronger than most of these other towns. In the first decades of the towns, Marion seemed to have the advantage as the junction town for railway lines, and indeed many Mennonites east of Freeman identified more with Marion than Freeman. The decision to locate South Dakota Mennonite College at Freeman in 1900 was likely what made Freeman rather than another town like Marion the center of the Anabaptist Russian-German settlement.

These geographical and demographic statistics of the Freeman community remind us that we are speaking here about a very small rural community. The population of South Dakota grew from a population of under 12,000 in 1870 to over 800,000 in 2010.[39] Even at the height of their populations, Turner and Hutchinson County had a population of less than 30,000, and today they have a population of just over 15,000. But the health and the vitality of rural communities can never be measured by

---

35. John D. Unruh, *Century of Mennonites*, 91.
36. Unruh, *Century of Mennonites*, 140.
37. Lavin et al., *Atlas*, 294.
38. Wikipedia "Hutchinson County," and "Turner County."
39. Wikipedia, "South Dakota."

their populations, but by the economic viability, ecological sustainability, and social cohesion of their agrarian cultures.

In the 1950s, most farms in the community were between one or two quarter sections in size. Though the industrialization of agriculture had begun in earnest in the years following World War II, the tractors and farm equipment were still small, and precluded being able to farm more than 160 to 320 acres. Still, the community was farmed quite intensively, with only rugged creek drainage areas untouched by tillage. Most farms had made the transition from horse power to tractors by 1950, but with the cost of machinery, the larger agricultural implements like combines and balers were often owned jointly by family members or neighbors, and they often shared the work of hay-making and harvest as well.

Most farms of this era were still diverse, with a variety of enterprises. Crop rotations were the norm, usually consisting of a rotation of corn, small grains, and hay, and with many permanent pastures still in use for livestock. The crop rotations and the use of plowing and cultivation controlled weeds, though weeds were also pulled by hand in the growing season. Most of the crops grown, both corn and small grain, were utilized on farm for feeding livestock. Excess small grains were sold at harvest. Ear corn not needed for animal feed was shelled by commercial corn shelling operations in winter, with the shell corn sold in town and the cobs used as bedding for animals or for household fuel.

In addition, most farms had a variety of livestock. Most of them had flocks of several hundred chickens, though some specialization of poultry operations began appearing. The sale of eggs from these flocks was a staple income. In addition, most farms also farrowed out a dozen or so sows a couple of times a year, both for on-farm use but mostly for sale as cash income. Some farms had sheep rather than pigs, or some of both. The manure from these livestock enterprises was often enough to fertilize the land, and the use of commercial fertilizers that needed to be purchased was only beginning.

Many farms also had small dairy operations of from a dozen to several dozen cows. In earlier years, the cream was separated and sold for cash income once or twice a week with the skim milk used in the household and fed to pigs, but in the 1950s more farmers began to have bulk tanks to sell whole milk that was picked up on the farm by trucks from the dairy cooperatives in the community. On some farms, cows were milked by hand into the 1950s. Some farms with more land in permanent pastures also had beef herds that were run on the pastures and then fed on the farm in winter. Both dairy and beef herds produced both heifers for replacement stock or sale and steers for on-farm meat and for sale. During the first half of the twentieth century, the weekly sale of cream and eggs provided the grocery money for most farm families.

In the era of the 1950s, farms of this description were economically viable, providing farm families with a comfortable living when supplemented by household garden and orchard production. Farmers were able not only to sustain their own lives but to produce food on a small scale for the larger society. On the other hand, they did not by themselves provide for future generations of farmers on the land. As we have seen already earlier in this chapter, this agrarian system depended on either the growth of the community's land base, or failing that on the exodus of the farm's children as they left the community for educational opportunities and careers out in the world. In other words, even the most successful era of the community economically did not hold the promise of a future for the agrarian culture.

In terms of ecological sustainability, much can be said in favor of the agricultural system of the community in this era. The farms needed few off-farm inputs to stay fertile. The combination of crop rotations and animal husbandry brought a strong degree of ecological sustainability to the community. The greatest ecological hazard of this agricultural system was the intensive tilling—plowing and cultivation—it required. This exposed the soil to erosion and the release of carbon from the soil into the atmosphere through oxidation. This not only threatened the fertility of the soil, but also contributed to global warming which is currently a grave threat not only to rural communities but to the global community as a whole. While the agricultural system of the community's golden years had elements of ecological sustainability, the seeds of ecological failure were also evident.

The agricultural system of the community's golden years did provide a strong basis for community cohesion and stability for several decades, manifested primarily through the strong congregational life of the churches of the community. Nearly all the members of the rural congregations were farmers who despite rivalries still did support and care for each other in informal networks of assistance and cooperation.

The two Swiss Volhynian churches of the East Freeman community I know best did experience their golden years from the 1940s through the 1970s. Salem-Zion Mennonite and Salem Mennonite churches had a combined membership of 972 in 1950, near the peak membership of

The Community in Its Maturity (1925 to 1975)

1,017 in 1970.[40] Both congregations built new houses of worship to replace the wood frame structures of the 1910s. The Salem-Zion church built an imposing circular sanctuary in 1957, and Salem Mennonite Church built a large brick sanctuary with fellowship hall and educational wing in 1966. When this structure was destroyed by fire in 1985, the congregation rebuilt the church on the same foundations, giving little thought to the fact that the membership of the church would begin to decline rapidly in succeeding decades.

While the membership of these congregations was dominantly composed of farmers, they were also highly educated and cultured. In World War II quite a number of young men who were drafted spent time in Civilian Public Service camps in lieu of military service. When they returned to the community to farm, they brought a broader perspective and experience to the community. After World War II, Mennonites continued to offer voluntary service programs to youth who were drafted, and increasingly young women also entered these service programs both within America and around the world through Mennonite Central Committee and other church programs. The young people who returned to the community continued to enrich the life of the community. In addition, many of the people who entered agriculture in the second half of the twentieth century were educated in church colleges or universities. A good number of the members of Salem Mennonite Church were more highly educated than I as their pastor, some of them as professionals, but some of them as farmers. This drive toward education was also undoubtedly fostered by the presence of Freeman Jr. College until its demise in the 1980s.

As a consequence of this social cohesion and education, the Freeman community also has excelled in the arts. The two Swiss Volhynian congregations described above both have large pipe organs in their sanctuaries. The Mennonites were instrumental in starting the Swiss Choral Society in the 1930s, which until recent years presented a large choral work to the community every year. The annual spring Schmeckfest celebration of the Mennonite ethnic cultures of the area presents a musical each year. And there have been many smaller vocal and instrumental groups that have performed through the years.

---

40. Kaufman, Centennial Sermons and Talks. (Membership Chart attached to Sermon XIII, "Our Golden Age.") See also Figure 14, Salem/Salem-Zion Membership, in chapter 7.

The achievement of the Freeman community in the mid-decades of the twentieth century was its ability to maintain the distinctive element of its agrarian cultures after having found an acculturation to American society. This achievement was fostered by the particular agrarian conditions that shaped the live of the cultures. These conditions were small, diversified farms in close proximity to one another on a clear and stable land base, and the persistence of shared labor and equipment as well as the strong component of human labor in the farming enterprise. In the golden era of the community, farmers and farm families still worked the land with their hands. They were not yet alienated from the soil and did not yet see the soil as inert dirt to be exploited as a medium for the production of commodities.[41]

Small farm of the 1950s

In this golden era, farming was seen as a vocation to which one is called, and not in the first place as a business. This turns out to be a key ingredient of genuine agrarian culture. In this era, however imperfectly, farmers still understood themselves to be caretakers of and partners with the land in the work of providing for the needs of their family and the human family. Indeed, they understood their calling theologically, as a tenet

---

41. See Figure 13, Small Farm of the 1950s.

of faith. This was not so much a matter of formal theological expression as it was a matter of lived faith experience. Mennonite farmers understood that their calling was to care for the Earth, God's creation, as part of a community of faith, so that both through their communal life and the produce of the Earth human life might be sustained and redeemed. They saw themselves as participants in the wider dominant society in which they lived as non-conformist communities of faith called to serve the needs of the human family through the produce of the Earth and the redeemed quality of their communal life. They acculturated to the dominant society in ways that facilitated this calling.

While the Freeman community still exhibited these characteristics of healthy agrarian cultures in this golden era, Mennonites locally and throughout the land began to recognize that the growing forces of urbanization in America and globally were a major threat to the survival of traditional rural communities like Freeman. The 1930s and 1940s saw a considerable effort to revitalize rural communities in America, both among Mennonites and also among other Protestant and Catholic churches as well. For instance, the National Catholic Rural Life Conference dates back to 1923.[42] After some years of discussion, a Mennonite Community Association was formed in 1945 with the aim of helping to form communities with the "values cultivated in face-to-face village life."[43]

Though this association was short-lived, it bore witness to a deep concern in that generation of Mennonite leadership and thought. Mennonite scholars like J. Winfield Fretz, a sociologist and church leader, and Melvin Gingerich, an historian, deplored the influence of urbanization on traditional Mennonite agrarian cultures. "Our former rural security is disappearing, we are becoming secularized, our community life is breaking down, and our culture is losing its distinctive qualities," Gingerich wrote in a 1942 article in the *Mennonite Quarterly Review*.[44] This point of view was challenged by other Mennonite leaders like J. Lawrence Burkholder, who pushed for a greater engagement with society by the church, and saw the rural community as a "romantic tendency" that ran the danger of identifying God's kingdom with "a particular cultural expression."[45] But how else can the kingdom of God be seen but as a particular cultural

---

42. Smith, "Celebrating 95 Years."
43. Toews, *Mennonites in American Society*, 196.
44. Toews, *Mennonites in American Society*, 101.
45. Toews, *Mennonites in American Society*, 196.

expression? The only issue is which cultural expressions of Christian faith we find compatible with our own theological perspectives.

Despite both the economic and ecological shortcomings of the agrarian cultures in their golden age of the 1950s, it was no small achievement for these agrarian cultures to exhibit the vitality and strength they had as non-conformed but acculturated sub-cultures in America. The Anabaptist groups had survived two World Wars with Germany with their pacifist faith largely intact. They had managed to preserve their land base as a community under private ownership but with a clear sense that it represented their communal identity as a people. They had adopted agricultural technologies that complemented rather than destroyed their communal values.

I believe that when I began work on this project, I had hopes of being able to describe the golden age of the community in its maturity in much more glowing terms, perhaps even as a paradigm for the community's future. That view likely reflected my nostalgic sentiments for the era in which I grew up. Still, this rural community in its maturity through the mid-decades of the twentieth century has much to teach us about what is required to preserve agrarian cultures as they adapt and acculturate to a powerful dominant culture bent on imperial expansion, growth, and wealth.

7

The Community's Decline under an Industrial Agriculture (1975 to 2025)

SYNOPSIS

THE INDUSTRIALIZATION OF AGRICULTURE began in earnest in America in the years following World War II, as American industry shifted its vast productive capacity from military weaponry to agricultural equipment. Unfortunately, the military mindset was not lost as industry shifted its production to agricultural implements. Just as weapons of war are developed to conquer, and if necessary, destroy the enemy, industrial agriculture sees Nature as an enemy to be conquered and made to bend to man's will. Of course, every form of agriculture has the potential for approaching Nature in this way, but most traditional agrarian cultures, and certainly the most successful and sustainable, seek to work in partnership with Nature, seeing Nature as a teacher and mentor in the production of the goods needed for human welfare.

The land tenure arrangements in the American Midwest made American farmers particularly susceptible to the intrusions of industrial agriculture. Settled on individual homesteads with the assumption of private ownership of the land, farmers as individuals were quite vulnerable to the forces driving the industrialization of agriculture. There were first the policies of government bureaucracies, which favored and rewarded those who adopted the industrial model. Next there was corporate control of both the inputs and the products of agriculture, with individual farmers forced to accept the prices set for both their inputs and their commodities. And finally, there was the technocracy of land grant universities, which dictated for farmers the practices required for industrial efficiency and production, often contradicting long established agricultural practices honed by generations of agrarian culture.

The methods and practices of industrial agriculture were slow to take hold in the larger Freeman community, bearing witness to the strength and resilience of the local agrarian and communal culture that had been practiced for several generations. However as communal restraints and faith perspectives regarding care for the land eroded, farmers began to buy into the methods of industrial agriculture. And once they had a foothold in the community, most farmers were eventually forced to accept the industrial methods if they hoped to remain in business at all. They after all had to compete against each other to stay in business, and the old communal values ceased to be operative. Faith became an individual, private matter, irrelevant to the forces of the dominant culture being imposed upon the community.

The end result of the industrialization of agriculture is the commodification of agricultural products for a global market while mining the soil for maximum production, the introduction of ever larger and more expensive and sophisticated agricultural equipment, the abandonment of animal husbandry except for concentrated animal feeding operations (CAFOs), and the enlargement of farms since the economy of scale demands ever larger acreage per economic unit. This effectively drove new and young would-be farmers off the land and out of the community and led to the dramatic demographic decline of the rural community across America in the past fifty years or more. School enrollments declined even as more and more schools consolidated, churches closed, and villages and towns lost their commercial viability and died. Rural communities lost control over their most essential asset—the land, and the community was confronted with its mortality.

THE INDUSTRIAL REVOLUTION

The Industrial Revolution is generally considered to have happened in the eighteenth and early nineteenth centuries beginning largely in Great Britain. While the Industrial Revolution had serious negative consequences for rural communities from its inception, agriculture did not begin to widely adopt industrial methods of production until the post-World War

II era, at least in America. Undoubtedly, the enormous industrial production required for the war effort had something to do with this. Industry, having geared up for the war effort, needed new markets for its goods and services, and agriculture was able to absorb and utilize this production.

Unfortunately, it was not just industrial equipment and methods that were foisted onto agricultural production, but the military mindset as well. Having conquered our enemies, we now determined that we could impose the same methodologies on Nature itself. Nature came to be seen as an enemy to be conquered by industrial methods of farming. One only has to watch a few advertisements on television to see how this works, with their militaristic images of conquering pests and weeds for agricultural production.

While I don't intend to present a full-blown account of industrial methods and mindsets, it may be helpful to outline some of the major innovations brought about by the Industrial Revolution and to see how they were applied in agriculture.

1. Industrial methods involved the replacement of draft and human labor with machines powered by water, wind, steam, coal, and later petroleum used to power internal combustion engines. In agriculture, this meant the replacement of horses and oxen and human labor with tractors, which is not in itself a bad thing.

2. Industry was driven to find economical and ever more efficient methods of production. Applied to agriculture this meant ever larger machines capable of farming more acres, which also meant that farms would grow larger and involve many more acres per farm.

3. Industry was interested in the uniformity of production, which meant each task of making something became more and more specialized. In agriculture, this involved the movement toward monoculture farming and away from the diversity traditionally associated with agrarian systems. This meant commodity production in field crops and the introduction of concentrated animal feeding operations, or CAFOs, for producing animals for meat. No longer would every farmer have some field crops and some animals for slaughter, and milk and eggs to sell, but instead specialize in just one or two agricultural enterprises.

4. Industry emphasized the division of labor. One person would no longer be involved in the production of a product from beginning to end as crafts people were. Instead a team was involved in producing products on an assembly line, with each person specializing in one function over and over. In agriculture, this reinforced farm specialization in the

production of commodities for the market. Farmers came to be seen as just one component of a food or commodity production system.

5. Industry depended on the money economy in the form of capital investment to fund the huge infrastructures required for industrial production. In agriculture, this resulted in farmers being dependent on loans from banks and government crop production programs for their annual operation and to finance the land and equipment required for their farms.

6. Profit became the bottom line for industrial production. Profit for investors and stock holders is the motive for industrial production. Industrial production that did not make a profit was abandoned. In agriculture, this meant the commodification of every farm product, and indeed of Nature itself with all its natural resources and systems. Witness the ubiquitous product number relentlessly attached to every apple that is sold! Farms that were not profitable were advised to grow or get out of business.

7. Industrial systems are based on analytical knowledge rather than on systemic knowledge. Industry depends on being able to analyze and control every step in a process, but pays little or no attention to the system as a whole through time. In agriculture, this meant that every problem, whether pests or weeds or animal diseases, required a technical fix that while temporarily solving a particular problem invited the possibility of long-term systemic failure.

8. Industrial production required the separation of consumption and production. Until the Industrial Revolution, the vast majority of people, whether peasant farmers or craftsmen, worked from their homes, and every home was both a unit of production and a unit of consumption. The Industrial Revolution removed first men and then women as well from the home, making it only a place of consumption, while productive work was done at the factory or the office or the field. In agriculture, this has led to the ironic reality that farm families are often as dependent on grocery stores for their food as their urban neighbors. Thankfully, many households in both urban and rural communities still maintain productive household gardens for domestic use.

Nearly all these innovations of the Industrial Revolution involved the creation and manufacture of new technologies and machines to accomplish their aims. This was no new development in human affairs. Ever since humans left the Garden of Eden, they have been devising new technologies to ease the burden of their lives here on Earth. The use and harnessing of fire and wind and water and stone occurred early in a variety of forms. Animal husbandry and gardening, the domestication of plants and animals for human use in the development of agriculture, came next. The technologies of metallurgy advanced military weaponry, and were later also adapted to agricultural use. Remember how the farmers of ancient Israel had to go to their enemies, the Philistines, to get their agricultural implements sharpened because the Philistines, who were more advanced in metallurgy, did not want the Hebrews to learn smithery of iron weapons and thus make their own (1 Sam 13:19–22)?

The problem is that every new technology devised by humans also has unintended consequences we do not foresee or understand when the technology is introduced. A dramatic example of this is found in the story of the Tower of Babel in Gen 11. Who would have thought that the introduction of a new construction technology—bricks instead of stones, bitumen in place of mortar—would have resulted in the disintegration of the unity of the human family and the confusion of their speech? But the new technology fostered our human desire to make a name for ourselves and to take God's place, as so many new technologies do. Such endeavors always inevitably result in confusion and dispersion and alienation. In the arc of the biblical story, the unintended consequences of the Tower of Babel were not reversed until the day of Pentecost in Acts 2, and the formation of the church as a new local community of humans living together toward a sustainable future.

Still, every new technological advance in human history also represents a more intrusive and destructive disruption of both human communities and natural systems. This makes the unintended consequences of new technologies always more dangerous and disruptive. Some of the unintended consequences of the technologies of the Industrial Revolution are the pollution of the environment and degradation of the soil, depletion of natural resources, an altered climate through the use of fossil fuels, the corporatization of society, an enormous societal wealth disparity between rich and poor, and a misplaced trust in technological fixes. While many of the goals and achievements of the Industrial Revolution were beneficial and laudable, we have to ask if they were worth the cost of these and many other unintended consequences.

Since the Industrial Revolution, still more intrusive technological revolutions have occurred. Humans have learned to produce energy by mastering the atomic structure of the Universe, and thus have the possibility of destroying the Earth as an unintended consequence. Note how once again with the development of atomic technology, the militaristic use of the technology preceded its peaceful use. Humans have also mastered the genetic code which lies at the heart of the myriad forms of life created by God on Earth. The recent introduction of genetically modified organisms (GMOs) into agricultural production has had immediate benefits, but the unintended consequences have still to be seen and understood. Now that we are on the brink of making the Earth uninhabitable for humans, many technocrats seriously dream of colonizing space, a total denial of our origin here on Earth. In the same way, the development of computers and information technologies and their application to agricultural production has immense promise, but the unintended consequences are still unclear. What are the implications of humans messing with God's created order, not just for the natural world, but also for the human community and the human spirit?

All of these technologies see Nature as inert matter to be manipulated and used by humans for their own purposes and desires. Criteria of faith and ethics for acting and human behavior have been replaced by analytical scientific knowledge that confines all of Nature and life to utilitarian ends. While it is easy for technocracy skeptics like myself to become paranoid and fail to see the positive aspects of technological innovations, the record of these innovations in unintended consequences implore us to be more thoughtful about the adoption of new technologies. Perhaps the Amish are ahead of us in this, evaluating new technologies on the basis of their effect on their communal life and faith heritage, accepting new technologies when they serve the welfare of the community and refusing them when they would have negative impacts on their life together. This is not to say that the Amish always make the right communal choices, but only to affirm the validity of their methodology of using criteria other than pragmatism and utility and profit in the adoption of new technologies.

THE VULNERABILITY OF RURAL COMMUNITY TO INDUSTRIALIZATION

We have already frequently noted how the Russian-German communities that came to the Great Plains in the 1870s had to forgo village life and settle on individual homesteads. This, along with the promise of ownership of land so long a dream of many of these immigrants, set the stage for the twentieth-century assault on rural communities by the dominant culture's adoption of the values and methods of industrialization.

Throughout history rural communities have had to address powers of dominant cultures in different ways. In the early years of the capitalist system and the Industrial Revolution in Great Britain, rural villages with their arts and crafts and subsistence lifestyles were threatened by enclosure movements, with land claimed by upper classes for wool production, thus dispossessing village people and driving them to cities to find work.[1] In the mid-twentieth century, rural communities in North America confronted three major powers and simultaneous threats to their existence.

First, there was government bureaucracy, the growing influence of federal government intervention in the agricultural system through programs designed to enhance the production of commodities for global markets. In the wake of the Dust Bowl of the 1930s, Soil Conservation Districts were formed. The federal government enacted the Agricultural Adjustment Act of 1933 to help conserve topsoil. When key provisions of the act were ruled unconstitutional, eventually the Agricultural Conservation Program administered by the Agricultural Stabilization and Conservation Service was enacted.[2] While these programs did much through the decades to preserve farmland, they were co-opted especially after World War II to maintain commodity production for global trade.[3] Marty Strange, then director of the Center for Rural Affairs in Nebraska, is quoted as follows: "Farm credit programs have been reshaped to fit the emerging farm economy in which a handful of farms dominate production."[4]

The net result of government agricultural policy has been to radically reduce the number of farms in America while increasing their size. "Since the mid-1930s farm numbers have steadily fallen from almost 7 million to less than 2.4 million today [1984], while average farm size has increased from less than 150 acres to over 500."[5] "Smaller and less established operations are more likely to be absorbed into the shrinking minority of larger operations in an increased concentration of farm ownership that parallels the earlier fate of other profit-seeking enterprises in the farm input,

---

1. Wallbank et al., *Civilization Past and Present*, vol. 2, 29–32.
2. Sampson, *Farmland or Wasteland*, 259–66.
3. Wessel, *Trading the Future*, 29–31.
4. Wessel, *Trading the Future*, 57.
5. Wessel, *Trading the Future*, 29.

food processing, and marketing sectors of the food economy."⁶ All this is due, James Wessel says in *Trading the Future*, to the fact that government programs have led to the "Boom/Bust Cycle" of farm income, with small producers caught in the Bust end of the cycle and forced off the land by larger operators able to withstand the fluctuations.⁷

The second *power* threatening rural communities in the twentieth century was the growing presence of corporations in agriculture. The twentieth century has seen the development of multi-national agribusiness corporate involvement in all aspects of the food system and agriculture. There were machinery companies producing agricultural equipment, always ready to develop and produce the next generation of farm equipment as farms grew larger. There were grain and milling companies that developed especially in the second half of the twentieth century to be agents for the global trade in commodities. Corporations like Cargill began to invest in vertically integrated production of food, owning and controlling every step of the food production process, from the field and the farm to the consumer table.⁸

In more recent decades, agrochemical companies have come to play a dominant role in the production of farm commodities, controlling access to fertilizers, herbicides, pesticides, and fungicides, as well as the genetically modified seeds (GMOs) that are required to be used with the chemical weed- and pest-controls offered. Corporations thus control every aspect of the dominant agricultural paradigm of commodity production. They control the price and availability of the inputs farmers require to plant and harvest a crop, as well as the price of commodities farmers produce. Farmers must now also become commodity brokers in a global market in an effort to sell the products they raise. And with their immense power and wealth, corporations work hand-in-glove with federal agencies in shaping farm policy to their advantage.

As I write this chapter in 2019, the power and dominance of multi-national corporate control over the global food system continues to expand. Monsanto, the American corporation that developed glyphosate herbicides in the 1970s and then went on to develop and mandate the sale of GMO-modified seed required to utilize the glyphosate herbicides, was bought by the giant German drug company Bayer in 2018. Opening the

---

6. Wessel, *Trading the Future*, 29.
7. Wessel, *Trading the Future*, 27.
8. Wessel, *Trading the Future*, 108–9.

January 2019, issue of *National Geographic* one morning, the first thing I saw was a full-page advertisement from Bayer, with the title: "How can we farm better." Here's the final paragraph of that advertisement:

> Alongside drones and robots, a combination of sensors, handheld devices, apps, and wearables, are making it easier to gather valuable information on everything from soil health to crop growth to the welfare of individual animals. All this technology, once mastered, could enable farmers to take even more targeted and timely action across even larger areas of land—significantly boosting efficiency. Armed with these new tools, farmers will have greater control over their resources than ever before, at a time when maximizing agricultural productivity has become a global priority.[9]

Though this advertisement uses the term *farmer* twice, it is clear that farmers no longer have any role to play in agriculture. Indeed, there is no human interaction with the soil, no tilling of the ground. The entire production process is controlled by machines and technology for the sake of greater efficiency over more land, and people have no more role to play as food producers. They are relegated only to the role of being consumers of the products the system produces. Nature is again portrayed as an enemy that requires us to be *armed* against. It is for me a portrait of a sadly technocratic dystopian future, and of course, it is a vision of the future that has absolutely no idea about, or at least takes no responsibility for, the unintended consequences of these technologies.

In recent decades, the organic movement has gained some traction as an alternative food producing system, appealing especially to educated urban consumers who know enough to be alarmed by the products of the industrial food system on their grocery shelves. However, the organic movement itself is always in danger of being co-opted by the power and wealth of agribusiness corporations. The dairy industry has experienced this kind of co-optation, with large organic dairies once again putting smaller dairies out of business.

The third *power* threatening rural communities in the twentieth century is technocracy (the rule of technology), already hinted at in the previous paragraphs. Land grant colleges were established in the United States in 1862 and 1890 by two separate Morrill Acts, named for the Vermont legislator who wrote the legislation. With this act, every state was

9. Bayer, "How Can We Farm Better?," 23.

entitled to form an agricultural college, in addition to liberal arts universities. In South Dakota, the land grant university is South Dakota State University. In 1887, the Hatch Act established state agricultural experiment stations. And in 1914, the Smith-Lever Act created the extension service, local offices that would disseminate the teaching and research of universities to local communities.[10]

As Wendell Berry reminds us in his account of the land grant universities, the Morrill Acts had the laudable intention of providing an education that was both practical and liberal for what was then the significant rural percentage of the American population.[11] However, as with government agricultural programs, the land grant colleges were soon co-opted to serve the interests of corporations invested in agriculture. In this way, land grant universities, instead of fostering rural community and its life, ended up becoming the agents for the technocratic interests of the corporations. Public funds designed to enhance and preserve rural communities were instead diverted into the coffers of corporations, and government bureaucratic extension agents became the propaganda representatives for the technocratic elite of the land grant universities representing the interests of agribusiness corporations.

Wendell Berry summarizes the effect of the land grant university contribution to the disintegration of rural communities this way. "The expert knowledge of agriculture developed in the universities, like other such knowledges, is typical of the alien order imposed on a conquered land. We can never produce a native economy, much less a native culture, with this knowledge. It can only make us the imperialist invaders of our own country."[12] In other words, land grant universities with their technocratic elite became still another colonial agent of the land on behalf of imperialist ambitions of the United States. For his part, Jim Hightower's conclusion is this: "Had the land grant community chosen to put its time, its money, its expertise, and its technology into the family farm, rather than into corporate pockets, then rural America today would be a place where millions could live and work with dignity."[13]

By now it must be exceedingly obvious that the three powers threatening rural communities in the twentieth century have all colluded

---

10. Hightower, "Hard Tomatoes, Hard Times," in Merrill, *Radical Agriculture*, 89.
11. Berry, *The Unsettling of America*, 154–58.
12. Berry, *The Unsettling of America*, 168.
13. Hightower, "Hard Tomatoes, Hard Times" in Merrill, *Radical Agriculture*, 106.

together to advance the imperial interests of the government, the profit interests of the corporations, and the research interests of the technocratic elite. Indeed, as we have seen, it is hard to talk about any one of them alone. Theologically, we might speak of them as another *unholy trinity*, like that described in Rev 12 and 13. Any one of these powers would have represented a grave challenge to the cultural integrity, the economic viability, and the communal survival of rural communities. With these powers acting together, rural communities across North America (and indeed around the world) have been by and large defenseless and helpless.

As for individual farmers in these communities, they have been even more vulnerable to disenfranchisement as their debts mounted despite their efforts to get big enough to exercise the economy of scale required to stay in business and hold onto their land. And clearly, using now conventional agricultural methods, farmers have little if any choice about how to farm, what to plant, how to raise animals, or how to market their produce, despite the fiction of private ownership so cherished by the American farmer. All of these decisions are made for farmers by government bureaucrats, corporate boards and investors, and university technocrats.

THE DECLINE OF THE FREEMAN COMMUNITY

I'd like to think that the Freeman community was able to resist the forces of agricultural industrialization outlined in the previous sections. It was perhaps slower to adopt the new technologies being foisted on rural communities by these forces. I remember my own father's wariness about signing up for government programs, and his resistance toward adopting the *bigger is better* mentality in the 1950s and 1960s. But of course, he was by then an older man who didn't need to compete to stay in business. The small Anabaptist cultures of the Freeman community have managed to maintain a strong minority cultural heritage. The strong educational emphasis of the community had something to do with this, but the heritage of non-resistance and peace was even more responsible for the maintenance of this ethnic identity. We took a certain pride in having this unique heritage that was so distinctive, being aware at the same time that it separated us from our neighbors as a minority that might be seen as subversive or unpatriotic.

The negative side of this is that our distinctiveness took on the character of ethnocentrism, where the preservation of the ethnic heritage that embodied our uniqueness became more important than the uniqueness itself. In other words, we often came to value our heritage more for its ethnic identity than for the faith convictions it had brought to us. So we often conveyed a certain disdain for the other groups around us, coming across to them as snobbish and self-righteous. It also prevented these Anabaptist subcultures from collaborating with other threatened agrarian cultures around them and around the world to resist the powers of the *unholy trinity*.

Unfortunately, the uniqueness we felt about our faith and ethnic heritage no longer impacted our life as an agrarian people. The influence of fundamentalism on our Anabaptist faith had made faith a private and individual affair between ourselves and God, and had undercut the discipleship and communal aspects of our Anabaptist faith, as noted in the last chapter. So while we clung to our ethnic heritage as the embodiment of our uniqueness, it no longer informed the way we farmed together cooperatively or communally, the way agrarian cultures typically supported the members of the community. While we saw ourselves as different from other cultures on Sunday morning at church, we began to compete with them and with each other when we returned to our farms on Monday morning. Our farms became more and more isolated business enterprises in our thinking, with little relevance to the faith perspectives that made us unique as ethnic enclaves.

About every five years, the United States Department of Agriculture publishes a census of all farms in the United States, with statistics collected at both state and county levels. In this census every producer of agricultural goods totaling $1,000 annually, whether urban or rural, is included. The census counts not only the number and size of farms but provides a quite detailed analysis of the agricultural products sold and how land is being used. Here we are mainly concerned with the number and size of farms in Hutchinson and Turner Counties, South Dakota, the counties of our interest. A comparison of the number and size of farms over the past century is revealing. Here statistics for these two counties will be documented for the years 1925, 1950, 1974, and 2002.[14]

In 1925, there were 1,728 farms in Hutchinson County with an average size of 290 acres. In 1950, there were 1,674 farms with an average size of 310 acres. In 1974, there were 1,266 farms with an average size

---

14. Data in the following two paragraphs from United States Department of Agriculture, Census of Agriculture Historical Archives, "Summary County Tables for South Dakota," for the years 1925, 1950, 1974, and 2002.

The Community's Decline under an Industrial Agriculture (1975 to 2025)

of 417 acres. And in 2002, there were 768 farms with an average size of 658 acres. The number of farms continued to grow in the 1930s, but the number of farms in 1925 was near the historic high in the 1935 census with 1,805 farms in the county. The number of farms began dropping off significantly after 1950 so that by 2002, there were nearly one thousand less farms than there had been in 1925. That's a pretty dramatic loss of farms for a seventy-five-year period. At the same time, average farm size increased from 290 acres in 1925 to 658 in 2002, an acreage growth of over 100 percent, from less than half a section in 1925 to over a section in 2002.

In 1925, there were 2,010 farms in Turner County averaging 187 acres in size, just over a quarter section. In 1950, there were 1,914 farms averaging 202 acres in size. In 1975, there were 1,319 farms with an average size of 302 acres. In 2002, there were 713 farms with an average size of 487 acres. As in Hutchinson County, the number of farms peaked in 1935 with 2,078 farms. The number of farms held fairly steady until the decades after 1950 so that again in 2002 there were more than one thousand less farms than in 1925. Farm size in Turner County grew from 187 acres in 1925 to 487 in 2002, again a growth of average farm size of over 100 percent. The smaller farms of Turner County reflect the climatic reality that the further west one goes in South Dakota, the larger the farms get due to less rainfall and a harsher climate. For example, the average farm size for the state of South Dakota was 1,352 acres in 2012, over two sections, compared to 640 acres in Hutchinson County and 484 acres in Turner County.[15]

Statistics for farms and farmers parallel the overall population trends in these two counties. The populations of these two counties peaked in the 1930 census, with a population of 13,904 in Hutchinson County and a population of 14,891 in Turner County. Again, in both counties, population held fairly steady until 1950, when there were 11,423 people in Hutchinson County and 12,100 in Turner County. Then came the precipitous decline to a population of 7,343 in Hutchinson County in 2010, and 8,347 in Turner County, a population decline of nearly half.[16] Meanwhile, during this same period, the overall population of South Dakota grew from 692,849 in 1930 to 814,180 in 2010.[17] This demonstrates a precipitous disenfranchisement of the rural population of South Dakota.

15. United States Department of Agriculture, National Agricultural Statistics Service, "County Summary Highlights, 2012."
16. Wikipedia, "Hutchinson County" and "Turner County."
17. Wikipedia, "South Dakota."

A final interesting statistic is that from 2002 to 2012, the number of farms increased slightly in both counties, to 802 in Hutchinson County and to 794 in Turner County. There was a slight decrease in farm size as well, down to 640 acres in Hutchinson County and 484 acres in Turner County.[18] This one decade does not undo nearly a century of decline in the rural communities of these counties, but perhaps these statistics indicate the beginning of a renewal or rebirth in the agrarian cultures of the area, as more small-scale, food-producing farmers begin to be established. But that's a story to explore in the next chapter.

BRINGING IT ALL HOME: A CASE STUDY

In this book I understand agrarian cultures to be very specific local neighborhoods bound together by a common environment on and a common care for the land, and often by a common heritage of faith and ethnicity. On the Great Plains, the most local and specific manifestation of an agrarian culture tends to be a church congregation, bound together by the people's proximity to one another on the land and by their common heritage of faith and ethnicity. As the pastor of five rural congregations, I can vouch for the fact that every congregation, however small or large, has a unique culture, even when, as here in the Freeman community, several congregations may share the same ethnic and faith heritage. Sometimes, as here in the Freeman community, these local agrarian cultures have a long history going back generations, reflected in the villages of origin that traveled together from Ukraine to make a new home here in America.

Salem Mennonite Church in rural Freeman is one such local agrarian culture. Rural by every measure, and still composed predominantly of farmers or people engaged in supporting agriculture, this congregation grew from a charter membership of 129 in 1908 to a peak membership of 578 in 1970. In 2018, the membership was 336, barely half the peak membership.[19]

---

18. United States Department of Agriculture, National Agricultural Statistics Service, "County Summary Highlights, 2012."

19. Salem Mennonite Church, Yearbook and Directory, 56. See Figure 14, Salem/Salem-Zion Membership.

MEMBERSHIP
Salem & Salem Zion
1874-2008

DECADE	SZMC	SMC	BOTH
1874	71 families		175?
1880	82 families		200?
1897			350
1908		129	
1910	220	158	378
1920	323	306	629
1930	364	369	733
1940	410	500	910
1950	433	539	972
1960	423	547	970
1970	439	578	1017
1980	429	546	975
1990	390	474	864
1999	386	434	820
2008	345	371	716

Compiled by S. Roy Kaufman from Yearbooks of Salem and Salem-Zion Mennonite Churches, and from other historical sources.

The original wood frame church of 1908 was expanded in 1917 and became a classic rural wood frame church with a steeple. A new brick structure was built and dedicated in 1966, with an imposing sanctuary and a large fellowship hall and educational wing. When this structure was destroyed by arson in 1985, a new very similar church was built on the same foundations and dedicated in 1987.[20] It is known locally as the *South Church*, as it is a daughter of the original Swiss Volhynian congregation established in 1880, Salem-Zion Mennonite Church, two and a half miles to the north, and known as the *North Church*.

---

20. See Figure 15, Salem Mennonite Church Buildings.

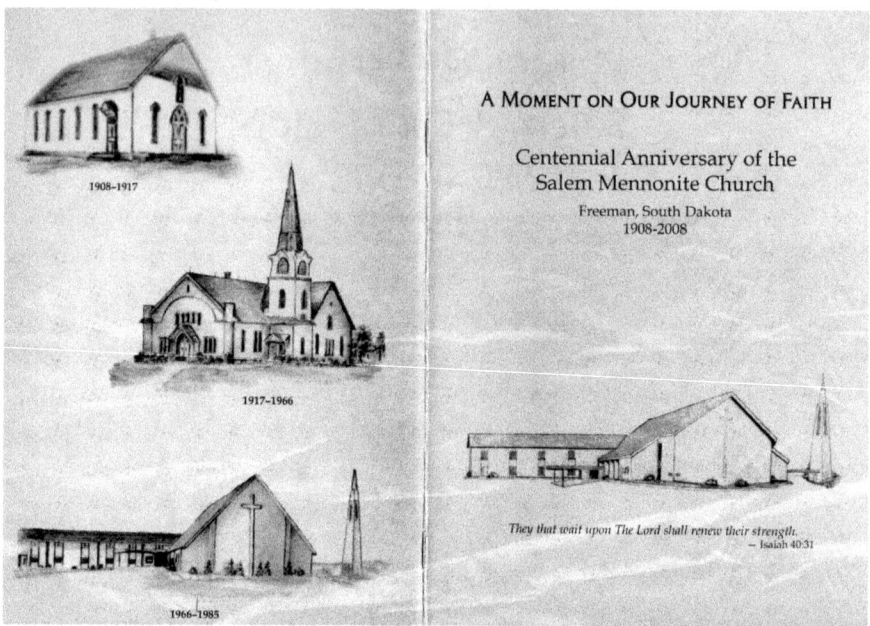

Salem Mennonite Church buildings

I was raised and baptized in this church. I served as a pastor for three rural congregations in Iowa, Illinois, and Saskatchewan, before being called to serve my home congregation in 1999. I served as lead pastor of the church until 2010, when I retired from full-time ministry.

In 2008 I was granted a four-month sabbatical from the church. The theme of the sabbatical was Renewing the Vision for Rural Ministry, and involved a trip to Israel/Palestine, as well as to Greece, where I first gained a vision for the role of a religious leader in the life of agrarian villages. One of the spiritual disciplines I followed on the sabbatical was to spend one day a week outdoors in a natural setting from sunrise to sunset, walking and journaling and reading. Engaging this discipline from mid-winter to spring in Indiana, Michigan, Iowa, South Dakota, Palestine, and Greece was challenging and revealing.

Returning to my ministry position at the Salem Mennonite Church, I resolved to be more intentional about engaging the spiritual discipline of walking. I planned and led four prayer walks for the church from June to September 2009, each walk scheduled for the early morning as the Sun rose in the east and the full moon was setting in the west. Salem Mennonite Church is built on the intersection of 281st Street and 443rd Avenue, so each walk involved an eight-mile pilgrimage around four sections in each quadrant around the church—southeast, southwest, northwest, and northeast. These sixteen square miles surrounding the church I defined as the church's neighborhood, and it lies in the north-central heart of Childstown Township.[21]

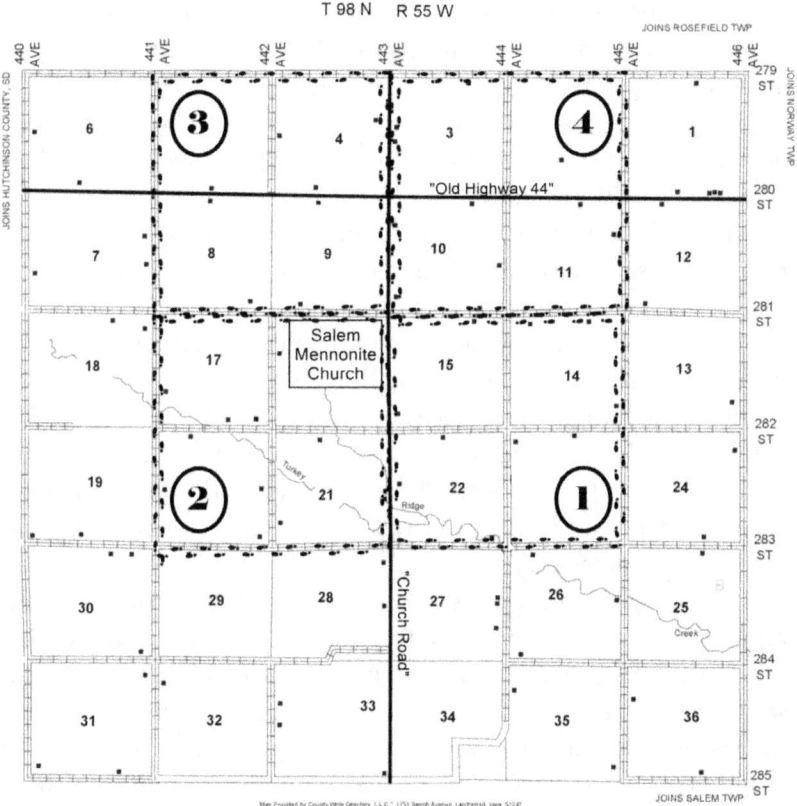

In preparation for these walks, I researched as much as I could about the area we were walking around in terms of land use, land ownership, watersheds and other ecological features, population, land use, and residency. These four studies as well as three introductory studies about prayer walks and the local history of the area were shared with both the walkers (four regulars, nine in all) as well as the whole congregation. Following the four

21. See Figure 16, Salem Mennonite Church Prayer Walks, 2009.

walks, I wrote a longer review of learnings I gleaned from the experience, from which I condensed an article published in *The Mennonite*.[22]

The situation of these sixteen square miles of agricultural land surrounding the South Church portrays in a microcosm the trends discussed earlier in this chapter for the larger Freeman community. One interesting discovery was that only 10 percent of the members of the church lived in these sixteen square miles. When the church began in 1908, it was located on the edge of the valley overlooking Turkey Ridge to the south, a location justified as being more accessible to members in the days of horse and buggy transportation. If indeed the bulk of Salem's membership once lived within the *parish* of the church's neighborhood, that was no longer the case in 2008. However their scattered status affected their communal identity as church members, it clearly had a detrimental effect on their cohesion as an agrarian culture. Being so scattered, members no long envisioned working their land as a communal asset to serve the welfare of the community.

The prayer walks revealed that of the 110 pioneer Swiss Volhynian homesteads established in the 1870s, thirty were located within the South Church neighborhood of sixteen square miles.[23] This statistic bears out the fact that the community was much more cohesive in terms of their land holdings in the first years of the community. The walks generated a good number of stories from the walkers about the trials and tribulations of these first homesteaders.

The prayer walks put us in touch with the local natural environment. Nearly all these sixteen square miles are part of the Turkey Ridge Creek watershed, and the creek itself was crossed on the two southern walks. While these walks revealed a lot of premier agricultural farmland suitable for cropping, it also revealed a lot of erosion from land that should perhaps not have been cropped, but rather kept in grass or hayland. And indeed, there were a good number of permanent pastures and hay-lands on the more rugged and steep sections drained by local creeks and waterways. There were no discernible plots of land that reflected the original ecology of the prairie. Both cropland and permanent pastures and hay-lands reflected a dominance of introduced or invasive crops and plants. While there were many evidences of native fauna (coyotes, foxes,

---

22. Kaufman, "Anatomy."

23. A map on exhibit at Heritage Hall Museum and Archives documents the original location of the homesteads of the Swiss Volhynian immigrants.

The Community's Decline under an Industrial Agriculture (1975 to 2025) 177

badgers, skunks, muskrats, and birds of all kinds), the dominant evident fauna was domesticated animals.

While no actual census was taken, the population of these sixteen square miles was estimated to be about 115 people, or 7.2 per square mile. Fifty-five built sites where people had lived were identified, which would have come out to 3.4 homesteads per square mile, about what one would expect when a quarter section was the size offered by the Homestead Act. There could have been additional building sites that we could no longer identify. Fifteen of these sites were completely abandoned. Forty of these fifty-five built sites were still occupied in these sixteen sections. Of these forty occupied sites, twenty-nine were operating farms, and the other eleven were rural residences for people who worked in town or in the city. The original fifty-five built sites likely all represented farms, so very nearly half of the original working farms in these sixteen sections were gone.

Except for the rural residences and the church and its cemetery, all of the land of these sixteen sections was agricultural. The land was farmed conventionally for the most part, producing corn and soybeans for the global market. There was a large multi-family dairy operation and a large multi-family cow/calf and beef-feeding operation. Most farms still had a few beef cows to graze the permanent pastures, but within about the past two decades nearly all the small local dairies that used to be common on every farm had disappeared. There were a few smaller confined animal feeding operations (CAFOs), mostly for hog production. There were a couple of organic farms in this neighborhood, including a small dairy selling raw milk, but for the most part, this neighborhood resembled rural neighborhoods across the Great Plains engaged in commodity-oriented, industrialized agriculture.

The land of these sixteen sections was owned by eighty-four parties, according to the plat maps for Turner County published for 2009.[24] Landholdings in individual plots ranged from ten to 1,026 acres. Half (forty-two) of these land-holdings were being farmed by those who owned the land, though not all these farmers lived in these sixteen sections. Thirty-four of the land holdings appeared to be property rented out by the owner, either to a family member or to another farmer. Half (seventeen) of these rental properties appeared to be absentee landlords, usually heirs of family property who inherited the land. Sometimes these rental properties were owned by outside investors who had bought land in the community.

24. Turner County South Dakota, *Directory*, 36.

Whenever the land is owned by people who no longer work the land, the community loses control over the use of the land. Farmers who rent land held by non-residents need to farm in ways that guarantee the owner their rental charges, and that means the land must be farmed within the conventional agricultural paradigm. Much of the same dynamic is true when the land is owned by fewer and fewer large owners, even when they farm the land themselves. Land tenure and land ownership patterns that reflect the community's engagement with the land are crucial to the survival of agrarian cultures. The communal land-base of the agrarian culture of Salem Mennonite Church has been seriously compromised in recent decades.

Salem Mennonite Church is a strong and vibrant congregation. It is the largest, strongest, and healthiest of the five rural congregations I served as pastor. While there is a good bit of theological diversity among the membership, the church as a whole has a strong and clear sense of its identity as an Anabaptist/Mennonite congregation, and a strong conference and denominational connection to Central Plains Mennonite Conference and Mennonite Church USA. Lois Janzen Preheim, one of the congregation's historians at the congregation's centennial, described the church this way when she married into it in the 1980s. "My first impression of Salem Mennonite was that this congregation was a 'cruise ship' firmly making its way across the prairie sea and that the individual, once on board, could trust that one would get to one's heavenly destination."[25]

While there is a good bit more ethnic diversity than there used to be in the membership, the congregation remains overwhelmingly European. Many members continue to have some connection to the Swiss Volhynian ethnic origin of the congregation and value that heritage, so that is often cited as an obstacle for people of diverse background to feel welcome in the church. Though not all members would describe themselves as pacifists, the congregation as a whole is clear about its identity as a peace church. A good number of the congregation's youth continue to engage in some form of voluntary service. Many families send their children to Mennonite schools—Freeman Academy, and also Mennonite colleges.

Despite all this, it would appear to me that the congregation has lost its identity as an agrarian culture. During the farm crisis of the 1980s, the congregation made an effort to address farm issues from a faith perspective, but little concrete action was taken beyond affirming

---

25. Salem Mennonite Church, A Moment, 31.

The Community's Decline under an Industrial Agriculture (1975 to 2025)   179

the value of farming as a way of life and expressing concern for farmers suffering in the crisis. There continue to be a few examples of machinery and labor sharing in the congregation, either within extended families or in neighborhoods. And there is an eager readiness to help farmers in distress when there is illness or accident that prevents a crop from being planted or harvested. Nevertheless, these are vestiges of an agrarian culture. When it comes to how the land is held and farmed, the church (community) has little influence or voice. Then it is every farmer for him or herself, and it is assumed that no one has a right to question the decisions farmers make. In other words, the community, in this case the congregation, has little if any voice or influence in questions of land tenure and land use. There is little sense of the land being held as a communal asset for the welfare of the community.

In saying this, I do not mean to disparage either the congregation or its farmers. The farmers were and are highly skilled entrepreneurs who operate with a high ethical and moral sensibility. The congregation likewise has a strong missional concern for the welfare of both the community and the society in which it lives. The failure, if such it be, is that both the congregation and its membership acculturated to the dominant culture in terms of agricultural practices. How the land is held and used, and how people farm, was no longer seen as relevant to the Christian faith or the mission of the church.

In many ways, this acculturation does not represent a loss of the congregation's stated identity. Agrarian cultures rarely articulate how land is held and used in formal or legal or theological terms. If the South Church was in its earlier years a more effective and healthy agrarian culture, that was because traditional patterns of communal and agricultural life that expressed the lived faith of this agrarian culture were still being practiced informally. The community had no mechanism for questioning or modifying its accommodation to the dominant culture's agricultural practices once these began to be introduced in earnest following the Second World War. Only now, in retrospect, can it begin to be seen how the congregation's life has been changed in questionable directions by this acculturation.

It would be easy to demonize industrial agriculture described earlier in this chapter as the culprit in the decline of the rural community, and I've been guilty of that. Indeed, the powers that drove the industrialization of agriculture were incredibly strong and seductive. It is also hard, indeed wrong, to fault the farmers of the community for choosing to engage the technical tools and methods that brought about agricultural industrialization. Standing alone as individual entrepreneurs, the farmers of rural communities had little alternative but to adopt the new methods and tools that were offered to them as the means to keep their farms and preserve their livelihoods. And when this pitted farmers against one another for control of more land, that was just the way things were.

Still, the more fateful choices that were made or not made were those of the rural communities and the agrarian cultures themselves. Specifically, the blame for the demise of rural communities lies with religious institutions and faith communities and their leaders like myself, who failed to preserve and articulate the communal and agrarian values of their heritage. In other words, there was in this communal and agrarian heritage the means to at least challenge the hegemony of industrial agriculture, even if they might not in the end prevail against it. Only a strong communal solidarity has the means through a combination of subversion and adaptation to challenge industrial agriculture.

As it turned out, the religious community and its faith heritage failed to equip itself and its members for this struggle, and industrial agriculture prevailed, mostly by default. We in the faith community simply did not rise to the challenge of dealing with the industrialization of agriculture. We divorced faith from socio-economic life, and made God's work of reconciliation in the world a matter of personal spiritual salvation for the future life. We lost the connection between God's work and our care for the Earth. We no longer understood our use of the land as the basis for our common life together, and let everyone make their own choices in the way that they held and used the land.

ASSESSING THE RURAL COMMUNITY'S CAPITAL

Rural sociologists Cornelia Butler Flora and Jan L. Flora, in their study of rural communities in America, describe seven forms of capital assets found in rural communities—cultural, human, social, financial, built, natural, and political.[26] At this juncture of our study of the Freeman community, it may be helpful to evaluate the capital assets of the community as the cultures that comprise it are all in radical decline as viable agrarian cultures. This will be a purely subjective exercise on my part, based on personal observations about the state and the health or ill-health of the Freeman community. I will give the Floras' definition

---

26. Flora et al., *Rural Communities*, 9–10.

The Community's Decline under an Industrial Agriculture (1975 to 2025)

of these seven forms of capital and offer a few comments on the state of these assets in the Freeman community.

1. "*Natural capital* is the landscape, air, water, soil, and biodiversity of both plants and animals. It can be consumed or extracted for immediate profit, or it can be a continuing resource for communities of place."[27]

The landscape of the Freeman community has been radically altered by the settlement of European colonizers arriving in the 1870s. The prairie landscape is irrevocably lost, although the vast vistas overlooking the plains for miles and miles remain. What was once a vast sea of grass populated by a diverse flora and fauna is now a variegated patchwork of cropland and pastures and hayfields. Whereas these fields used to be fenced, the fences of small farms are increasingly disappearing to be replaced by quarter- or half-section fields stretching from one section-line road to the next.

In the same way, the small farmsteads that used to dot the vast landscape with their small groves of trees are rapidly disappearing. Natives returning to the community to visit, like my ninety-year-old brother, are often lost as the landmarks they remembered from their youth have disappeared to make room for a few more acres of corn and soybeans. In place of these farmsteads there are instead the occasional large confined animal feeding barns (CAFOs) and the huge steel grain bins used to store grain until it is sold. The biodiversity of flora and fauna that characterized the original prairie landscape has been replaced largely by monoculture crop-land.

As noted above, there is evidence of soil erosion and many fields show deepening gullies as the water-ways that used to be installed in the fields succumb to the need to cultivate fields with large unwieldy farm equipment ill-designed for working around the uniqueness of particular landscapes. Fertilizers and seeds can be placed with GPS precision, but the machinery cannot navigate the intricacies of the landscape.

The primary natural capital of the community is its topsoil. Efforts are made to preserve this asset through minimum and no-till cropping methods, and increasingly in recent years through the planting of cover crops to hold the soil in the off-growing seasons. Because of the use of commercial fertilizers and chemical pest and weed controls as well as the use of large, heavy machinery, the soil is often largely compacted and does not have the biological vitality and complexity of native prairie soils.

27. Flora et al., *Rural Communities*, 10

It is also then ineffective in absorbing rain water. The soil is no longer a living organism, but has indeed become inert dirt used as a medium to produce crops. Though there is still considerable soil loss due to wind and water erosion, this prime asset of the Freeman community does remain strong, and could likely with different agricultural paradigms be restored to something close to its pristine prairie quality in a century or two.

2. "*Human capital* is the skills and abilities of each individual within the community. It includes potentials . . . and acquired skills. . . . Formal and informal education contribute to human capital. One's health and leadership skills are also part of the human capital."[28]

The human capital of the Freeman community is numerically seriously depleted. The population of the town of Freeman has held relatively stable, from a high of 1,462 in 1980 to a current population of 1,306.[29] However, the population of the surrounding countryside has been seriously eroded in recent decades, to something nearly half what it was in the 1930s.

On the other hand, the population of both the rural areas and the town has grown increasingly diverse. Some fifty years ago, the vast majority of family names in the community reflected the Germanic origin of the community as German immigrants from Russia. Today, while the population remains predominantly European ethnically, that population is much more diverse. Recent decades have seen a significant minority of families of Hispanic origin in the community, many of whom work on the large dairies or other industrial-sized agricultural enterprises of the community.

One would expect that the increased diversity of the population would enrich the human capital of the Freeman community. Unfortunately, that has not always been the case. The community, both in town and in rural areas, has struggled to integrate newcomers into the fabric of the community. Rural residents especially struggle with this. New non-farm residents of former rural farmsteads are attracted by the economy and location of the farm-place rentals, and have jobs in trucking or in the city. Yet, they are scarcely integrated into the community itself, and their human capital is largely lost to the community. The diversity of socio-economic class and lifestyles has not made it easy to integrate this diversity into the established social structures of the community. This of course is the responsibility of the established residents of the community,

---

28. Flora et al., *Rural Communities*, 9.
29. Wikipedia, "Freeman."

but both as individuals and as congregations, the established structures of the community have failed, with the resultant loss of an immense human capital for the community. Each of the residents of the community do, after all, bring an immense range of skills and abilities to the community.

Within the established structures and churches of the community, the quality of human capital is rich. In this respect, the rural community continues to reflect its traditional strength in nurturing its youth for productive roles in society. The educational system is strong, both in the public and the private schools. Many young people go on to university or trade schools. The community continues to instill in its youth a strong work ethic. The unfortunate thing is that the community often loses this wealth of human capital by failing to provide opportunities for its youth to remain in or return to the community and to make their contribution of human capital here.

3. "*Social capital* includes the networks, norms of reciprocity, and mutual trust that exist among and within groups and communities. It contributes to a sense of a common identity and shared future."[30]

The social capital of the larger Freeman community traditionally resided in the small agrarian cultures of Russian-Germans who came to the area in the 1870s as village and church entities. We have seen in chapter 5 how this social capital was compromised by the subtle village and religious rivalries that afflicted each of these groups and often prevented them from working together for the common welfare of the larger Freeman community.

Social capital of the community was further compromised by the ethnocentrism that afflicted each of these groups, but particularly the Anabaptist/Mennonite sub-cultures. Those with an Anabaptist identity often see themselves as a minority persecuted for their pacifist faith. This created a suspicion and a defensiveness among the Anabaptist groups towards their neighboring communities. It fed into an ethnocentrism and emphasis on ethnic identity that prevented them from working cooperatively with the other agrarian cultures present in the larger community and in neighboring communities. Instead of cooperation, there was an aloofness and defensiveness that bore witness to an insecure identity. Speaking for myself as a member of this culture, we didn't know how or where we fit in relation to other cultures. We were afraid to relate to them, and were uncertain about our ability to engage other cultures in an open,

30. Flora et al., *Rural Communities*, 9.

respectful, non-defensive, inter-cultural manner. Then we justified our insecurity and lack of engagement on the grounds of theological differences. In the process, we squandered an immense reservoir of potential social capital.

The development of Freeman Jr. College and Academy as a parochial Mennonite school may illustrate this dynamic of squandered social capital. Though the school does represent a cooperative effort of the various Anabaptist groups in the community, it often presented itself and was seen by the larger community as an attempt to offer a superior alternative to the public schools. So while the school did contribute to the social capital of the community in many ways, it also deepened the division between Mennonite and non-Mennonite elements of the community. While the school was always open to all in the community, and while many did avail themselves of the junior college training, there has always been a fairly deep divide in the community regarding public versus private education. In recent decades the huge spring ethnic fair sponsored by Freeman Academy, Schmeckfest, has begun to bridge this divide, as the Mennonite community can no longer put on this event by themselves and engages the local community to help them.

The potential social capital of the Freeman community is also hampered by the influx of new and more diverse rural and town residents, as noted in the discussion of human capital. The community as a whole has struggled to incorporate a more diverse population and to form reciprocal engagements and mutual trust between traditional, ethnic residents and new, more diverse residents.

4."*Cultural capital* includes values and approaches to life that have both economic and noneconomic implications. Cultural capital can be thought of as the filter through which people live their lives, the daily or seasonal rituals they observe, and the way they regard the world around them."[31]

The thesis of this book is that the Freeman community was planted and grew up as a collection of small agrarian cultures. The agrarian aspect of their culture was defined by the rural village economy they had formed in Europe and brought with them to America that viewed the land and its use in agriculture as basic to the community's life. Particularly among the Anabaptist-related groups of the Freeman community, their distinctive cultural heritage remains fairly strong and clear. However, in recent

---

31. Flora et al., *Rural Community*, 9.

decades the particular agrarian element of that heritage has largely been lost. The land and how it is used and held is no longer understood as a community asset but instead as a private inheritance.

In their chapter on cultural capital, the Floras ask, "What happens when one group is technologically and militarily superior and attempts to impose its cultural capital on another group with a very different legacy?"[32] The example they cite is the imposition of the dominant American culture on traditional Native American cultures throughout American history. The example in this book is the imposition of the industrial agricultural model on the village agrarian cultures of the Freeman community. As I have tried to argue, that imposition has seriously depleted the agrarian cultural values of the larger Freeman community.

The Floras describe cultural capital in terms of *legacy*, which they define as "what families, communities, groups and nations pass on to the next generation."[33] A good example of legacy is given in a two-person drama written by Doug Nopar for the Land Stewardship Project of Minnesota. In this drama an older farm couple is confronting their legacy as they approach retirement. The husband thinks of legacy primarily in terms of the estate he will be able to pass on to his children. The wife, whose family had farmed the land generationally, is interested in preserving the agrarian heritage of the farm. The husband's legacy can easily be achieved by selling the land to the highest bidder. Then the couple is approached by a young couple who want to rent the farm as a small food-producing operation. That's an attractive legacy for the wife, but it's a messy solution to their retirement. What will their legacy be? What cultural values or capital are reflected in each of these choices?[34]

While there are many notable exceptions, it seems the prevailing legacy accepted by many famers in the community, often by default, is the sizeable financial asset represented in their estates. Perhaps many farmers wish their land could be preserved as a family-operated agricultural unit, but they despair of anyone having the capability of being able to buy and manage their farms. And following the dominant agricultural paradigm, they are likely correct. But this illustrates the way land has ceased to be seen as an asset for the welfare of the community and is now only seen as a personal estate.

32. Flora et al., *Rural Community*, 26.
33. Flora et al., *Rural Community*, 25.
34. Land Stewardship Project, "Opportunity Knocks."

The Freeman community as a whole retains a strong reservoir of cultural capital in the groups and churches that comprise it. Ethnic celebrations like Schmeckfest every spring bear witness to the desire and effort to retain the values and culture of our ethnic heritage, and to build on that heritage by including the whole Freeman community, especially in the musical productions for which it is famous. How the loss of the communal, agrarian elements in that heritage will affect the larger Freeman community in the long run remains to be seen. But at least the loss of those communal agrarian values needs to be acknowledged and taken into account.

5. "*Financial capital* consists of money that is used for investment rather than consumption. *Investment* means using a purchase or a financial instrument to create additional value."[35]

The Freeman community is rich in financial capital in the form of its farmland. A cursory internet exploration of farmland for sale indicated two quarter-sections for sale, one near Freeman listed for $7,000 an acre, and another near Hurley for $6,700 an acre. Both of these sales would total over one million dollars. It is impossible for a new farmer to purchase a quarter like this and pay off the investment with the produce of the land. Land at these prices can only be purchased by those who have money to invest in land, usually investors from outside the community, or by large established farmers whose operations can absorb the investment. In either case, the potential for financial capital to be available for community development from farmland is small under current land tenure and investment models.

The town of Freeman is home to the Freeman Community Development Corporation, a local non-profit organization "dedicated to promoting the economic vitality of the community and promoting the highest quality of life for residents and those who visit the Freeman community."[36] The FCDC has received significant contributions from estates and recognizes the importance of agriculture to the community. It will likely be a significant resource for the future revitalization of the Freeman community. Already it is assisting in the formation of a current new endeavor—a possible butcher shop and meat processing plant.

The current financial wealth of the agricultural community around Freeman has obscured in many ways the cultural decline of the

---

35. Flora et al., *Rural Communities*, 9.
36. City of Freeman, "Freeman Community Development."

community. It has enabled the community to maintain and build services and institutions that bring growth and stability to the community. The health and educational institutions in particular are strong in the Freeman community relative to other neighboring small towns, and the same is true of retail and financial services. Still, I have to reflect on the decision of Salem Mennonite Church to rebuild a large structure in 1985 because it was financially able to do so, only to have some members talk now about merging with a neighboring church because of declining membership. The financial assets obscured the actual demographic and cultural decline of the community.

6. "*Built capital* [is] factories, schools, roads, restored habitat, community centers, and the like, all of which contribute to building other capitals for communities."[37]

Considering that the land around Freeman was all virgin prairie when the first European settlers arrived here in the 1870s, the community is rich with built capital. Most obvious are the farmsteads and the towns of the community, and the roads connecting them all. We have seen how the railroad led to the thriving of the pioneer community in the 1880s, although the tracks running through Freeman have long disappeared. Still, nearly every section line has a graded gravel road maintained by township boards, and many county roads are paved, as well as the state and federal highways running through the community. While some of this infrastructure is aging and even crumbling, a significant investment is made to maintain it.

The rural dwellers as well as local towns are likewise served by a considerable additional public infrastructure. While initially the farmsteads had to fend for themselves and were isolated, Rural Free Delivery mail service was brought to rural areas by the US Postal Service in the late nineteenth century. The early twentieth century saw the development of rural telephone service, often established by local township companies, that connected rural farmsteads with local towns and beyond. The mid-twentieth century saw the delivery of electricity to rural farms through the National Rural Electric Cooperative Association (REA for short, locally) established in 1942. Later in the twentieth century, rural water systems were also established to bring treated water to rural residents and farms, and farms no longer had to rely solely on their own wells. And early in the twenty-first century, fiber-optic telecommunication infrastructure

---

37. Flora et al., *Rural Communities*, 9–10.

for connecting to the World Wide Web was installed throughout the local rural community.

We've already noted the building of local churches in town and in the countryside. Freeman has new and modern K–12 public schools, and Freeman Academy built a new gymnasium within the past decade. The Freeman hospital built in the 1950s served the community well until medical services were consolidated into urban medical centers, but the Freeman Regional Health Services maintains a strong local medical clinic, an emergency room, a swing bed facility, and a nursing home as well as apartments for the elderly. Salem Mennonite Home for the Aged was begun in the 1950s and is currently in the process of establishing a new and enlarged campus in the southeast corner of Freeman. The Freeman Community Development Corporation has land for an industrial park along US Highway 81. The community has a strong and vibrant museum that studies and celebrates the unique history of the community in Heritage Hall Museum and Archives.

Whatever the future holds for the Freeman community, and however it may change in future decades, there is a strong built infrastructure in place to facilitate the changes and innovations that may be required. On the other hand, as someone who walks the quiet, country lanes of the community regularly, I am appalled at the waste of built capital evident in the countryside. Not only are there many abandoned farmsteads, but even the existing farms all have built capital wasting away in the form of large hayloft barns, silos, paved feedlots, a multitude of smaller farm structures, and outdated agricultural implements and equipment. All this built capital was simply abandoned in place when new agricultural technologies made them obsolete, and now most of those classic barns are slowly yielding to disuse, disrepair, and the ravages of time. I have to wonder about the judgment future generations will have on the agricultural economy of the second half of the twentieth century so oblivious to waste and ruin.

7. "*Political capital* is the ability of a group to influence the distribution of resources within a social unit, including helping set the agenda for what resources are available, and who is eligible to receive them."[38]

Political capital would be exercised in a rural community like Freeman through city councils, school boards, township boards, and county supervisors, in additional to state and federal political legislatures and

---

38. Flora et al., *Rural Communities*, 10.

officials. At the most local level, there would seem to be a good measure of political capital within the Freeman community, meaning that local residents do have the ability to influence the distribution of resources, tax revenue, and local spending. At the state and county levels, local communities struggle to maintain some measure of influence against the influence exercised by urban centers and agricultural corporations. Local residents struggle to control the establishment of confined animal feeding operations (CAFOs) in their neighborhoods, which also often tear local neighborhoods apart. In the same way, organic farmers struggle to deal with aerial spraying and the drift of chemicals onto their properties as legislatures relax environmental laws in favor of corporate interests.

Political capital depends in large measure on the cohesiveness and vitality of the rural community. When the rural community is fractured and depleted by individualism, rivalries, and ethnocentrism, it loses the ability to exercise a significant degree of political capital. Locally, that tension can often be felt between rural and town residents of the community, who each tend to pursue their own interests, sometimes at the other's expense. It is difficult for rural and town residents to pursue a common agenda that serves the interests of both.

This is a very superficial, subjective, and highly biased portrait of the larger Freeman community. But perhaps it begins to describe the current status of the Freeman community using sociological criteria. This portrait may be useful as we begin to explore the future and perhaps the rebirth of the Freeman community in the coming decades. The agrarian cultures that characterized the Freeman community for the past century and a half are no longer operative as they once were. There may be continuities between those cultures and the new agrarian cultures that begin to emerge. Nevertheless, the future agrarian cultures will also have a much different character than those of the past.

PART III

Toward the Rebirth of the Community

8

The Community's Movement toward Revitalization (2000 to 2050)

SYNOPSIS

RECENT YEARS HAVE SEEN the beginnings of a movement toward the revitalization of the Freeman community. As the economic, ecological, and energy crises confronting the dominant culture of American society deepen, it is increasingly evident that the industrial agriculture model that has prevailed in America for the past decades is unsustainable. Energy costs increase, the federal costs of subsidizing industrial farming are becoming prohibitive, and the effects of global warming caused in part by agriculture are gradually changing the climate and making the costs of industrial agriculture much greater. The realities of these developments are slowly percolating through the fabric of rural communities like Freeman, leading even proponents of industrial agriculture to have second thoughts about the wisdom of their methods.

Several developments are contributing to the beginning of a transformation of rural communities like Freeman. Young adults who left the community for professions and who in their urban environment are confronting the deepening crises of the dominant culture are seeking to return to their rural roots and coming home to raise their families. They bring with them not only the energy and vision of youth, but also the benefit of their education and worldview. This indeed is characteristic of the Freeman community. Many of the now aging farmers are themselves persons with higher education degrees and in many cases with international experience in a variety of agrarian settings around the world, a consequence of the emphasis on service prominent in the Anabaptist/Mennonite faith of the community.

In addition to the beginning of a demographic reversal, recent years have seen the development of a number of alternative agricultural models. Some of these are simply small, niche-market-oriented enterprises, like a vineyard of an acre or two on a farm, or poultry or small animal production. Others are more thoughtful and thoroughgoing enterprises, transforming farms into full-scale organic islands in the sea of industrial agriculture and developing local markets in nearby urban centers for the produce of the farms.

Still another indication of change might be found in the formation of faith-based organizations like Rural Revival at Freeman, dedicated to the formation of a local food system and to working at land tenure issues and the transfer of land to the next generation. There are indications that the churches of the rural community are re-awakening to the role they can and should play in shaping the agrarian culture in which they live rather than simply pouring their resources into urban ministries and denominational programs, worthy as these might all be. Faith-based care for the land and communal values are once more re-asserting themselves as the primary contribution of the church to the community in which it lives.

THE THREE E CRISIS: ECONOMY, ENERGY, ENVIRONMENT (ECOLOGY)

At the surface, the dominant culture of America appears to be strong and stable in the first decades of the twenty-first century. The United States remains the pre-eminent political and military power of the world. Despite occasional setbacks, the economy continues to grow, at least measured by the growth of the stock market. Great work has been done in undoing some of the most egregious ecological disasters of recent decades. Many corporations are beginning to introduce products and ways of operating that limit greenhouse gases and mitigate the threat of climate change. Technological advances continue to be introduced on every front, not only in the ubiquitous information and communication front, but also in controlling Nature, from agriculture to conservation to human health and reproduction. There seem to be no limits and few constraints on the dominance of American society both domestically and internationally.

Nevertheless, economic growth remains the primary preoccupation and goal of American society. Every quarter, and often in between, news casts focus on the Gross Domestic Product, and grave concern is expressed if GDP growth is less than 2 or 3 percent annually. At the same time, any rational person can see that continued economic growth in a finite world is impossible. Economic growth is ultimately sustained only through the use and exploitation of natural resources and human labor. Natural resources have a finite limit, and human labor involves the hidden cost of injustice and inequality and exploitation, and the bill for that cost will eventually come due, as the history of past empires assures us.

Economic growth requires an inordinate amount of energy consumption. Though great strides have been made in the direction of renewable energy, notably wind and solar, the primary energy source contributing to economic growth in America is still fossil fuel. Though obscured by the development of hydraulic fracturing (which bears its own unacknowledged environmental risks) to extract the oil reserves, fossil fuel is a limited resource that will only grow more costly in the future. More seriously, the use of fossil fuel as the primary energy source for a society like ours is one of the main contributors to greenhouse gases that lead to global warming and ultimately to climate change.

Not least, continued economic growth also involves environmental risks of the first order. These risks involve not just pollution and resource depletion and waste management, but more fundamentally the risks to environmental and human health by the introduction of technical fixes designed to assure short-term economic success that leads to economic growth. But the greatest environmental risk of unrestrained economic growth is the economic disparity it fosters. Economic growth always comes at the expense of the poor, creating a class of impoverished people whose lives are hopelessly mired in dependence and who usually live at the most vulnerable natural settings of the world. While dated, being published in 1980, Kirkpatrick Sale's book, *Human Scale*, still provides a comprehensive and trenchant critique of the American preoccupation with bigness and growth.[1]

It is traditional and agrarian cultures that bear much of the burden for the growth of the American economy. Indeed, the resurgence of white nationalism so ably exploited by people like President Donald Trump bears witness to the alienation and resentment felt by rural cultures at

---

1. Sale, *Human Scale*. See especially Part II, "The Burden of Bigness."

their exclusion from the dominant urban culture of American society. As Howard Zinn pointed out years ago in *A People's History of the United States*, the American elite have since America's founding done an excellent job of pitting dispossessed elements of society against each other so that the elite may continue to exploit them all.[2]

It is evident that the American Empire is living on the edge of a precipice. Weighed down with massive debt, fettered by political deadlocks, buried under the weight of its waste, struggling to maintain a position of prominence on the global stage, threatened by environmental crises and climate change, hampered by the vast disparity of wealth between rich and poor, eaten from within by drug abuse, torn by racial divisions, fractured by rampant individualism with each demanding his or her rights at the expense of the community, fearful of immigrants waiting at our borders, and now in early 2020 confronting the global coronavirus pandemic, the only question is whether the empire will suddenly implode and fall apart in massive social disintegration, or whether sufficient ameliorating reforms will be made to enable a transition of a more stable and humane social order. While justice would seem to require the former, the latter would perhaps involve less social upheaval and violent conflict.

What this means is not just that rural communities are among the victims that perpetuate an unsustainable society. It means that rural communities like Freeman are required for a societal movement into a sustainable future. That is true first of all in the most basic sense of providing a local food system for the population. But just as important, healthy rural communities provide the social stability and structure required for the society at large if there is to be movement toward a more sustainable future. However useful they might be, governmentally mandated reforms, corporate business restructuring, and technocratic solutions cannot fundamentally change the trajectory of American society toward disintegration and chaos. And at the other extreme, individuals alone can do little to effect widespread change, however clearly they might envision the future. It will be again, as it always has been in the past, the role of local communities to create a new social order reflecting the ecological, social, and spiritual conditions required for the future.

---

2. Zinn, *People's History*. See especially ch. 4, "Tyranny is Tyranny."

RE-ENVISIONING THE RURAL COMMUNITY OF FREEMAN

This chapter is intended to describe the first indications of a movement toward the revitalization of the rural community of Freeman. Such a revitalization is crucial given the economic/energy/environmental crises the United States, and indeed the global community as a whole, confronts in the twenty-first century. But in order to mark movement toward a revitalization of rural communities like Freeman, it may be important to describe what we might or should be moving toward. What do we (I) envision the revitalized rural community of Freeman to look like a generation from now, say the mid-twenty-first century?

I envision the larger Freeman community (western three-fourths of Turner County, eastern third of Hutchinson County) with a repopulated countryside in 2050. There are advantages for agrarian cultures to have residents living in villages and going out to tend flocks and fields, but there is currently a transportation and communication infrastructure in place to make a dispersed population living on scattered farms surrounding the small towns and villages of this area workable.

By repopulated countryside, I mean that I envision four or more agricultural enterprises or farms on each section of land. Given the ecological constraints of this environment, there was some wisdom on the part of the United States government in providing for a quarter section of land for homesteaders in the Homestead Act. A quarter section (160 acres) is small enough that a farm family can provide attention and care for the whole, while also allowing for a wide variety of agricultural enterprises on it, from gardens and groves and orchards, to small tilled fields for feed crops, to pastures and hay fields for livestock.

I envision a landscape with a significant portion of the land restored to prairie in the form of native grasses or hay and grassland for livestock. We cannot in this environment escape the ecology of the prairie in a sustainable view of the future. The small farms would have a large proportion of their land in hay or grassland and have a strong livestock component, either for meat or dairy production. On a rotational basis, a small percentage of the land would be tilled to raise grain crops for animal feed and for human consumption, along with the permanent gardens and orchard groves.

The small farms of the community will be linked together in local agrarian cultures encompassing no more than a couple of hundred people, and that may indeed be much smaller neighborhood associations.[3] These local agrarian cultures may at first be structured around historic religious congregations with ties to particular areas of the community. They might also be cooperative associations or organizations formed within specific neighborhoods to engage in particular economic enterprises. Whether or not they are strictly faith-based, these neighborhood associations would be the center for much of the social and cultural life of the community. They would meet the social and economic needs of the neighborhood in the form of cooperative labor, shared agricultural equipment, and joint processing and marketing of farm produce.

While the ethnic heritage of the historic congregations of the community should be known and studied and celebrated, these rural congregations will look quite different in the future. They will learn to welcome and include all the diverse residents of the rural community and celebrate their heritage and identity while also maintaining their own heritage and performing the traditional religious functions of worship, education, and fellowship. In addition, these congregations will actively pursue relationships with all the other agrarian cultures and faith communities around them locally, regionally, and globally, for the purpose of collaborating in the revitalization and maintenance of rural communities everywhere.

Most importantly, rural congregations and assemblies of all denominations and faiths will see the economic and social life of the larger community as central to their faith mission. While connections with area and denominational structures are important both for communal identity and cooperative endeavors, rural congregations will invest their human, cultural, and financial assets in the development of the local community. Central to every faith perspective are not just issues of spiritual welfare and eternal destiny, but also the way in which the community lives together both internally and in relationship to other communities, and especially in the way the community cares for the land as the basis for its life here on Earth.

These more strictly agrarian cultures of the countryside will work with the local towns (one thousand to ten thousand population) like Freeman and Parker, and villages (one hundred to one thousand population) like Marion, Bridgewater, Hurley, and Menno, to become an economically and socially self-sufficient rural community. The towns and villages and the rural residents will work together collaboratively to provide for

---

3. I'm reminded of Wendell Berry's term for this kind of association, "The Membership," described in ch. 11 of his novel, *Hannah Coulter*.

the needs of the whole community. The farms will provide the food and agricultural produce, and the villages and towns will provide the processing cooperatives and marketing mechanisms for that farm production. In addition, the towns and villages would provide the primary and secondary educational institutions and the medical, financial, and retail services needed by the community. Everything produced in the Freeman community would be used locally and marketed in the nearby urban (10,000 to 100,000 population) centers of Yankton and Mitchell, and the metropolitan (plus 100,000 population) center of Sioux Falls.

I envision the Freeman community itself developing all the processing facilities required for the produce of the land—the food, fiber, and fabric required by the community and for sale to urban areas. In addition, I envision the Freeman community developing the manufacturing industries required for both household needs and for much of the minimal, small-farm equipment needed to serve the modest agricultural enterprises of the community. In the same way, the Freeman community will develop the renewable energy systems required to serve the energy needs of the local rural and town/village community. While some of these small manufacturing and energy industries may not be the first order of business for the community, the viability of the rural community depends on its ability to become largely energy and economically self-sufficient over a period of decades.[4]

I envision the Freeman community as a place where traditional arts and crafts can be learned and practiced. Agrarian cultures provide opportunity for a broad range of arts and crafts that by now have been largely lost in this era of mass-produced consumer goods. Both rural and small-town residents would find opportunity and resources to establish household crafts and industries that would serve both the needs of the community and profitably be sold in nearby urban areas. In addition, music and drama and art and literature can be developed that give rural residents the opportunity to participate in endeavors of human creativity rather than simply being entertained as consumers.

In other words, I envision the larger Freeman community (as defined above) as an economically and socially self-sufficient community with a population of fifteen thousand to twenty thousand town, village, and rural residents. The various small cultures and the community as a whole would seek to become less and less dependent on the dominant

4. Sale, *Human Scale*, makes the case for community self-sufficiency in Part Four, ch. 10, of his book.

culture and economy of American society. This would not be so much a withdrawal from or rejection of that dominant culture, but simply a means of being able to function as a community without a large dependence on that culture and economic system. Youth would be intentionally trained and educated to provide all the services needed by the agrarian cultures of the community. Only when rural communities are largely independent from the structures and institutions of the dominant culture are they able to retain control over their land and the agricultural heritage basic to the community's life.

I envision the Freeman community planning intentionally about how it will retain its independence and self-sufficiency for the future. The community will decide together how to live, establish broad policies for land use, and devise land tenure procedures that provide for the generational transfer of land. The community will provide resources and structures that enable its youth and new residents to become landed members of the community, but also plan intentionally for how to limit economic and population growth in ways that ensure that the community will not outgrow and deplete its land base. In this way, the community would also foster the stability and health of the larger American society and model a progressive, sustainable, just, and humane future to a dominant culture obsessed with wealth and power, and characterized by oppression, exploitation, waste, and ecological devastation.

This is not a particularly radical vision for the future of the Freeman community. It retains the paradigm of small diversified farms around small towns and service centers that marked the early development of the community. But it does return agriculture to its primary function of raising food, and away from industrial, commodity-oriented agriculture. It requires the formation of a local food system that integrates rural farms and small towns into a vibrant, largely self-sustaining community. It seeks a third way between the extreme individualism of the dominant culture and the radical communitarianism that may thwart individual initiative and achievement and has sometimes characterized the Anabaptist cultures featured in this study.

ATTITUDINAL CHANGES IN RURAL COMMUNITIES IN THE PAST FORTY YEARS

I've hinted that I grew up in a fairly conservative home, theologically and culturally. My father, Harry Kaufman, resisted acculturation, particularly in the way he farmed. He was not uninformed politically, but participated only marginally in the political process (voting), and was highly skeptical about governmental involvement in agriculture, particularly policies adopted under the administration of Franklin D. Roosevelt. He supported local community improvements like the township telephone companies and the development of a local hospital and museum in Freeman, but deplored and resisted the industrialization of agriculture that began in earnest during the final decades of his life. Interestingly, he fairly early in the 1960s adopted soybeans into his crop rotation.

In my young adult years, I was deeply influenced in my intellectual development by my oldest brother, Maynard Kaufman, then a professor of religion and environmental studies at Western Michigan University in Kalamazoo. While on the other end of the spectrum theologically, there was an interesting congruence of suspicion about the direction of the dominant culture in America between father and son. From my brother I gained the intellectual tools to articulate an agrarian vision and critique the developments occurring in rural communities across the country.

Coming into pastoral ministry in rural congregations of the Great Plains in the early 1970s with these perspectives, I fairly early assumed a critical stance toward the dominant agricultural paradigm operating in the congregations I served, and which were occurring also here in my home community of Freeman. Before long, during the farm crisis of the 1970s and 1980s, I was a speaker at church conferences and events designed to address the crisis in rural America. I often presented biblical studies that helped to explain the current dynamics of rural America and to point toward avenues of rural revitalization.

While the rural congregations I served at the time supported my extracurricular ministries within the broader church, I also early on learned to temper or camouflage the more radical implications of my thought in the local settings. My church members were after all mostly farmers, folks who made their living from the land, and who themselves were often struggling for financial survival. These were folks who quite uncritically participated in the industrialization of agriculture, and indeed were quite enthralled with the latest agricultural equipment and technology and quite sure that these advancements or progress would ensure the future. Of course, there was even then the occasional organic or *natural* farmer in the area who resisted the inevitability of the future and who was grateful and eager for my biblical critique of current agricultural systems, but I could see the disinterest and even contempt my congregants had for these alternative farmers.

While the change has been slow and often painful, there has been a significant shift in the attitudes of farmers in recent years. Aware of their dependence on governmental subsidies for the survival of their farms and of the urban resistance toward bailing out farmers, and burdened with debt and the uncertainties of a global market for their commodities, farmers today look with some measure of respect at their peers who try and succeed to farm in alternative ways, seeking out niche markets for some part of their farm produce. This is particularly true when the farm community is made aware by organic farmers of the huge economic advantages to be had once the transition to organic production is achieved. An article on organic farming, part of a series on Rural Alternatives published by the local newspaper, *Freeman Courier*, confirmed the economic viability and profitability of organic farming.[5] Though these local organic farmers continue to face a lot of questions, they certainly have the attention and often the respect of their peers.

It is this attitudinal change over the past couple of decades that demonstrates the possibility of a revitalization of the Freeman community. Obviously, there will be no whole-sale shift from conventional to organic agriculture. Indeed, such a dramatic shift would likely be highly disruptive to the community. But this shift in attitudes creates space for the development of new agricultural and community paradigms to emerge. In recent years, the USDA farm bill has also made provisions for organic and sustainable farming enterprises. The growing realization of the unsustainability of conventional or industrial agriculture and that there are better ecological and economic alternatives lead to this attitudinal change in rural communities that begins to make space for community revitalization.

Agrarian cultures are by nature conservative. These cultures bear to the current generation the wisdom of past generations of human experience and belief, socially, theologically, and agriculturally. When techniques of industrial agriculture were being introduced, they were

---

5. Kaufman, "Conventional Crops."

presented as aids to the traditional agricultural paradigm, for instance in the form of labor-saving devices, and not as challenges to it. The full range of implications attending the introduction of new technologies was not presented or explored. A new agricultural paradigm was put into place without the participants being aware of it. Indeed, industrial agriculture continues to present itself as central to the preservation of the family farm in farm advertisements that show idyllic farm scenes even while it effectively destroys the family farm. This accounts for the way in which farmers have resisted agricultural paradigms that challenge industrial agriculture. Farmers believe they are conserving their traditional culture by resisting current new agricultural paradigms, and ironically see practices like organic farming as foreign to their tradition.

Meanwhile, the dominant culture has also undergone a shift. It is now understood that several different perspectives can co-exist without canceling each other out. Rather than either/or, in the dominant culture, it is now more often both/and. Acculturated as we are to the dominant culture, this also enables people in rural communities to see and accept the co-existence and perhaps even the compatibility of the various agricultural paradigms that are currently being utilized and explored.

In any case, there has been a significant attitudinal shift in rural communities in recent decades, and that does create space for new ways of understanding the agricultural enterprise. This may seem like a very small and indeed a preliminary step in the re-formation of struggling rural communities, but in fact it represents a huge and essential step. It creates a sense of fluidity within agrarian cultures. It invites an exploration within those cultures of the traditions of the past, and an evaluation of the methods, techniques, and technologies currently in use or proposed for use in the future.

CHANGING DEMOGRAPHIC REALITIES

Much of this chapter relies on anecdotal and subjective observations about the Freeman community and the agricultural scene, and may thus be as much a matter of wishful thinking as it is of reality. For instance, I began attending Salem-Zion Mennonite Church, where I am now a member, in 2010, when it had virtually no children to come forward for a children's story. Now there are sometimes nearly twenty children present. The parents of these children represent mostly children of the congregation who made the choice either to return to their home community to raise their families, or to marry and stay in the community. Most of them are engaged in some agricultural endeavor, even if it is not the family's sole or primary income. Many of them bring back educational, service, and life experiences gained in their years away from the community. While highly acculturated to the dominant culture, their values are shaped by that culture's awareness and critique of the limitations of its commitment to growth and exploitation. They are for the most part families very aware of the problems of global warming, climate change, injustice, and the dangers of the industrial food system, and are integrating these perspectives with the faith heritage represented by the church and the agricultural heritage of the community.

At the same time, I'm aware that the neighboring, sister congregation I last served as pastor has experienced the reverse demographic. While I was there as a pastor in the first decade of this century, there were large catechism classes of new members being baptized every year. Many of these young adults left the community, and this congregation is now suffering from a lack of children. Children's Christmas programs and Summer Bible Schools are held jointly between the two churches, and this congregation that twenty years ago had both a cherub and a large junior choir now has neither. As a pastor, I'm very well aware that every congregation goes through natural cycles of membership growth that ebb and flow. Perhaps there is really no new demographic reality yet at work in the Freeman community.

One aspect of the continuing demographic reality of the Freeman community is the way the agrarian culture is informed by both educational and service experiences. Since World War II, the Anabaptist congregations of the Freeman community have had a strong emphasis both on education and on Christian service to meet human needs. When there was a draft, this emphasis was fed by the need to find alternative service in lieu of military service, but even since the Vietnam era, the Anabaptist congregations have continued to send a strong number of youth into service both in North America and around the world. Those returning from these terms of service, which often involved rural development work in a variety of cultural settings, have brought back a rich wealth of perspectives and ideas relevant to the development of the Freeman community with its agrarian cultures. Many of the most innovative agricultural entrepreneurs through the years as well as recently represent this kind of personal history.

Statistically, neither Turner County nor Hutchinson County demonstrate a demographical rebound currently. Both counties declined in population from the 2000 to the 2010 censuses. Turner County had a very small population increase in the estimated 2018 population, but not enough to bring the population back to the 2000 census level. This is true even though Turner County is part of the Sioux Falls Metropolitan Statistical Area which continues to see significant growth.

With 618 square miles, Turner County has a higher population density of 13.5 per square mile, than Hutchinson County, with 814 square miles, nine per square mile. In 2018, Turner County had 3,470 households, and Hutchinson County had 2,862 households.[6] In the recently released five-year USDA Farm Census for 2017, Turner County had 757 farms averaging 519 acres per farm, and Hutchinson County had 775 farms with an average size of 588 acres.[7] This means that around a quarter of the households in these two counties were farms.

The population of both counties peaked in the 1930 census, with 14,891 residents in Turner County and 13,904 in Hutchinson County.[8] Assuming relatively equal population density across the counties, this means that the western three-fourths of Turner County had a population of around 11,200, and the eastern third of Hutchinson County a population of about 4,600, for a total of 15,800 residents in what I am defining as the larger Freeman community. In the 2010 census, Turner County had a population of 8,347, and Hutchinson County a population of 7,743.[9] Using the same criteria employed for the 1930 census, the western three-fourths of Turner County had a population of about 6,200, and the eastern third of Hutchinson County a population of about 2,600, for a total of about 8,800 residents in the larger Freeman community in 2010. The population of the community can nearly double before it reaches the population density it had in 1930, and that would still be well within the population projected earlier in this chapter for the revitalized Freeman community.

All this means that even though the Freeman community as a whole has not yet seen a significant demographic shift in its population, the potential for re-populating the countryside is very real. In addition to

---

6. US Census Bureau, "Quick Facts."

7. United States Department of Agriculture, National Agricultural Statistics Service, "County Summary Highlights, 2017."

8. Wikipedia, "Turner County," "Hutchinson County."

9. Wikipedia, "Turner County," "Hutchinson County."

providing a place for its own youth who may still be in urban centers, the community has the possibility of capitalizing on the yearning of many other youth to return to the land and engage in farming. The work of organizations like Dakota Rural Action in South Dakota, the Land Stewardship Project in Minnesota, and the Center for Rural Affairs in Nebraska all bear witness to the interest many young families in American society have in finding a place on the land where they can live and farm and raise their families. We are on the cusp of a major demographic shift in American society from urban to rural, and we have the various forms of capital as a rural community to facilitate that demographic shift.

PIONEERS OF NEW AGRICULTURAL PARADIGMS

While much of this chapter has reflected subjective and wishful thinking about the future of the Freeman community, there are in fact a good number of concrete and ongoing initiatives in the Freeman community that point the way toward revitalization. Some of these are small, by-the-way enterprises that farm families explore alongside their primary commodity-oriented farming operation or off-farm jobs. Others represent more thoroughgoing enterprises in which the whole farming operation stands in stark contrast to the industrial farms which still dominate in the community's landscape.

A decade or two ago, a local farm family planted an acre vineyard near their farmyard. When the grapes are ready to harvest they invite their friends and neighbors to come and help collect and stamp out the grapes, which are then sold to a local winery that produces a local label identifying the source of the wine. Another farm family with several children works with their college-age daughters to manage a Community Supported Agriculture operation on their otherwise conventional farm in order to finance their college education.[10] This same family has also had a broiler slaughtering operation that sells chicken to friends and neighbors. Another farm family with college-age children engaged them to raise and sell sweet corn for the same purpose. A couple living on a farm place at the edge of town have a dozen or more goats they raise for sale. Still another young farmer has a goat herd he rents out to local farms who need their wood lots cleaned up of brush and undergrowth. A local farmer initiated a Community Garden in Freeman for the sole purpose

---

10. Kaufman, "A Local 'Local Food' Enterprise."

of raising fresh vegetables for a local Food Pantry operated by a local church. Churches in the community help tend and pick the vegetables throughout the summer.[11]

These are just a few of many local initiatives that contribute to the development of a local food system. The town of Freeman began a once-a-week summer farmers market a few years ago, now administered by a local non-profit, Rural Revival. This is one of the outlets for sale of local farm produce as well as baked goods and jams and jellies. A few intrepid souls venture out to the highways and byways to seek out surviving wild plum and chokecherry stands for use in making those jams and jellies.

Agricultural operations with a more thoroughgoing alternative to conventional agriculture include a conventional organic farm; in other words, an organic farm raising conventional crops like corn and soybeans for a premium organic marker. This farm is a small family corporation involving two brothers and includes a strong livestock component, as well as a poultry and berry operation. The field crops are sold on contract at a price considerably higher than the conventional crops, and the demand for organic crops is very large.[12]

Another farmer has transitioned his farm to grass more than twenty years ago. He manages a cow/calf operation using paddocks on which the cattle graze on a rotating basis, while hay for winter is also put up on other paddocks. The feeder calves sold on the market as drug-free are the primary income of the farming operation. While not organic, the farm avoids the chemical inputs of conventional agriculture as well as the soil erosion to which field crops are prone, while retaining and building organic matter in the soil and sequestering the carbon lost in conventional farming.[13]

About fifteen years ago, another local family came home from years of community development service abroad and took over a family farm that had recently been transitioned to organic by the farmer's father. Almost by accident, the family discovered there was a strong demand for raw milk in the area, as there are strong health benefits to consuming raw milk. They built up a dairy selling raw milk on routes primarily in the Sioux Falls area as well as locally. At a certain point, the state agriculture department was engaged to work out the legalities of selling raw milk. The cows are grazed on grass, and to compensate for the lack of green

11. The anecdotal examples given in this paragraph are based on personal experience and knowledge of the community.

12. Kaufman, "Conventional Crops."

13. Kaufman, "Grassland Farming."

grass in winter, a barley-seed-fodder feeding system was installed on the farm.[14] The milk customers also buy the grass-fed beef and free-range eggs the farm produces.

The nephew of a local farmer who grew up away from the farm and this farming community wanted to raise buffalo and sell their meat. He built a fence to contain the buffalo on his uncle's farm, bought young buffalo who grazed throughout the summer and were harvested on site in fall. However, he found that the main market for his product was not local, but in Florida, where he and his partner lived. In addition, he found that the slaughtering restrictions for his animals was constrictive and inadequate. So his operation is currently on hold.[15]

Meanwhile, this young man and two others, one a local farmer and entrepreneur, recently formed a new company, Prairie-to-Plate. They purchased a Mobile Slaughtering Unit and planned to build a more permanent processing facility in the local city industrial zone. This USDA-inspected facility would serve local livestock producers raising animals for local use or sale. These farmers now have to wait months for openings in the few slaughtering facilities and butcher shops remaining in the region.[16] Unfortunately, financing for this operation proved difficult, but Rural Revival is currently exploring the formation of a local cooperative to carry through with this project.

In 1968, several related farmers joined forces to create Rural Manufacturing, a locally owned and operated manufacturing plant on the edge of Freeman that produces livestock handling equipment of all kinds. The plant employs a couple of dozen workers. It is a prime example of the kind of integrated rural community endeavor that creates community self-sufficiency by providing the manufactured equipment needed for local agricultural endeavors.[17] In 2018, Rural Manufacturing celebrated fifty years of successful business.

This is a small sampling of the kinds of local business initiatives that I consider indicative of a revitalization of the Freeman community as a collection of agrarian cultures working together to serve the needs of the community and the larger society. While there is some networking among a number of these businesses and farms, they are primarily

14. Kaufman, "Midwinter Grazing."
15. Jeremy Waltner, "Where the Buffalo Roam."
16. Jeremy Waltner, "Idea Men."
17. See www.ruralmfg.com.

family-owned business initiatives. It will be interesting to see the multiplier effect as these and other pioneer efforts toward a new agricultural paradigm emerge and begin to collaborate with each other and other interests in the community.

CULTURAL SHIFTS THAT SUPPORT RURAL REVITALIZATION

Recent decades have seen a couple of major shifts of attitudes and practices in the dominant culture that have a huge significance for rural communities, particularly as they move toward different agricultural paradigms. Interestingly, these cultural shifts do not begin in rural communities. Instead they mostly reflect urban trends and dominant cultural perspectives within American society. Alternatively, they are shaped by the institutional religious establishment, which itself is often only responding to the broader cultural shifts in society. To understand the Freeman community's possibilities for revitalization, it is important to understand these cultural shifts and how they play themselves out in rural communities like Freeman.

The Foodie Phenomenon

Recent decades have seen a spate of books on food and the industrial food system in the United States. Two representative books that I liked were *Animal, Vegetable, Miracle* by Barbara Kingsolver, and *The Omnivore's Dilemma*, by Michael Pollan.[18] Novelist Kingsolver describes her family's attempt to live for one year on what they could produce on their farm. Pollan follows two components of our food, corn and cattle, from their farm production to our tables. Books like these not only support a local and natural food system, but also expose the weaknesses and dangers of the dominant industrial food system both in terms of health and in terms of environmental sustainability.

While these books and others like them have not succeeded in changing the industrial food and agriculture system fundamentally, they have sparked a strong interest in local food systems, particularly in the remaining urban middle class of consumers. Two of my daughters live in large urban centers, and they and their peers are very conscious of their

18. Kingsolver, *Animal, Vegetable, Miracle*; Pollan, *Omnivore's Dilemma*.

food choices. They have found ample alternatives to the prepared and fast-food offerings of the industrial food system. Urban centers, at least in the Great Plains region, are surrounded by small food-producing farming operations that serve this urban, middle-class clientele. It is refreshing to visit the large farmers markets in the Twin Cities and to see the vast quantities of fresh produce for sale, often raised by new immigrants to America like the Hmong people.

Thus far, rural communities like Freeman have not participated very strongly in this huge shift in the dominant culture. Indeed, there has often been resistance to local food systems. Farmers and small-town people often no longer trust what the Earth produces, and prefer the processed products so readily available in their grocery stores. Local farmers with produce to sell often find rural markets locally to be slim pickings, combined with skepticism about, for instance, drinking raw milk, or paying a premium for organically-produced produce. Most rural residents are looking for bargains at the grocery store and have little interest in paying more for locally produced or organic food.

This is beginning to change as rural farmers see their peers open up new markets for the food they produce in the surrounding urban centers. And this brings us to the central point to be made. The primary impetus for rural revitalization in communities like Freeman is and will be the demand for local food and produce in the surrounding urban areas! There is of course a huge irony in this, that it will be urban consumers who bring farmers and agrarian cultures back to their roots and their reason for existence. But hey, those of us interested in rural revitalization will take it anyway. And indeed, the shift to a food-producing agriculture does have to work economically, and the urban demand for healthy, high-quality, environmentally sound food provides the needed economic rationale.

Acceptance of Climate Change as Reality

The environmental movement as a distinct cultural development on the global scene probably owes its origin to the air pollution caused by the burning of coal in the Industrial Revolution of the eighteenth and nineteenth centuries. As humans gained the capability of significantly damaging the natural environment by their economic activity, the environmental movement was born in an effort to protect the environment and human health. Air and water pollution, soil contamination and erosion, the exploitation of Earth's mineral resources, and destruction of Earth's natural resources have all led to countervailing environmental efforts.

Early environmentalists would include Henry David Thoreau, whose book *Walden* was first published in 1854, and John Muir, through whose efforts national parks were born early in the twentieth century and who founded the Sierra Club in 1892. Aldo Leopold's *A Sand County Almanac* was published in 1949, and Rachel Carlson's *Silent Spring* in 1962. The environmental movement was solidified institutionally in the 1960s and 1970s. The first Earth Day was observed on April 22, 1970, and the Club of Rome published an early scientific analysis of the Earth's health in *The Limits to Growth*, in 1972.[19]

By the 1980s and 1990s, the terms *global warming*, and *human-induced climate change* began to be used. There was now a recognition that human economic and political actions not only had deleterious effects on specific environments and the humans that lived in those environments, but that human activity was threatening the whole global ecosystem, with the real possibility that we would make the Earth uninhabitable for humans. It is this awareness along with other factors that account for the many apocalyptic movies and books that are produced in recent years.

Throughout the twentieth century the concerns of environmentalists have been confirmed and documented by scientific studies showing the negative effects human activity, including the release of greenhouse gases into the environment, was having on the environment and human health. The United Nations adopted the Framework Convention on Climate Change at the Earth Summit in Rio de Janeiro in 1992. The Paris Agreement of 2015, a meeting of the Framework Convention, seemed to move toward actions to limit greenhouse gases significantly, but the United States has subsequently pulled out of this agreement.[20] Indeed, despite solid scientific evidence to confirm indications of global warming leading to climate change, the established political and economic powers of the United States have strongly resisted changing the exploitative and dangerous practices of the status quo. Yet by the end of this second decade of the twenty-first century, even die-hard skeptics and climate change deniers are having to yield before the growing scientific evidence and popular cries for action to deal with global warming.

---

19. Thoreau, *Walden*; Leopold, *Sand County Almanac*; Carson, *Silent Spring*; Meadows et al., *Limits to Growth*.

20. Wikipedia, "Global Warming," "United Nations Framework."

Conservative by nature, and indebted to the powers that drive industrial agriculture, the people of rural communities have often been among the most skeptical resisters to the growing evidence of climate change. This is partly a defensive stance growing out of the recognition that industrial agricultural practices have contributed significantly to global warming. Not only does their use of fossil fuels to power tractors and make fertilizer and pesticides add to atmospheric carbon, but tilling the soil itself opens the soil to oxidation, releasing carbon into the air. That's what has made agriculture a major contributor to global warming. So if I'm a conventional farmer, I'm going to be pretty skeptical of criticisms that fundamentally undermine my agricultural operation.

However, in the past decade or more, it has become evident that while industrial agriculture contributes to global warming, *regenerative* or *natural* or *organic* farming methods actually restore and store carbon in the soil. Carbon, a key greenhouse gas, can be sequestered in the soil naturally by farming! This process is now described in numerous articles and books, including "Beating the Big Dry," an interview with Johannes Meier, a leader in a Bruderhof farm in New South Wales, Australia.[21]

For rural communities on the cusp of revitalization, these new understandings are game-changers. They enable rural communities to move toward natural or regenerative agricultural paradigms and away from industrial agriculture. Of course, it will still take time for opinions to change in conservative rural communities, but when clearly profitable and healthy alternatives to the existing agricultural system are increasingly practiced in their communities, the change could happen fairly quickly, perhaps even in the space of a generation.

Clearly, the environmental movement has significantly shaped the dominant culture of American society. Petrochemical companies continue to exploit the Earth for petroleum, but energy companies are increasingly moving toward renewable energy systems, particularly wind and solar. Business-oriented administrations may cancel previously enacted environmental protections, but many businesses themselves are beginning to recognize both the public and the economic advantages of keeping those protections in place. In so many ways, these shifts in the dominant culture are paving the way for the revitalization of rural communities as well as they transition away from industrial agriculture toward regenerative and natural farming systems.

21. Meier, "Beating the Big Dry." See also Land Stewardship Project, "Carbon's Crisis," and Shaw, "Fostering Healthy Soil."

A Theology of Creation Care

As a young pastor influenced by and committed to both agrarian, communitarian values and ecological principles, I often felt quite lonely, like *a voice crying in the wilderness*. Yes, I was given forums to share my views and was recognized as having something important to share. But the dominant cultural/theological framework of most Christian denominations, including my own Anabaptist/Mennonite church, rarely if ever recognized creation care as important. Indeed, it seemed often to be viewed as a distraction from the real mission of the church, or even more, a sinister intrusion of secularism into the spiritual work of the church. Until recently, particularly in evangelical circles, the environmental movement was seen as worshipping creation instead of the Creator, and thus dismissed.

While I was often discouraged about my own church's lack of interest in environmental issues, I took courage from writers in the wider Christian world who were making connections between Christian faith and care for the environment. The 1980s saw the publication of books like *A Worldly Spirituality*, by Wesley Granberg-Michaelson, then associated with the Sojourners community. Professional theologians were writing theological treatises that specifically addressed ecological issues, as among many others in German Jürgen Moltmann's *God in Creation*, published in 1985.[22]

The rural crisis of the 1970s and 1980s provided a context for the church's incorporation of Earth stewardship into its concern. In 1980, the Regional Catholic Bishops of the American Midwest produced a statement on land issues, *Strangers and Guests: Toward Community in the Heartland*. In 1974, the Church of the Brethren published a report on a study committee on the church and agriculture: *This Land: Ours for a Season*.[23]

In the second half of the twentieth century, American churches of all denominations still had very large and wealthy constituencies in rural America. Some, like the Mennonite Church, were predominantly rural. So the rural crisis was strongly felt and addressed by both denominational leaders and organizations like Mennonite Central Committee. There were annual meetings in a number of states and regions to discuss farm issues. Environmental issues were always a delicate part of these

22. Granberg-Michaelson, *Worldly Spirituality*; Moltmann, *God in Creation*.

23. The Heartland Project, *Strangers and Guests*; Church of the Brethren, *This Land*.

conversations, because raising environmental issues caused by agriculture felt like blaming the victims, in this case farmers, for the devastation of rural America. But they were nonetheless a part of all those discussions. In 1987, Faith and Life Press of the General Conference Mennonite Church published *Hope for the Family Farm: Trust God and Care for the Land*, a collection of essays (the second chapter written by this author) on stewardship of the Earth.[24]

In the 1990s, Mennonite churches began to address environmental issues more directly. In 1991, Art and Jocele Meyer published *Earth-keepers: Environmental Perspectives on Hunger, Poverty, and Injustice*, based on their work with Mennonite Central Committee on these issues.[25] In 1989, two major Mennonite conferences (who have now merged into Mennonite Church USA) established an Environmental Task Force, which in 1995 organized a Creation Summit. The papers from the conference were published as *Creation and the Environment: An Anabaptist Perspective on a Sustainable World*, edited by Calvin Redekop. The Environmental Task Force work is continued today in the Mennonite Creation Care Network, which publishes an online newsletter.[26]

In 1995, the two Mennonite conferences that today make up Mennonite Church USA adopted a new confession of faith. Articles 5 and 6 on "Creation and Divine Providence" and "The Creation and Calling of Human Beings," as well as article 21 on "Christian Stewardship," all present fairly integrated and adequate statements of ecological and creation care concerns into the essential framework of the Mennonite articulation of faith.[27] I finally began to realize that I was not alone in my concerns for creation care and agrarian life. I may still regret that the church has addressed these concerns belatedly in response to societal ferment and prompted by a secular environmental movement rather than creatively leading the way for communities and societies in caring for God's Earth. But, I guess, better late than never.

Beginning in 2014, the seminary where I received my training, Anabaptist Mennonite Biblical Seminary, in Elkhart, Indiana, began sponsoring an annual Rooted and Grounded conference dealing with environmental issues. The conferences increasingly focused on the

---

24. Platt, *Hope for the Family Farm*.
25. Meyer and Meyer, *Earth-keepers*.
26. Redekop, *Creation*; Mennonite Creation Care.
27. Mennonite Church, *Confession of Faith*, 25–30, 77–80.

concerns and interests of urban environmentalists, and less on agrarian issues. This reflects the changing demographic and cultural ethos of the Mennonite Church in the twenty-first century. But conferences like this do keep the concern for creation care on the agenda of the broader church, and most of the topics have application for agrarian communities as well. The major papers (including one by this author) and a number of presentations from the first conference in 2014 were published in *Rooted and Grounded: Essays on Land and Christian Discipleship*.[28]

Rural communities in the Mennonite Church are finally positioned to integrate the theological perspectives of their faith on creation care and community life into the practical revitalization and re-formation of their agrarian cultures. The Anabaptist movement's care for creation throughout history was a largely practical and lived-out expression of their faith and discipleship. It was expressed theologically, if at all, in Anabaptist motifs of discipleship and humility. When agrarian cultures of the twentieth century confronted the assaults of the dominant culture of industrial agriculture, it had no tools to articulate its resistance to these assaults. Now rural communities do have the theological tools to buttress the new agricultural and communal practices that can lead to their revitalization.

RURAL REVIVAL: A SMALL START

About ten years ago, in 2009, I was approached by a local activist and community organizer asking if there could be a forum for discussing rural issues in the community. We began meeting monthly on Sunday afternoons in my office at Salem Mennonite Church—a small group of a half dozen or so interested people. After I retired as pastor, we met for a time at Salem-Zion Mennonite Church, and finally we moved our meetings to a meeting room at the public library in Freeman, to make it a less *Mennonite* group. In July 2012, we finally incorporated as a non-profit organization in the state of South Dakota. Throughout this time, Dennis Lehmann, the community organizer who originated the idea, gave leadership to the group.

While we saw ourselves as faith-based, we didn't articulate a strong parochial or theological identity, hoping to broaden our appeal to people who might not be religious or Mennonite. For much of its existence, Rural Revival, the name we eventually chose for the group, represented a

---

28. Harker and Johnson, *Rooted and Grounded*.

gathering of like-minded farmers and community members for support, networking, and collaboration. Eventually we adopted a mission statement: "promote and enhance local food markets; provide information and tools for thoughtful generational land transfers, and educate the community on a diverse set of rural issues."[29]

Over the past seven or eight years, Rural Revival has sponsored several public meetings, two or three a year. Regarding generational land transfer issues, Rural Revival had several public programs with lawyers and financial managers to identify and explore possible options aging farm families might choose for their farms. We also sponsored the drama, "Look Whose Knockin'," that explores the legacy farm families may wish to consider when passing on their farms.[30] Regarding a local food system, we sponsored a Thanksgiving feast featuring local foods produced by community members. We assumed responsibility to manage the local summer farmers market in Freeman. We have sponsored public meetings related to a variety of agricultural enterprises, and currently feature a local farm enterprise at our monthly meetings.

Despite sponsoring these events, we have often as a group felt we had little impact on the agricultural community. Most of our members represent alternative agricultural enterprises in one way or another, and while we have been open to conventional farmers participating with us, we rarely attracted these farmers to our meetings. So we have remained largely a support group for the small number of alternative farmers represented in the community. But that in itself is a significant service to the revitalization of the Freeman community.

Rural Revival, as part of its informational/educational goal, has collaborated with the local weekly newspaper, *Freeman Courier*, to publish an occasional column entitled Rural Alternatives. In this column we report on a wide variety of initiatives taken by local farmers in their farming operations, and that stand out in some way. A good number of these were already described in the *pioneers* section of this chapter. Other columns have dealt with planting fall cover crops, a small family goat operation, a small heritage hog operation on grass, the return of a Freeman native to take over her large family farm leaving behind a growing career as a music professor, and a conventional strip-cropping initiative.

29. Rural Revival, "Mission."
30. Land Stewardship Project, "Opportunity Knocks."

From our founding, one of the issues that came up again and again was the need for a local meat slaughtering and processing facility. Quite a number of farmers, including more conventional farmers, have a small number of livestock they want to slaughter both for their own use and for possible direct sale to purchasers in some kind of niche market. The nearest small butcher shops are now more than fifty miles away, and are usually booked months in advance. But the group never knew how to proceed with our dream. We are hopeful that a cooperative can be established to develop a butcher shop and meat processing facility in Freeman.

Within the past year or two, Rural Revival has also ventured more directly into the generational land transfer and land tenure arena. A non-resident native of the community, along with his three siblings, inherited a small acreage at their parents' death. This heir, along with one brother, wanted this land farmed organically, and rented their shares to a local organic farmer to begin the three-year transition to organic production. Another sibling wanted to sell his portion, so the first heir, along with several partners including Rural Revival, are purchasing another quarter of the property to be added to the half already committed to organic transitioning.

This concrete involvement in local land has led Rural Revival to begin exploring how it can expand its mission to include the formation of a regenerative community farmland trust. Such a trust would represent an effort to regain control of local land on behalf of the community by providing land-owners with a mechanism to keep their land in the hands of a new generation of local farmers. It would make land available to a new generation of farmers, with preference given to those who are interested in developing a local food system. The community farmland trust would have the intention of revitalizing the rural community in the development of a local food system, preserving the land in local control for agricultural use, and resourcing farm families in the generational transfer of farms and the support of a new generation of farmers.[31]

While this community farmland trust idea is still in its formative stages, it may represent the most concrete step toward the revitalization of the Freeman community. Land in the community is often sold at auction to the highest bidder, who is often an outside investor. The community needs to regain control over its land as the fundamental resource it has as an agricultural community. A community farmland trust is one

---

31. Rural Revival, "Proposal for a Community Farmland Trust."

way to remove farmland from the speculative market and make it available to young farmers who otherwise could not afford to make the major investment the purchase of land and establishment of a farming operation requires.

My own vision for Rural Revival was always that it might become the vehicle through which all the churches and faith traditions (agrarian cultures) of the Freeman community might come together to work for the re-formation of the community. At this point none of the congregations, including those to which most Rural Revival members belong, have adopted Rural Revival as a non-profit with which they want to identify and in which they might invest their missional resources for the welfare of the local community. I am still hopeful that as local congregations (the agrarian cultures of the community) learn more about what is required to rebuild the community, they will begin to cooperate together through Rural Revival or through other associations to engage this mission.

The Freeman community is a long way from being re-formed. Groups like Rural Revival often feel it is quite a hopeless endeavor, despite their efforts. Change in rural communities comes only slowly and incrementally. Nevertheless, the developments described in this chapter indicate that the process has begun, and that the potential for significant growth and change is possible in the Freeman community that had its beginnings nearly 150 years ago on what was then virgin prairie.

9

The Re-formation of an Agrarian Culture

SYNOPSIS

AS AGRARIAN CULTURES LIKE those around Freeman begin to re-form and take new shape, there are several things that will be required. The assumption is that the old agrarian cultures that had sustained the community for a generation or two in the early and mid-twentieth century have by and large passed from the scene and cannot be helpfully resurrected. We cannot simply go back to the past, however much we must still learn from it. So with the triumph of industrial agriculture it will now be necessary to re-create a new agricultural paradigm and a new agrarian culture. What will be required for that to happen?

First, the agrarian cultures of the Freeman community will need to build a new relationship with the land on which they live. We have allowed the dominant culture to define our relationship to the land as a private possession, as an imperial asset, and as an inert medium on which to grow crops and livestock for a global market. We need to recover a view of the land as a divine gift given for the sustenance of the whole human family, the place of our common life together as a people, and most importantly, as our partner and teacher in the agricultural endeavor. We need to learn again to live within the opportunities and constraints that this particular land opens up for us. This will involve the formation of agricultural paradigms quite different from those currently operative.

Second, the agrarian cultures of the Freeman community need to recover their cultural and communal identity. Only by having an alternative identity and set of values, practices, and beliefs to the dominant culture will the cultures of the community be able to develop sustainable relationships with the land and the dominant culture of American society. This means first defining the cultural heritage unique to each of the traditional and new cultural groupings that emerge in the future. Cultural groupings cannot work together unless they each know who they are and what from their past or from the values of their culture they bring to the table for the re-creation and re-formation of the community as a whole. Each culture of the community, whether traditional or newly-emergent, needs to clarify the beliefs and values it holds so that its gifts can be offered to the larger community. Then all the cultures of the community need to create venues in which common goals can be pursued for the community as a whole.

Third, the agrarian cultures of the Freeman community need to rebuild reciprocal, healthy, and mutually beneficial relationships with the dominant American society. In their acculturation to American society, the agrarian cultures have come to allow the dominant society to define the values, customs, and practices of their lives. This has put them at the mercy of the exploitative tendencies of the dominant culture and undermined their future. Agrarian cultures will always be vulnerable to the more powerful institutional forces of the dominant culture. Relations with the dominant culture will always have a subversive element, undermining the exploitative and oppressive values of the larger urban society. At the same time, rural communities depend on the dominant culture of urban society for the market of their produce. Agrarian cultures must forge healthy reciprocal relationships with the dominant culture.

COMPONENTS OF A STABLE AND VIABLE AGRARIAN CULTURE

Chapters 4 through 7 of this book were an attempt to document the birth, growth, maturity, and decline of the agrarian cultures that comprise the Freeman, South Dakota, rural community, specifically the three Anabaptist cultures that came to this area from Russia in 1874. The last chapter attempted to place this community in the broader context of the dominant culture of American society in the twenty-first century and began to explore the possibility of the community's current rebirth or reformation.

This chapter will be an attempt to step back and begin to discern the lessons that can be learned from the story of this specific community with its various agrarian cultures. The premise is that there is something paradigmatic about the history of a rural community that can help us learn what brings about its fragmentation and decline and decay, and what may also establish it on viable and solid ground, both literally and metaphorically speaking. We have seen that the health and welfare of rural communities depend on the health and vitality of the agrarian cultures that comprise the community. So this chapter will seek to lay out what we may learn from the story of the Freeman community about what makes for healthy and vital agrarian cultures.

At the outset, we should be sure we know what we are talking about. My dictionary defines culture as the "integrated pattern of human knowledge, belief, and behavior that depends on man's [the human] capacity for learning and transmitting knowledge to succeeding generations."[1] Several aspects of this definition deserve attention. First, culture represents an "integrated pattern of behavior." Culture represents a whole way of thinking, working, and relating that people in that culture take for granted as the *normal* or *right* way to do things. Second, culture depends on the human capacity for learning. Acculturated people have learned how to live within or fit within a particular cultural context. And finally, this learning among humans is also transmitted generationally, from one generation to the next.

My old college sociology textbook talks about culture in terms of behavior or folkways or customs, in terms of artifacts or tools used by the group, and in terms of the belief or value system held by the group.[2] Folkways or behavior or customs have to do with all the ways we learn how and what foods to eat, how to relate to one another within the group, and all the myriad ways people learn how to act appropriately within that culture. Language itself is a part of the folkway of a culture. Artifacts or tools are the physical objects used within a particular culture to serve particular needs. Working in a museum that includes tools from earlier eras, we are frequently puzzled about the utility of a particular tool since we no longer know the cultural context in which it was used. And of course,

---

1. *Merriam Webster's Collegiate Dictionary*, 10th ed.
2. Bell, *Social Foundations*, 33–34.

beliefs and values have to do with what a particular culture understands to be right or wrong, sacred or profane, worthy or unworthy, ethical or unethical, appropriate or inappropriate, shameful or exemplary.

On top of this general understanding of what culture is, we need to understand what is unique about an *agrarian* culture. What makes a particular culture agrarian? The word *agriculture* derives from the Greek word for field, ἀγρός (agros), and the Latin word for cultivation, *cultura*. Agriculture literally means the cultivation or the culture of the field. Agriculture refers to all the ways humans interact with Nature in the domestication of plants and animals for human use. Human use of Nature in agriculture is typically at some level a communal endeavor, however much individualism and private property are extolled. In other words, societies or communities decide together on the folkways and practices, the tools, and the values or beliefs that will govern their use of land. So human communities that work together to utilize Nature for human purposes form agrarian cultures. Alongside and perhaps at the heart of all the other cultural practices a human community engages, an agrarian culture includes also the practices and tools and values that govern their use of the land.

Culture is learned, but it is learned not formally, but through absorption, by the experience of growing up and living in it. Even when someone enters a culture as an outsider in a cross-cultural experience, one learns about that new culture by absorption, by living in it, however much he or she may have read and studied about the culture. So it is not surprising that most of us are rarely aware of our native cultural context. We have a largely unconscious and surely an uncritical awareness of the culture in which we were raised or are living.

Cultures are inherently conservative. Cultures are typically resistant to change, and often change only when external forces threaten the culture with disintegration. Yet at the same time, cultures may also be observed to be changing all the time. Cultural change happens by and large unconsciously and barely perceptibly, which is why cultures seem to be changeless. This type of cultural change is most often initiated by respected innovators within the culture who adopt a new practice or tool or value, and when that innovation is adopted by more and more members of the community, cultural change occurs. Only in hindsight or in retrospect, if this ever happens, will a culture consciously be aware of the changes that have occurred.

The Re-formation of an Agrarian Culture

The middle four chapters of this book were an attempt to chronicle the birth, growth, maturity, and decline of the larger Freeman community and the small half dozen or more local agrarian cultures that built the community. Successful and sustainable agrarian cultures need to always tend three relationships simultaneously—their relationships with the particular land they inhabit, their relationships with the other agrarian cultures around them that together build rural communities like Freeman, and their relationships with the dominant culture and larger society in which they live.

The central chapters of the book demonstrated the ways in which these local agrarian cultures failed to develop sustainable agricultural methods on their land and indeed are gradually losing control of their land to outside interests. It might seem that these cultures simply outgrew their land base, as so many agricultural communities do. But the problem was not simply the size and growth of farms that depopulated the community. It was that the land that for thousands of years had been a fertile and sustainable prairie ecosystem was transformed into a cultivated agricultural system that was not sustainable. And even more to the point, this agricultural system no longer served the welfare of the rural community but rather the economic and imperial interests of the larger society around it. Unless the Freeman community is able to relate to its land with a more sustainable, community-oriented agricultural system, it is likely to continue to decline and die.

The central chapters of this book describe the struggle the local agrarian cultures of the Freeman community have had in relating to one another. They were too often driven by an insecure ethnocentrism that prevented them from working together for the welfare of the community as a whole. In the mature years of the community, there was indeed a fairly high degree of cooperation and interdependence among these local agrarian cultures. When the community began to decline, the local cultures became more isolated and defensive of one another and also lost the ability to function themselves as healthy local cultures. Unless the local cultures themselves are able to be revitalized and to work together with each other to revitalize the community, the Freeman community as a whole will continue to struggle and lose its character as a rural, agricultural community.

The central chapters of the book explain the inevitable acculturation that occurs when local, foreign cultures come to a new land and a new dominant culture and society, particularly one as vital and imperial as

American society has been for the past two centuries. Yet agrarian cultures depend for their survival on their ability to define themselves over against the dominant culture and to find ways to collaborate in healthy reciprocally beneficial ways with that dominant culture. When they allow the dominant culture to dictate the terms of their social and economic life within a rural community, they will inevitably lose their identity and ultimately their cultural life. Unless the agrarian cultures of the Freeman community find new and reciprocal ways of relating to the dominant culture, the community as a whole will struggle to survive, becoming simply the exploitable asset of the dominant culture of American society.

The agrarian cultures of the Freeman community are at a crucial time in their nearly 150-year history on this land. These cultures cannot simply return to the past, as we have seen, for there is no unfettered *golden age* in which they were doing everything right, even in the best years of the community's maturity as a relatively vital and successful rural community. The local agrarian cultures need to re-invent themselves, both as local cultures and as agricultural entities, in order to build a renewed rural community.

BUILDING A NEW RELATIONSHIP WITH THE LAND

A proper and healthy relationship with the land begins with the awareness that the land is a divine gift given for the welfare of all humanity and all creation. For too long, we have thought of the land as a commodity that we can use for our own benefit. We have seen the land as an economic resource, a repository of exploitable commodities we can use with impunity and without consequence. In fact, however, the land is alive, filled with living organisms. And being alive, there is something holy about the land. We cannot treat the land like dirt without destroying both the land and ourselves.

It is this character of the land as a living reality that allows us to enter into a relationship with the land, to have a conversation with the land. Relationships imply mutuality, a partnership in which each party has something to say and something to learn. In the modern era, we have learned to dissect Nature and the land. We can take it apart and look at its component parts analytically to see how it is made and what makes it tick. This has allowed us to replicate many natural functions and to suppose that we don't really need the natural processes of Nature or the land.

Helpful as our scientific knowledge about Nature and the land might be, it is not a conversation either with Nature or with the land. It is at best a monologue, a conversation with ourselves about Nature or the land. It does not understand Nature or the land as a conversation partner, as having something intrinsic to say to us.

So how do we have a conversation with the land? How do we listen to the land? What do we say to the land, and what can we expect the land to say to us? This type of relationship demands a holistic rather than merely an analytical or scientific understanding of Nature and the land. It requires us to see ourselves and the land intricately woven together. It requires us to see the relationships between healthy human communities and healthy land. We need to know something more than how something was made. We need to know its place within the system of life that sustains both the land or creation as well as the human community. While analytical, scientific knowledge can indeed help us understand systems of life, we need the deeper encounter—a conversation with the land and with Nature as a whole, as a living system. And this type of knowledge comes from experience more than from analysis. It is the type of knowledge honed through generations of experience in specific agricultural contexts in all the agrarian cultures of humanity.

The first conversation an agrarian culture must have with the land when it comes into a new place is to inquire about its native or aboriginal ecosystem. Agrarian cultures need to mimic that native ecosystem if they hope to establish a sustainable life in that place. It's why coastal or riverine communities establish fisheries, and mountain or plains communities tend to be pastoral. It's why annual crops tend to be planted in temperate zones, while tropical agriculture tends to specialize in fruits and nuts. In order to adapt successfully to a particular ecosystem, the agrarian cultures that come into that ecosystem need to mimic as closely as possible the characteristics of that ecosystem in the agricultural practices they develop. Agrarian cultures always need to learn from Nature about both the possibilities and challenges as well as the constraints and limitations of the ecosystem in which they are living.

The Russian-German agrarian cultures that came to the Freeman community were moving from one temperate zone to another, and so could fairly easily transplant the agrarian wisdom of their past into the ecosystem of the Great Plains of North America. However, these cultures didn't pay enough attention to the grasslands, the prairie ecosystem of the Great Plains. They were too eager to retain the annual cropping patterns of the agriculture they had known rather than to listen to the land and mimic the ecology of the grasslands more intentionally in their agricultural practices.

This became critical when industrial methods of monoculture, commodity-oriented, industrial agriculture became established. This agriculture has not only destroyed the prairie ecosystem, but has also gone a long way toward destroying the soil itself. The use of large equipment and the loss of soil tilth due to chemical fertilizer, herbicide, pesticide, and fungicide use has made the soil impermeable even when tiled.[3] In my community I observe that this has led to increased run-off and soil erosion as well as increased untillable acres that have become sloughs. Low places that my father and I consistently planted and cropped in the 1960s with only a little effort in draining them are now seldom worked and usually drown out when they are planted.

An agriculture that respects the prairie ecosystem (listens to the land) would immediately return to some form of animal husbandry for the use of the land along with grazing and hay-making. In this way, farmers would end the wasteful, unhealthy, and unethical practice of using confined animal feeding operations (CAFOs) for raising and caring for their animals. Minimal field cropping might be done for animal feed and perhaps some cash crops, but annual crops would be highly diversified and rotated, with the land kept in cover crops throughout the year.

When the agrarian cultures came to the Great Plains, they often planted trees around their farms for protection from the weather. Trees typically did not grow on the Great Plains except along creeks and rivers due to grazing and periodic prairie fires. With intentional grazing and with prairie fire mitigation, orchard and nut and tree planting in the form of silviculture may be possible.[4] Still, unless global warming increases prairie rainfall significantly from its current twenty-to-twenty-five-inch-per-year average, it doesn't seem to me that the Great Plains has a great future as a forested ecosystem.

The recent book by Gabe Brown, *Dirt to Soil*, is perhaps the best current guide for listening to the land, particularly in the Great Plains region. In the Introduction, Brown identifies five principles of soil health: limited disturbance, soil armor, diversity, living roots, and integrated

---

3. Brown, *Dirt to Soil*, 51–52, 128–30, discussing water infiltration.
4. Discussed in Shepherd, *Restoration Agriculture*.

animals.⁵ These principles are implicit in the agricultural practices I have briefly outlined here, and farmers who listen to the land in this way will be engaging in regenerative agricultural practices that will not only restore the land but also increase the carbon in soil, actually sequestering carbon back in the soil where it belongs. In this way, agriculture can contribute to ending global warming instead of fostering it.⁶ Agricultural practices taught by the land will return farmers to their original, primary, and historic vocation, that of stewarding and caring for the land and its life, and providing food and fiber for themselves, their families, their community, the larger society, and the world.

However, the land has something to say not just to the farmers who work the land, but also to the communities in which these farmers live. The land needs to inform rural communities about the optimum human population this particular rural setting can sustain in a healthy way. How many dispersed farm families can this land sustain economically as food-producing units? Then the rural community as a whole needs to work together collaboratively to achieve that optimum human, agricultural presence on the land.

We have already seen how the Freeman community outgrew its land base even before industrial agriculture expanded farm size exponentially. Few if any agrarian cultures have seriously worked at learning how to live on their land base for the long haul. Almost always they have spun off other communities, as the Amish are doing in the United States, instead of learning to live on their land. Living sustainably on the land involves family planning, to be sure, so that the human population will not outgrow the land's ability to provide for the community. But it also involves community organizing, so that the gifts and resources of the human community can serve the welfare of the local community. In the Freeman community and in most rural communities, too many individuals left or were forced to leave the rural community to live and find work elsewhere in cities and urban areas where there are industries or opportunities. This was particularly true of persons with unique or different gifts or personal identities.

Traditional agrarian cultures, on the contrary, found ways to use the diverse human abilities found in village life to form self-sustaining village economies. This reduced even if it did not cease the agrarian culture's growth beyond its land base. Of course, there should always be room

5. Brown, *Dirt to Soil*, 1–3, and ch. 7.

6. Brown, *Dirt to Soil*, 44–49. For other articles on carbon sequestration see sources at ch. 8, note 21.

for some in the community to move to the city or join other communities, as well as openness to receiving urban refugees or transplants from other rural communities. These types of exchanges are what keep rural communities vital and engaged with the larger world. Nevertheless, rural communities need to do a much better job than they have done at keeping and employing and using all the diverse human gifts to be found in its agrarian cultures. Never again should youth be given this message, as my generation was in this community growing up in the second half of the twentieth century: *There's no future for you here. It's a hard life and you can't expect to make a decent living here. Indeed, there's no room for you here on the farm. Get an education and leave as soon as you can!*

A part of the rural community's listening to the land in this way involves taking responsibility for land tenure. Currently, with land as private property being the dominant paradigm for land ownership, land tenure issues are left haphazardly to land owners or individual farmers. This almost guarantees that the community will outgrow its land base as we saw in the land tenure patterns of the Freeman community. It worked well to find farms for all one's sons and to marry daughters to other farmers for about two generations, as long as there was plenty of land. But then the community either had to expand its land base as it did in the third generation, control its population, or begin to lose many of its youth.

One alternative to land as private property is to hold land as a communal asset, held in trust for the welfare of the community as a whole. In such a model the community itself might come to own some or much of the land, removing it from the speculative land market, enhancing opportunities for generational land transfers, and providing mechanisms to oversee the stewardship of the land itself. Community farmland trusts are rare but not unknown. Rural Revival in Freeman is in the process of forming such a farmland trust.

The Community Farmland Trust of Rural Revival is seeking to become a community-based non-profit that would seek to regain control of the land on behalf of the community. It would purchase or receive land deeded to it, and extend long-term, inheritable leases to a new generation of farmers willing to use regenerative farming practices. While using regenerative agricultural practices and being engaged in at least some aspect of a local food producing system, leaseholders would be free to engage in the agricultural pursuits that suit their interests and abilities, earn equity for capital improvements they might make on the land, and be able to transfer their lease to heirs. Such a land trust would preserve the best features of current land tenure models (individual initiative and use of the land) without the prohibitive economic risks of private land ownership. It would enable communities to retain control over the land and how it is used along with a mechanism for generational land transfers.[7]

As rural people and rural communities, the land is our teacher. We learn from the land both the limitations and the opportunities, the constraints and the possibilities of our life together on the land. Above all, we never forget that the land is not ours to do with as we please. It is a gift we receive from the Creator for the welfare of the whole human and natural community of life as well as the whole world. In the Judeo-Christian tradition, we affirm that the land belongs to God, and that we are but stewards, aliens and tenants, on the land. "The land shall not be sold in perpetuity, for the land is mine; with me you are but aliens and tenants" (Lev 25:23). This is a perspective radically foreign to the way the dominant culture of American society sees the land, but it is basic to the future of humankind and the whole Earth, as well as the health of agrarian cultures.

RENEWING RELATIONSHIPS WITHIN AND BETWEEN AGRARIAN CULTURES AND RURAL COMMUNITIES

The Russian-German immigrants came to America as communal groups, for the most part, agrarian cultures that already had a long shared communal history. This communal history was reinforced among the Anabaptist groups theologically, by their strong commitment to mutual aid and accountability as a key mark of the church that formed their identity. It is what American society finds so remarkable about the Amish—the way the will of the individual is subjected to the will of the community. It is how groups like this define their conformity to their sub-culture and their nonconformity to the dominant culture around them. Taken to the extreme, such communalism can often do violence to the individual in the community. Rather than finding ways to include and incorporate individuals with unique ideas or identities, communities may repress or even exclude such individuals. Yet when freely chosen by the members of the community in communities that respect and celebrate the uniqueness of each person, this is one of the ways agrarian cultures and rural communities are able to maintain their sub-cultural identity within the larger society.

7. Rural Revival, "Proposal for a Community Land Trust."

In their assimilation into American society, we saw how the Anabaptist groups lost some of their strong theological commitment to community through the influence of fundamentalist theology in the 1920s and 1930s. The emphasis on correct doctrine and personal salvation tended to water down the Anabaptist emphasis on discipleship and mutual aid. This made the agrarian cultures of the Freeman community more vulnerable to the individualism so characteristic of American society, with its emphasis on individual rights and freedoms.

The first step in rebuilding a strong rural community that cares for the land regeneratively and relates to the dominant culture positively is for each agrarian culture in the community to recover and reclaim its unique heritage. Strong rural communities need all the agrarian cultures within it working together and contributing their gifts. If the local agrarian cultures have lost their identity and heritage, they need to rediscover and redefine who they are in order to contribute to the community. Groups that are insecure and unsure of their unique identity tend to reflect the values and ethos of the dominant culture and have little to contribute to the building of a strong rural community. Such groups often have internal conflicts and are pulled in different directions by strong individuals bent on exercising their power. On the other hand, when groups are guided by the values and beliefs of their heritage and a common vision for their future, they can contribute to the rebuilding of a strong rural community.

The *groups* and *agrarian cultures* referred to in the previous paragraph are in the Freeman community the historic Anabaptist, Reformed, and Lutheran congregations as well as other denominational, faith-oriented, inter-faith, non-profit, governmental, business, and educational entities of the community. In a rural community, most of these entities will have some agricultural components and agrarian interests. All of them contribute to the health and vitality of the rural community by virtue of the unique gifts and perspectives they bring to the table. But there will be no table and nothing to bring to the table if these various groups and entities have not identified the unique gifts they have to offer.

While I cannot speculate about the gifts other agrarian cultures in the Freeman community may bring to the table, I can speak to the gifts the Anabaptist congregations can offer to the Freeman community. The *Prairieleut* of Hutterite background bring a cultural tradition going back nearly five centuries to Moravia. They offer not only the communal heritage of their Hutterite brothers and sisters in the faith, but also the heritage

The Re-formation of an Agrarian Culture

of innovation and crafts and industry reflected both in early Hutterite history and in the innovations of current Hutterite people and colonies.

Likewise, the Low German Mennonite congregations offer an agrarian heritage that goes back nearly five centuries to the Low Countries of Holland and Belgium. Throughout their sojourns through northern Europe and into Ukraine, these people were innovators in making marginal land productive agriculturally by draining swamps, breaking the steppes, and improving livestock and crop lines. Low Germans from the colonies of southern Ukraine bring an experience in self-government within a dominant empire, while those from Volhynia bring the experience of living successfully as agrarian villages under the hegemony of a ruling class of land-owners.

As for the Swiss Volhynian congregations, they too bear a long cultural and ethnic heritage going back to their origins in Switzerland, again nearly five hundred years ago. This heritage undoubtedly informed the animal husbandry of these cultures. As former Amish congregations, these cultures also bear the communal heritage of the Amish faith that defines itself over against the dominant cultures of the world by patterns and structures of non-conformity and communal cohesion, seeking to establish as a community the behaviors, tools and values that preserve the integrity of the culture.

I must hasten to admit that the Anabaptist congregations representing these agrarian cultures today hardly reflect their heritage. They do bear some allegiance to their Anabaptist heritage theologically, particularly the sense of communal identity and adherence to the historic peace stance of Anabaptism. However, all these current Anabaptist congregations are oblivious to their agrarian heritage over the past centuries. Aspects of that agrarian heritage may survive in a few of the behaviors, tools, and values that are practiced, but these are for the most part unconscious remnants of a cultural life that no longer really informs contemporary agricultural practice.

But this is precisely the point I am trying to make. In order for these Anabaptist congregations to participate positively in the rebuilding of the Freeman community, they need first to recover and clarify the distinctiveness of the theological, ethnic, and agrarian cultural heritage of their past. Then, having identified some of the behaviors, tools, and values of their past, they can discern the gifts they may bring to the table for the restoration of the Freeman community as a collection of agrarian and small-town cultures. What aspects of their cultural heritage are relevant and important in the development of a sustainable rural community? How can the gifts of their heritage complement the gifts present in the other agrarian and small-town cultures of the community? How can all these cultural groupings work together in complementary ways that include all the diversity present within each culture as well as in the rural, small-town setting of Freeman?

Hopefully, the first fruit of such a discernment process in congregational settings will bring a re-vitalization of that agrarian culture itself. In the Anabaptist congregations this would involve a reclamation of their communitarian roots and a renewed agrarian vision of creation care in regenerative agricultural practices already discussed throughout this book. In this way, congregations would not only be prepared to bring their gifts to the larger community but also begin modeling for the community what a renewed rural community would look like.

I grant that it may be unrealistic to expect that all the local congregations representing the diverse cultural heritages of the community would simultaneously engage the laborious and painstaking process of recovering and clarifying their heritage. Most of these local congregations are struggling for survival and preoccupied with institutional maintenance, and they often face chronic conflict within their congregational life. However, if even one or two local congregations of the community had the foresight and courage to engage this process of self-discovery, it might have a catalytic effect on the other groupings of the community as well.

Speaking theologically, there is ample warrant for Christian congregations to engage such a process of re-claiming their heritage in order to participate more effectively in the restoration of their community. The church in the New Testament is seen as a leavening agent within the wider society in which it lives, bringing the leaven of God's love into the dough of the larger society. This is indeed the mission of the church born through the life, death, and resurrection of Jesus of Nazareth as a new community or humanity gathered in every place by God's Holy Spirit. The primary mission of rural congregations is the revitalization, restoration, and redemption of the larger communities where they live, through both their congregational life and their agricultural practices. The gospel that informs this mission is borne through the ethno-cultural heritage reflected in every congregation and its journey through history.[8]

---

8. The dynamic of the mission of Christian congregations is discussed in Kaufman, *Healing God's Earth*, ch. 13.

Native American wisdom suggests that we find our way into the future not by looking ahead as we moderns tend to do, but by looking back at where we have come from. We can only figure out how to live in the future by understanding our journey to this time. This perspective is also intrinsic to the museum work I do at Heritage Hall Museum and Archives. A quote from the museum's newsletter attributed to Lois Lowry says, "That's why we have the museum, Marty, to reminds us of how we came and why; to start fresh and begin a new place from what we had learned and carried from the old."

Rural communities in southeast South Dakota should make a special effort to develop community-to-community relationships with the Yankton Sioux Nation, whose people were dispossessed by the arrival of European immigrant communities. As the Dakota nations begin to reform their traditional cultures in new ways, we have so much to learn from them about how to live here on the Great Plains. The local peace group I relate to, Freeman Network for Justice and Peace, has established a relationship with the Wagner Area Horizons Team, a local anti-racism non-profit in Wagner, South Dakota, on the traditional Yankton Sioux Reserve. We meet together once or twice a year to share our work and establish relationships. While these are not yet community-to-community relationships between the Freeman community and the Yankton Sioux Nation, they have the potential for becoming this in the future. We who are settlers and colonizers on this land need to explore reparations with the communities we dispossessed so that in the future we can live together in sustainable ways on this land we share.

Once a number of local agrarian cultures (congregations) have identified the values, behaviors, and tools they can offer the community for its revitalization, the community needs to create an inclusive venue where all the diverse groupings in the community can bring their gifts and resources. A non-profit similar to the current Rural Revival group I have described elsewhere in this book might be the best vehicle for this purpose. It must be in any case a venue where all the local agrarian and small-town groupings can feel welcome and able to bring their gifts to the table, including all the Christian congregations of the community as well as representatives of other faiths and indigenous, traditional cultures and all the secular non-profit, governmental, business, and educational groupings of the community.

Such a community-wide effort to re-vitalize the community may prove challenging to the Christian congregations of the community, who have tended to engage such a mission only on their own terms theologically and institutionally and have been wary of making common cause with others who may not share their faith or their particular denominational loyalties, and this of course includes the Anabaptist congregations of my own heritage. However, it is important for rural congregations to understand that their mission is not institutional maintenance or the imposition of Christian faith on others. It is to own their own faith and gifts, while also giving themselves to the community for its life and its future, even if and when it might not serve the institutional life of the congregation in the short term.

Vital agrarian cultures working together create vital rural communities. Rural communities take different shapes in different contexts. Perhaps there are places where the agrarian culture itself forms the rural community. This may be particularly the case in traditional villages of many societies around the world. Here on the Great Plains, the human presence is much more scattered and atomized. In part this reflects the settlement pattern dictated by the Homesteading Act, but it also reflects the carrying capacity of the land itself which defies intense or dense human presence. So here, the human presence took the shape of the small agrarian cultures, Russian-German congregations of Anabaptist, Reformed and Lutheran heritage, that simultaneously settled the land in the 1870s.

These agrarian cultures spanned the eastern third of Hutchinson County, and the western three quarters of Turner County, from the James River to the Vermillion River, and from Turkey Ridge to Wolf Creek. Fortuitously, the town of Freeman came to be settled near the center of this geographical area and became the dominant service settlement for this area. So this has become the rural Freeman community, and its health and future depend on the health and the vitality of both the traditional Russian-German cultures that settled in this area in the 1870s, as well as the diverse cultural groupings that have developed and will still take shape within the town of Freeman and in the surrounding area.

REBUILDING RELATIONSHIPS WITH THE DOMINANT CULTURE OF AMERICAN SOCIETY

Building reciprocal, healthy, and mutually beneficial relationships between rural communities and the dominant culture of American society is a project fraught with pitfalls and dangers for rural communities. This is due primarily to the immense power imbalances that exist between rural communities and the dominant culture. Dominant societies typically function on the basis of power and control exercised through economic and political institutions designed to increase their wealth and influence. As the term implies, a dominant culture is designed to exercise hegemony over a particular area. In our era of history, these are the nation-states that make territorial claims over a particular area. While dominant cultures depend on the raw materials, particularly food and fiber, that are provided by rural communities, they don't particularly have the interests of rural community in their purview. They are interested in getting as many of these raw materials as cheaply as possible, and in order to do so they work to control both the land and the means of production, in this case, the farms that make up these rural communities.

In contrast, the primary concern of a healthy rural community is care for the land and the people who make up the rural community. Agrarian cultures are by nature both communal and ecological, designed to take care of the land and its people. While healthy rural communities engage in their activities in order to provide the raw materials needed by themselves and the dominant culture, their primary interest is not profit but the quality of the products they produce and the health and vitality of both the land and the community that produces them. This always makes rural communities vulnerable to the much greater power of the institutions of the dominant culture, as we have seen throughout this book. Yet, at the same time, rural communities cannot escape the responsibility of striving to establish reciprocal, healthy, and mutually beneficial relationships with the dominant culture in which they live.

Throughout history, rural communities have resisted the depredations of dominant cultures in a variety of ways. Agrarian societies have sometimes resorted to violent revolution against their dominant urban neighbors or imperial overlords, as in the Jewish rebellion against Rome in 64 CE, and in the Peasants' Revolts of central Europe in the 1520s. Such efforts have usually resulted in failure at great cost of human suffering on the part of those agrarian societies. An agrarian society is simply no match for the power of its imperial overlords.

More often, and more successfully, agrarian societies have used subterfuge and subversion to thwart imperial policies that threaten rural communities. This might involve the creation of underground economies that by-pass or undermine the conventional or dominant structures of the imperial power. It might involve agricultural workers sabotaging the estates of large landowners or corporations who threaten their land and communities. It would be a fascinating study to explore the ways agrarian societies have survived imperial depredations by these means throughout history.

In our time and in our context, there are also legal and political endeavors, including demonstrations and civil disobedience, to mitigate imperial policies of the dominant culture that favor the intrusion of corporate interests threatening the welfare of rural communities. The actions at Standing Rock by Native American tribes and their allies to thwart the development of oil pipelines on Native lands is a current example of such efforts. Such tactics are worthy of emulation and support by rural communities, being peaceful, orderly, and politically-sanctioned. However, the record of broken treaties and governmental policies sanctioning the exploitation of rural assets is not encouraging in terms of bringing the structures of imperial power to heel.

Most of the strategies described here thus far represent efforts to challenge or mitigate or change the power of the dominant culture as a whole. The intent is often to reform or change the dominant culture itself, weaning it away from the more oppressive and abusive and egregious effects of its abuse of power. While such efforts are worthwhile and important and sometimes do succeed in reforming dominant cultures and making them more humane and just, rural communities also need more immediate and productive relationships with the dominant culture. Often these relationships, mostly economic and cultural, can be formed with urban communities within the dominant culture.

The previous chapter described the cultural shifts within the dominant culture with regard to food, and the way in which urban consumers are looking for and demanding local food that is raised regeneratively and humanely. The last chapter also acknowledged the way in which urban communities are often leading the way in dealing with the ecological crisis. These, I believe, are the communities of shared values and practices with whom rural communities might establish reciprocal, healthy, and mutually beneficial relationships. Sometimes these relationships might be direct producer/consumer arrangements, as in community supported agriculture and farmers markets. Sometimes they might be community-to-community relationships in the form of producer/consumer cooperatives. Sometimes they might be shared-value or faith-based relationships, for instance, between rural and urban congregations of the same denomination.

As is evident for observers of contemporary life, rural and urban, all these relational arrangements are already being practiced and put into effect in a variety of contexts. Currently, however, only a small fraction of the rural or urban population is participating in these alternative economic and cultural exchanges. While the kind of relationships envisioned here will always involve only a minority of the population and be somewhat subversive or beneath the radar of the formal economy, there are immense opportunities for rural and urban communities to build and foster these kinds of relationships beneficial to both urban communities as consumers and rural communities as producers. In this way the worst effects of the formal economy in exploitative, abusive, and oppressive policies and practices can be mitigated, and rural communities can be rebuilt on the basis of strong, regenerative agricultural practices in partnership with urban communities that share these values with their rural neighbors.

Given the imbalance of power between rural communities and the institutional structures of multi-national corporations, government bureaucracies, and technocratic think-tanks, it will be more productive both for rural communities and for the larger society if informal, community-to-community relationships can be established between rural and urban populations. Political action to change and reform the institutional structures is important and sometimes productive, but the immediate need is for rural communities to forge these informal economic and cultural relationships with urban communities that share these communitarian and ecological values.

On the other hand, it is very difficult for rural people or even local, rural cultures (the congregations that are focus of this book) to forge such alliances on their own. It would be done most effectively when the people and agrarian cultures of a local community join together to develop these relationships. Rural communities have enough critical mass to establish cooperatives and cultural alliances with their counterparts in urban areas.

The other factor that makes relationships between rural communities and the dominant culture so fraught is the way the values and practices and behaviors of the dominant culture have infiltrated rural communities. We have examined throughout this book the way in which agrarian cultures have to acculturate and assimilate into the dominant cultures where they live. Yet at the same time, in order to function as a healthy agrarian culture, they must also retain and be clear about their agrarian identity. The communitarian and ecological values characteristic of agrarian cultures are in danger of being lost in most rural communities throughout the land. So for healthy, reciprocal, and mutually beneficial relationships to be forged with urban communities of the dominant culture, rural communities need to reclaim their identity as alternative, agrarian cultures.

The difficulty for rural communities comes in the struggle to maintain this dual identity, a primary agrarian identity that is also able to be at home in and work within the values and behaviors and practices of the dominant culture. This involves not just being clear about one's primary identity, but also able to know how and when to engage the values of communities within the dominant culture in ways that foster the health and well-being of both. This is of course the challenge that has always confronted Christians and other people of faith when they live as they always do within a dominant culture that does not share their faith values. *How to be in but not of the world* is how it is often characterized in Christian terms. The same dynamic confronts agrarian cultures of whatever faith orientation or value system as they live within a dominant culture.

Self-realization and the priority of individual rights are perhaps the primary values of the dominant culture. Beyond this, identity is found primarily in the institutional structures of nationhood or nationalism, which presumes the validity of domination through the exercise of power. Yet within the dominant culture, there are also strong strains that call for justice within the social order and the preservation and conservation of the Earth. It will be communities with these values within the dominant culture that agrarian cultures will seek to engage in healthy and reciprocal relationships for the benefit of all.

It is often said that farmers feed the world. This may not be true of industrialized agriculture that specializes in commodity production, or at least, it is not done in a way that produces healthy food in sustainable and humane ways that also build rural communities. The production of food does nevertheless remain the primary function and vocation of agrarian cultures. Agrarian cultures not only confront the challenge of developing and maintaining a regenerative agriculture that produces high-quality food. They also confront the challenge of making that food available to urban consumers in ways that build the health and vitality of both rural and urban communities. This may best be accomplished through rural/urban community cooperatives and alliances that feed not only the families of both, but also the cultural vitality of both urban and rural communities.

10

The Role of Religious Faith in the Formation of an Agrarian Culture

SYNOPSIS

REVIEWING THE LIFE STORY of the rural Freeman Mennonite community, it is evident that religious faith is a key component in the formation and sustenance of a healthy agrarian culture. Religious faith in this case means Christian faith, and specifically the Anabaptist/Mennonite expression of Christian faith. Yet this is not an appeal to religious exclusiveness. Any religious faith, including also non-Christian faiths and in particular the religious practices and beliefs of traditional cultures, will foster the life of an agrarian culture. This is true even and perhaps especially when as in Native American cultures there is no distinct or separate religious life apart from daily life, in other words, little or no separation between sacred and profane, holy and common. So how does religious faith foster the life of an agrarian culture?

First, religious faith involves an ethic of care for the land based on an understanding that the world is the creation of God and ultimately belongs to God, just as we ourselves are created by and belong to God. Religious faith disallows the objectification of Nature and understands all human interactions with one another and with creation as I/Thou relationships. It is not that we cannot learn useful things about Nature as object of scientific analysis, but in the end, a healthy agrarian culture will act always on the premise of this primary relationship with God and creation and others as inter-related and dynamic and alive—a living system.

At their best, agrarian cultures understand that they are called by the Creator to participate in the unfolding of creation and life for the welfare of the whole creation, to reflect within creation the divine image and principle of love through which God is bringing all things to fulfillment.

Second, religious faith asserts the priority of communal values over either individual or dominant societal values. Within the dominant culture of American society, a primary value is individualism, the maturation and full expression of one's individual potential. Such a value, worthy as it is, undermines communal values, both familial and other face-to-face relationships. At the other extreme, the dominant culture of American society demands allegiance to the state, along with all the attendant powers and ideologies that support the institutional structures of American life. Religious faith is often subverted in support of either individualism or the institutions of imperial power. However, at its best, religious faith will always assert the priority of communal values and in this way foster a strong and vital agrarian culture.

Third, Christian faith, along with other traditional religions, emphasizes the centrality of the table and food and hospitality and plenty in human life within creation. The Table is central in Christian liturgy, with Jesus as the host. Eating and drinking together is always a sacral act, and it is foundational to the agrarian culture that finds its central role to be participating with creation in the provision of sustenance for the life of the community. Every step in the process of bringing food to the table and consuming it together is holy, and the community that understands and acts with this in mind is well on the way toward being a healthy agrarian culture.

RELIGIOUS FAITH AND AGRARIAN CULTURE

Religious faith clearly played a major role in the origin and development of the three Anabaptist groups that came to America from the Ukraine in 1874 and settled in the area that later became the Freeman community. They came here for many reasons, not least of which was the promise of freedom and free land. But they were also motivated by a search for a place where they could practice their non-resistant faith and engage in their vocation as people of the land. They understood themselves to be a minority culture, a small group or remnant of people who sought in the midst of a world of oppression and domination and exploitation to be faithful to God's calling for all humanity. They believed they were to live peaceably as communities, caring for the land on which they lived, and in both of these ways bearing witness to God's intention for humanity.

The Anabaptist faith that brought these agrarian cultures to America emphasized discipleship—following Jesus in daily life, guiding the way they lived together, the way they organized their common life, and the way they cared for the land. While they did not have the language to speak about this theologically, the way they cared for the land and its life reflected the reverence they felt for the Earth as God's creation. Their agricultural practices were imbued with an ethical sensibility growing out of their faith in Jesus. While they shared the Christian hope for a better and eternal life to come and understood themselves to be sojourners or pilgrims here on Earth, their faith called them to live now as citizens of that rule of God's love to which they were pledged.

The Anabaptist faith of these cultures also affirmed that their life together as a church was the primary manifestation of their Christian faith. Each person of course must own the faith for him or herself (hence adult baptism upon confession of faith), but in the end, faith and salvation were understood not just as an individual but as a corporate reality. What Jesus accomplished through his life, death, and resurrection was the formation of a redeemed community that could function as a witness to God's intention for the world. Despite the struggles and failures of the church as a human community, Anabaptists believed that it was through this frail, often broken vessel that God was working to redeem both the world and creation itself. Whether or not such a faith was warranted, such a faith nonetheless informed the lives of these agrarian communities as they came to this new land. Their identity was communal rather than individual. Mutual care and the welfare of the community as a whole took priority over individual wants and fulfillment. There was an intention to seek the common good of the community, humanity, and creation in all of the decisions and choices that were made.

The Anabaptist emphasis on discipleship and community became the basis for the practice of peace and nonviolence. Given their vocation and communal identity, Anabaptists repudiated all the power dynamics implicit in the larger institutional structures of society, which inevitably lead to domination, oppression, and exploitation of both the human and natural communities of life on Earth. Anabaptists resolved to live alongside and within the institutional structures of life as families and communities living in a close and dependent relationship to the land.

Seldom have Anabaptist communities of faith been able to live up their high ideals of nonviolence and empowerment within their communities, but these ideals do explain the Anabaptist commitment to nonviolence and their repudiation not only of warfare itself, but of all the coercive manipulations used by the economic, political, and technocratic institutions of imperial power.

Anabaptist nonviolence is not however a repudiation of power as such. Every person and community has an immense reservoir of power. The question is whether such power will be used to dominate others and creation, as is the norm in imperial cultures of the world, or whether that power will be used alongside others, to empower and release the power every person and potential has. Of course, within families and communities, personal power may also be abused to control and manipulate others. But in such contexts, such power is easily recognized as being dysfunctional and inappropriate, disempowering rather than empowering others. But within the dominant, imperial cultures of the world, power over others is somehow sanctioned and seen as the goal of power, even by those who are disenfranchised and disempowered. The culture of Anabaptist communities does not disavow the use of power, but affirms that it is only appropriate and useful when it is used to come alongside and to empower all others within the human and natural communities of life in nonviolent, non-coercive ways.

These key Anabaptist faith perspectives—discipleship, community, and nonviolence—were values these agrarian cultures brought with them to America, and these perspectives informed their birth and growth to maturity. These perspectives are evident in the social structures that first engaged their energy as pioneers, the establishment of churches and schools. They are evident also in many of the agricultural practices adopted by the immigrants—small farms in close proximity to neighbors, shared agricultural labor and equipment, small-scale and community-sustaining skills and crafts, humane animal husbandry, labor-intensive production of crops, and cooperative processing and marketing of farm produce.

These are values of Anabaptist faith that were lost in large measure as these agrarian cultures began to decline in the second half of the twentieth century. These cultures did not lose their faith, but the agrarian practices that grew out of them were abandoned. Their agricultural practices were no longer shaped by their faith. There began to be a disconnect between the way these communities worshipped on Sunday and the way they farmed the other six days of the week. Now their agricultural practices were determined by the dominant culture of industrialized agriculture, mediated by multi-national corporations, government policies, and technocratic specialists. Now they were no longer motivated to act for the welfare of the community as a whole, but it was each farmer for him or herself, in competition with all the others. Vestiges of communal life were left to programs of mutual aid and church insurance programs, and the peace position became relevant primarily as a political stance against warfare, which grew weaker with each passing generation.

The beliefs people espouse do matter in the way they work themselves out in the life of the community. Picking up the fundamentalist beliefs of correct doctrine and life in the hereafter as the central tenets of Christian faith in the 1920s minimized both discipleship and community as basic Christian understandings. It was not wrong and perhaps was even necessary for these agrarian cultures to find their place in the American theological scene. But we should not imagine that there are no consequences when the core values of a particular culture are shifted. In this case, it meant the weakening of the link between their faith and their agricultural practices and communitarian interests. And that eventually has wrought the near fatal destruction of these agrarian cultures (congregations).

The way forward, then, is to reclaim the faith values and beliefs that nurture and sustain an agrarian culture. The way forward is to reground the life of the community in the faith perspectives that undergird and sustain agrarian cultures. In the manner of slow cultural change, that will be a long process—from articulating and owning the faith perspectives briefly outlined here, and then gradually shifting the agricultural practices and community behaviors to fit with those values and beliefs.

All this may seem to be an apology for the Anabaptist/Mennonite expression of Christian faith. But I have described how Anabaptist/Mennonite faith forms the basis for agrarian culture as an example and not as a claim to religious exclusivity. In fact, every Christian tradition bears within it the values espoused here, even if they are not always articulated or practiced as a matter of course.

The Eastern Orthodox tradition is highly incarnational in its theology, understanding that everything within creation and particularly all humanity bears the image of God. It is the particular calling of humanity to manifest that divine presence in its own life, and to call forth or reveal that divine element in all that God has created. Eastern Orthodoxy finds its strength in local parish settings of agrarian villages in traditionally Eastern Orthodox countries, as we experienced living among and working with the Orthodox Church of Crete in the early 1970s. These Orthodox perspectives are beautifully articulated by current Ecumenical Patriarch Bartholomew of Istanbul, Turkey, in his book *Encountering the Mystery*.[1] Patriarch Bartholomew has come to be known as the Green Patriarch for his espousal of environmental issues.

Roman Catholicism has seemed for much of its history to provide religious sanction for imperial powers, beginning with the Roman Empire and continuing through the Holy Roman Empire of European lands. Yet Roman Catholicism in the early thirteenth century produced Saint Francis of Assisi, the patron saint of ecology. In our time, the pope who took his name, Pope Francis, proclaimed the encyclical *Laudato Si*, a vigorous proclamation of ecological theology.[2] On the North American scene, 2018 marked the ninety-fifth anniversary of the National Catholic Rural Life Conference, begun in 1923.[3] Throughout these decades, Catholic Rural Life, as it is known today, has provided pastoral support for rural Catholic parishes whose churches dot the landscape of the Great Plains, many with European immigrant roots very similar to those of the agrarian cultures discussed in this book.

Protestant denominations have not historically been interested in agrarian or environmental issues. Mainstream Protestant denominations in the United States often assumed the role of civic chaplains to the established order, as can be seen in the fortress-like Anglican, Presbyterian, United Church of Christ, and Methodist churches that dot the downtown districts of most American cities and towns, many of them now relics. However, in recent decades many Protestant theologians have been articulating ecological concerns in their writing. Organizations like the Center for Theology and Land in Dubuque, Iowa, associated with the Lutheran Wartburg Theological Seminary but functioning ecumenically, has produced training for rural pastors and resources for rural congregation.[4] Evangelical Protestants, meanwhile, were primarily engaged in spiritual matters and debates before becoming embroiled in conservative politics in recent decades. However, groups like the Evangelical

---

1. Bartholomew, *Encountering the Mystery*.
2. Francis, *Laudato Si*.
3. Smith, "Celebrating 95 Years."
4. Jung et al., *Rural Ministry*, an excellent resource for rural pastors and congregations.

Environmental Network provide resources and teaching and social action for evangelical churches on environmental concerns.[5]

These sketchy outlines show how every tradition of Christian faith carries within it the theological perspectives that can help to shape agrarian cultures that bear those traditions. Though I don't have the expertise or experience to do so, I'm confident that the same theological underpinnings for ecology and agrarian life can be articulated in Muslim and Jewish traditions as well as the other major religious faiths of the human family. I did experience this in a Muslim setting during visits in 2008 and 2015 to the Muslim village of At-Tuwani, south of Hebron. This tiny Palestinian village facing Israeli occupation and surrounded by illegal Israeli settlements expresses its Muslim faith in its deep devotion to and care for the marginal land it inhabits.

The same can be said for the traditional aboriginal cultures that persist throughout the world on every continent. Native American nations did not develop formal religious institutions, nor, until recently, formal theological perspectives.[6] Yet religious faith informed every aspect of their daily life. They lived close to Nature and understood themselves to be an integral part of the web of life. This was expressed in their prayers to the Creator, acknowledging the divine presence in every direction and every season of life. They understood that the plants and animals that sustained their lives offered their life to the human community, and they received these gifts gratefully. In recent years I have often experienced the Lakota invocation of *mitakuye oyasin*, (all our relations), an expression of the relatedness of all humanity and also the way humankind is related to everything that is.[7]

European dispossession of Native American peoples from their land in recent centuries bore witness time and again to the integral relationship Native Americans had with the land on which they lived. The notion that land could be possessed, bought and sold, was not only foreign but repugnant to the Native American spirit. Perhaps the most classic expression of the cultural conflict between Europeans and Native Americans related to the land is the speech given by Chief Sealth in 1854 when white settlers at Puget Sound sought to sign a treaty with Chief Sealth's people.

5. Evangelical Environmental Network.

6. Recent Native American theological writings include Kidwell et al., *Native American Theology*; Treat, *Native and Christian*; and Heinrichs, *Buffalo Shout, Salmon Cry*, which includes essays by both Native and settler writers.

7. Kidwell et al., *Native American Theology*, 48–51.

> How can you buy or sell the sky, the warmth of the land? The idea is strange to us. If we do not own the freshness of the air and the sparkle of the water, how can you buy them?
>
> This we know. The earth does not belong to man; man belongs to the earth. This we know. All things are connected like the blood which unites one family....
>
> Whatever befalls the earth befalls the sons of the earth. Man does not weave the web of life, he is merely a strand in it. Whatever he does to the web, he does to himself.
>
> You may think that you own Him [God] as you wish to own our land, but you cannot. He is the God of man and His compassion is equal for the red man and the white. This earth is precious to Him and to harm the earth is to heap contempt on its Creator. Continue to contaminate your bed, and you will one night suffocate in your own waste.
>
> So if we sell you our land, love it as we've loved it. Care for it as we've cared for it. Hold in your mind the memory of the land as it is when you take it. And with all your strength, with all your mind, with all your heart, preserve it for your children and love it ... as God loves us all.[8]

AN ETHIC OF CARE FOR THE LAND

Religious faith provides a framework for an ethic of care for the land. Common to all religious faiths is the awareness that the Earth belongs to God, the Creator. Those who live close to Nature cannot help but experience awe and wonder at the mystery of creation and life. Here we are as humans, intricately woven into the fabric of life that moves through the millennia and eons of Earth's existence. However much science can teach us about how life has taken shape here on Earth, we still confront the ultimate mystery of finding ourselves as self-conscious creatures bound up with the unfolding of life and creation over which we have no control and which persists despite all that we have done to it in our efforts to control our destiny. We cannot sprout the seed upon which our lives depend. All we can do is plant and tend it.

The Judeo-Christian creation story in Gen 1 speaks about this in terms of our creation by God on the sixth day along with all the other creatures of the land, as the culmination of God's creative act. We are created, that story tells us, in God's image, and yet our lives are dependent

---

8. Chief Sealth, quoted in Granberg-Michaelson, *Worldly Spirituality*, 29–30.

on the green plants God created on the third day of creation. In other words, however aware we are of ourselves and our place within creation, however conscious we are of our relationship with the Creator, we are inextricably linked to all the processes of life and creation in which we live. The only appropriate response we can have to this mystery is awe and worship of the Creator, who deigned to place us in this way within the fabric of life.

It is in the nature of systems of domination and oppression and exploitation to objectify everything outside the self. The institutions and structures of society that characterize the history of civilization are based on the utility of the Earth, other forms of life, and other people. Everything is to be available for human use, for the service of the self. Nothing outside the self has intrinsic worth. Everything derives its worth only from its utility for the self, for the human presumed to be the center and end of all the world. So those who exercise power and dominion in human history presume the right to use the Earth and all its forms of life including other humans for their own ends, in order to extend and preserve their power and the institutions and structures they represent.

This tendency toward objectification present in the rise of civilization with its realms and empires was only intensified with the rise of science and technology that began with the eighteenth-century Age of Enlightenment. Basic to the scientific method is analysis of the world in which we live. In an effort to understand ourselves and the world in which we live, we have learned to take things apart to determine cause and effect. In the process, we have penetrated the secrets not only of all living forms but also the very atomic structures and genetic codes by which everything is made. While the scientific method has served us well in coming to understand how things work and enabling us to manipulate these processes, it has failed in helping us understand how things fit together and work together in living systems. Science is a good tool for analysis, but not so good at synthesis. Or at least, it has not been.

The result is that we have forgotten how to see ourselves as a part of living systems. We have forgotten to see ourselves in relation to all the other people and all the other forms of life and indeed the Earth itself, to say nothing of the Creator who made us. We have come to imagine that we are the only actors on the stage of life, whereas in fact we are but one bit player and indeed played upon more than player. We may imagine ourselves to be masters of our own fate and indeed masters who rule other people and other forms of life and the Earth itself. And while we may indeed do much to disrupt the systems of life as we see in the current global climate crisis, we are powerless to manage these living systems on which our lives depend.

Our calling as humans is not to manage the world. It is rather to grow in our understanding of our place within the drama of life and creation in which we find ourselves. While it is useful to understand how things work and how things are made, the real challenge for us as humans is to find our place in relation to all the other forms of life and to the Earth itself. It is to see ourselves within that web of life and to see how our every daily act plays itself out in relation to all the other forms of life including also the Creator. For it is the Creator and not we ourselves who is at the center of this drama of life and creation. However much we may seek to dominate and control creation or other forms of life or other people, all these efforts are destructive of both creation and self. Our lives only take on worth and meaning as we forsake self-assertion and understand our role in the world and our relation to all that is.

This means we must see everything that is as having intrinsic worth, not merely objects upon which we act, but as subjects to whom we relate. We can never understand the mystery of God's creative process, but we should never fail to ponder God's care for every creature and every form of life, however useless or transitory it might seem to us. Why has this stone or this bit of Earth assumed this shape and come to us in this place? What is the place and role of all those forms of life that grow in this place? Everything in creation is precious to God, every form of life, every sparrow that falls (Matt 10:29–31). And if it is so for God, so it should be for us who are made in God's image!

This does not prevent or forbid human use of creation or human involvement in the processes of life through agriculture and other endeavors. But it does mean that in such efforts we will be instructed by all the relations of life and creation, and not by that which serves self-interest or greed or other forms of domination and control. We will acknowledge the ways in which our own sustenance depends on the living sacrifices of other forms of life and yet may also nourish that whole web of life within which we live. We will honor and respect every life we encounter, treating all creation with the dignity it has as God's creation.

This is our calling as humans because we are made in God's image. God has deigned to put within every human person God's image of love, and it is our privilege to reflect this image of love in all our interactions and relationships with other people, with all creatures and living things, and indeed with all the elements of creation. In this way, God invites us to participate with God in the unfolding of life and creation. We are honored to reflect God's presence and character in all the ways we relate to others and other forms of life.

This is the ethic of reverence and care we are called to live out in all our relationships. It is the ethic rooted in the religious or spiritual sensibility of the human family, capable of worship for the God who has created us this way and in this way placed us within God's creation. Those who work most intimately with Nature as farmers, those who till the soil and tend the creatures of God's Earth, are the most natural heirs of this ethic, for they are daily in contact both with other humans, the creatures and all forms of life, and all creation. They are privileged by their daily labor to observe all the relatedness of life and to facilitate and enhance its unfolding. But it is not the duty and calling only of farmers. It is the calling given to the whole human family. To all humans is given the calling to tend and care for the Earth (Gen 2:15), the garden God intended for our dwelling.

Though in our day it is no longer often used, stewardship is another way of speaking about this ethic of care and reverence for the Earth. A steward is one charged with the care of the property of his master, the master's household. The language of stewardship reminds us that the Earth belongs not to us but to God, the Creator. It reminds us that God dwells in this creation as a home God made for God's self. And it reminds us of our calling as stewards to care for this Earth which is God's home.

These ethical perspectives are by and large foreign to our thinking as modern people who believe that our future depends on our ability to manage and exploit the Earth and its life and its people. It is foreign even to many who still work the land as farmers in the industrial model of agriculture. But it is not far distant from anyone, whether living in rural or urban settings. Indeed, I wish to think that it is a perspective still the experience of everyone now and then, when we are overwhelmed with the beauty of a sunset, with the majesty of a tree, with the power of a storm, with the antics of a pet, with the miracle of a seed sprouting from our planting. What we all need is to cultivate and tend these moments of divine awareness so that they more fully shape the daily choices we all feel constrained to make.

In the context of this chapter, these are the ethical perspectives that will assure vital and strong agrarian cultures, human communities living and making their living close to the land. We are the privileged caretakers of the Earth which is our home and the home where God may dwell. Our calling as humans is to tend the garden and to see how we can facilitate the unfolding of life and creation here on Earth. How can the daily choices of our lives put us in harmony with the ongoing life of creation?

Like most traditional societies, the agrarian cultures that came to the Great Plains to form the Freeman community in the 1870s were not theologically articulate. Traditional cultures express their faith in practice rather than in theological treatises. As noted in the previous chapter, Mennonites did not begin to speak about creation care theologically until very recently. But the reverence they felt was expressed in the care with which they planted the seeds and tilled the soil, and in the way they tended the livestock and animals in their care. This is not to deny that there were at times abuses and gross mismanagement in agricultural practices, but the mindset of farmers in these agrarian cultures was deeply reverent toward the Earth and the world of Nature in which they lived. Today, practices such as the use of pesticides and herbicides and fungicides and confined animal feeding operations might seem to contradict this reverence for life. But I've found that even farmers who engage these practices experience wonder and awe at the mystery and sacredness of Nature in which they are privileged to live, whether it is the animals and crops in their care, the flight of a hawk, the deer that inhabit the woods, or simply the regeneration of the Earth in spring after a long, cold winter season.

REASSERTING COMMUNITY AND THE COMMONS

In the creation story of Gen 2 God declares that it is not good for the human to be alone (Gen 2:18)! After creating all the animals, a suitable companion had still not been found for the man, so a woman was created from the man so that they might live together. The human was created for community, to live in families, extended families, and communities, all of whom would together share the blessings of living on God's Earth. Perhaps God intends for the human to be a social creature because God in God's own self exists as a community of Father, Son, and Holy Spirit in traditional, trinitarian Christian understanding.

Community implies communion, sharing together the means of human livelihood. And indeed, until the rise of human civilization, human communities lived upon the Earth as a Commons. All that was required to maintain life and community was available to all—the air, the water, the land, the plants and animals upon which human life depend. Today, communities barely share the air as a Commons. Everything else required for life and human community has been commodified, brought under the stern rule of law and property and money and economy. It is a process that began with the dawn of agriculture and urban life—human civilization. Once there was an excess of agricultural production, more than one family could eat, the question became, *Whose is it*? Now food, and eventually all the means of production, the water and the land required to produce the food, were bartered and bought and sold.

Of course, even after the rise of civilization, much of the Earth remained a Commons. The Earth was simply too big and too bountiful to be brought under any human rule and economy, even that of powerful empires. There would always be some place where human communities might live outside the domain of human rule and economy, enjoying the Commons of the Earth. And wherever human communities could establish just and fair terms with those who held power and wealth, the Earth could still be a Commons for those human communities who continued to live on the land and produce the food needed by those living in the city.

Still, working in the Commons for the common welfare of the whole human family became more and more problematic. Today there is no corner of the Earth that is not claimed and ruled by one or another nation-state. The institutions and structures of the powers that rule human life prefer to deal with individuals rather than with communities, for communities have much more bargaining power than individuals. So the powers of imperial societies seek to disempower communal structures and to atomize and fragment the population into isolated family or individual units. It is the way a population can be led to produce the commodities the market requires and to become unquestioning and docile consumers. It is a process documented in the earlier chapters of this book in the story of the Freeman community.

The result is that we live in a highly individualistic culture. The needs and desires of individuals are researched to determine how they might best fulfill their role as consumers in society. The emphasis on individualism in American society is not altogether misguided, of course. Individuals do have the right to self-expression and self-fulfillment, and in recent decades American society has bent over backward to assure that the needs and desires of every citizen, if not the resident aliens, can be met. Individuals in American society are not only masters of consumer society. They also now have the right to define themselves, including their gender and sexuality, without regard to either biology or cultural heritage. American society and the media continually extol the achievements of individuals who against all odds have managed to make a name for themselves and to succeed in whatever artistic or economic or personal or legal agendas they wish to pursue. And for this we can be grateful. It is a cultural achievement of no small magnitude.

Yet the reality is that all this also weakens and destroys the traditional bonds of community and culture that have been the strength and legacy of the human family through the ages. Communities, whether rural or urban, are fragmented and broken and dysfunctional. They no longer play a strong role in defining our identity or our self-worth. Or, conversely, cultural identity also becomes a venue for identity politics that pits one oppressed group against another in the interests of the powers of the dominant society. It is only communities whose cultural identity is weakened and diluted that are prone to become party to the racist ideologies characterizing American society.

In place of genuine cultural community and heritage, the dominant culture of American society offers us the false, idolatrous ideologies of nationality and capitalism and globalism and militarism for our allegiance and our identity. We are called to find our identity in allegiance to the nation-state, the achievements of Wall Street, the multi-national corporations that keep our grocery shelves stocked with foreign produce, and the deadly power of military technology like drones divorced from the risks of the battlefield.

Throughout history, there have been efforts to curb the destructive structures and institutions of imperial powers in favor of local human communities. The Tribal Confederacy of early Israel from 1200 to 1000 BCE was one such effort. The Mosaic Covenant envisioned a society of free landholders—small, agrarian villages scattered throughout the hill country of Palestine—as alternatives to the rule of the Canaanite city-states under imperial hegemony. These villages were called to eschew centralized governmental and religious institutions and form instead egalitarian communities living in alliance with one another. They were to remain agrarian cultures, living on the land as on a Commons. Indeed, it was made clear to them that the land belonged to God, and that they were no more than aliens and tenants on God's land (Lev 25:23).[9]

---

9. See Kaufman, *Healing God's Earth*, ch. 7, for a discussion of early Israel as an agrarian society.

The Role of Religious Faith in the Formation of an Agrarian Culture 253

How well the people of Israel actually lived out this vision of agrarian life is an open question. Clearly it ended around 1000 BCE with Israel's choice to have a king and to become a nation like the nations around them (1 Sam 8:20). But at least the vision was there, and apparently some effort was made to live it out during the two hundred years of the Tribal Confederacy. And to be sure, it has remained in the consciousness of both Jewish and many other agrarian cultures ever since. There are alternatives to being swallowed up by the imperial cultures of humanity. While individuals are usually powerless to withstand the power of imperial cultures, local communities working together in subversive ways have a chance to live out the ethical and economic vision held out to us by the prophets of the Old Testament.

In the New Testament, the crowning achievement in the ministry of Jesus of Nazareth was the formation of a new community we know as the church—local congregations of "surrogate kin groups"[10]—bound together with other local congregations in an inter-cultural, international, ecumenical association of egalitarian communities. Jesus' ministry among the rural villages of Galilee suffering under Roman imperial rule and Jewish temple hegemony was an effort to release the communal vitality of local agrarian cultures from all the demons of imperial rule that possessed them.[11] After Jesus' death and resurrection, local communities of faith—Christian congregations—sprang up as alternative communal manifestations throughout the Roman empire, in both rural and urban settings.[12] These are the roots of the local agrarian village cultures that emigrated from Russia to America in the 1870s to form the larger Freeman community.

Christian congregations clearly began as radical, subversive communities of faith, providing an alternative identity for their members to the imperial identities under which they were living. Why else were Christian congregations persecuted by officials of the Roman Empire for the first three centuries of Christian history? But so often throughout history, religious faith is co-opted by imperial power to sanction and bless imperial endeavors. This is what happened when Christian faith was first

---

10. Kaufman, *Healing God's Earth*, 197, based on Hellerman, *Ancient Church as Family*, 3–25.

11. Kaufman, *Healing God's Earth*, ch. 12; see the story of the Gerasene demoniac in Mark 5:1–20.

12. Kaufman, *Healing God's Earth*, ch. 13.

legalized and then made the official religion of the Roman Empire early in the fourth century CE.[13] Now the Christian church lost its character as an alternative, subversive community of faith. Nevertheless, in local communities, particularly in rural contexts, the alternative social and communal character of Christian congregations continued to nurture and empower an alternative communal identity throughout the centuries.

In the American experience, Christian faith has also been sometimes co-opted to bless and sanction the United States as an imperial power. We have seen this in the way that mainline Protestant denominations assumed their favored role as *chaplains* of American society in the eighteenth and nineteenth centuries and into the early twentieth century. Currently, the conservative Christian churches of the Religious Right have assumed this role in American society. Today Christian faith in more liberal progressive circles is co-opted to further and bless the extreme emphasis on individual rights within American society. None of these co-optations is completely without warrant, for there are many elements in American society, despite its overall imperial nature, that are in harmony with some values of Christian faith. Indeed, this is also true of most of the empires of history.

Despite all this, the most faithful expression of Christian faith and indeed of most religious or spiritual systems is to be found in their communal expression and character. Religious belief nearly universally calls out the altruistic nature of humanity. We live not for self alone, but for those near and dear to us, and ultimately for the *common good*. Religious faith, Christian faith, calls us to seek not our own good or our own welfare alone, but the good of the community as a whole.[14]

Within the Anabaptist/Mennonite faith, this communal emphasis works itself out in mutual aid and service to humanity. Mennonite congregations typically have mutual aid ministries that seek to serve the needs of all within the community, though in too many the emphasis is on meeting the needs of their own membership and sometimes fails to be extended to the larger communities where they live. Sometimes, as in Hutterite colonies, this concept of mutual aid extends to eschewing private property and holding all things in common.

---

13. Kaufman, *Healing God's Earth*, 112–16.

14. Phil 2:1–4 is but one of many expressions of this self-less character of Christian belief.

This book has documented the way in which mutual aid was also practiced across communities of like faith but in widely divergent geographical settings, as in the aid Mennonite and Amish communities in the eastern United States offered to Russian-German immigrants for their move to America, and the assistance and loans given to the struggling new Anabaptist communities on the Great Plains. Similar mutual aid can be seen in the development of Mennonite Central Committee, the service arm of Mennonite denominations in the United States and Canada. The initial impetus for the development of Mennonite Central Committee in 1920 was the plight of Russian Mennonites suffering from famine in the Soviet Union.[15] Since then, for the past century, Mennonite Central Committee has extended emergency and development aid to many communities of many faiths throughout the world, especially those suffering from war and colonial oppression.

This book has also documented the way the failure to practice mutual aid within the traditional agrarian cultures of the Freeman community contributed to the community's decline. As farmers acculturated to the individualistic ethos of American agriculture, they lost the sense that their land and farms were communal assets. Extended family land ownership patterns and the shared labor involved in producing and marketing agricultural produce were lost as farmers accommodated their operations to the global market economy.

Healthy agrarian cultures require a faith-based commitment to the welfare of the rural community. This doesn't necessarily require communal land ownership patterns, though that may be helpful in the form of community land trusts. It does require that those involved in agriculture recognize the need to work together in the production, processing, and marketing of agricultural products. Only in this way will rural communities have the strength to operate in a sustainable way within the structures of a dominant imperial culture based on the exploitation of the land and the people who live on the land.

The agrarian cultures of the Freeman community have the theological grounding and the cultural heritage to reclaim a communal approach to their agricultural endeavors. We have within our memory and in our congregational practices the mindset of mutual aid that would enable a community to work together for the welfare of all within the community while also serving the needs of the larger society and world in which we

---

15. Smith, *Smith's Story*, 551.

live. What we need to do is to reinvent the agricultural practices that serve these ends in the production, processing, and marketing of the food and fiber needed for our community, our society, and our world.

RECLAIMING THE AGRICULTURAL TASK: RAISING FOOD TO SUSTAIN LIFE!

Agrarian cultures and rural communities thrive when they are engaged in the task central to their life—raising food to sustain life! The struggle of rural communities for survival might most simply be explained by their abandonment of this central mission. Though lip service in American society is given to farmers feeding the world, the reality is that most commodity-oriented agricultural production, at least here on the Great Plains, is no longer engaged in food production. Some of the commodities produced for the global market are used to feed people, of course. But farmers are by and large several steps removed from the actual production of food that people eat. Few farmers raise food for themselves and their families and fewer still raise food sold directly to consumers. This reality has enormous consequences not just for the farmers themselves, but for the rural communities in which they live.

Traditional agrarian cultures throughout the world and throughout history understand food to be sacred. It is sacred because it is the stuff of life; it is what sustains human life. It is sacred because its presence is always perceived to be *gift*, something given to us in a sacred and mysterious process of growth. We plant seeds and till the plants for food, but we have no ability to make seeds grow or plants produce their crop. We breed and tend animals for the food products they offer to us, but their lives are always a gift given to us and for us.

People of faith typically *give thanks* with a prayer, however perfunctory, at the beginning and sometimes after a meal. However much the people at the meal may have labored in the production and processing and preparation of the meal, they receive the food as a gift, not as a right. Eating itself then becomes a sacred act. If the food is scarce in times of famine or war, that only increases the sacredness of the meal which is shared generously with all at the table. And when guests appear at the door they are invited to the table, regardless of how much or little food there may be. The means of life are sacred and through some miraculous means there is always plenty for all.

Perhaps in all religious faiths, but certainly in Christian faith, the Table is central and sacred. In addition to water baptism as an initiatory rite, the Lord's Supper or Communion is the universal and essential mark of Christian faith, as the community gathers around the Lord's Table to commune in the body and the blood of their Lord. Though instituted at the Last Supper of Jesus with his disciples before his death, the Lord's Supper is deeply rooted in the ministry of Jesus. Throughout his ministry, Jesus assumed the role of a host and officiated at the meals with his disciples.

An itinerant teacher and healer, Jesus traveled around Galilee with his disciples, a band of men and women who traveled with him. When evening came, the group would gather, likely in some quiet place, and the group would take stock. Perhaps someone in a village they passed through had given them some eggs or a chicken or some fish. Perhaps the women whom the Gospels portray as supporting Jesus (Mark 15:41) had bought a few basic provisions for the meal. Whenever the food was gathered and prepared, we find the same ritual. Jesus *took* the bread, *blessed* it, *broke* it, and *gave* it. These are the four verbs used not just at the Last Supper when the Lord's Supper was instituted, but also at every meal recorded in the Gospels, including the mass feedings of Mark 6 and 8. Jesus received the food as gift, gave thanks for it, broke or shared it, and gave it to all at the table. Everyone, all the hangers-on, were always welcome, no questions asked, and there was always enough for all.

This is the true meaning and significance of the Lord's Supper. It is a celebration of God's provision for us, for all humanity. Through human labor, the work of our hands, God provides through the Earth the food, all that is required for our lives. In these daily acts of *taking*, *blessing*, *breaking*, and *giving*, Jesus modeled the sacredness of food, the daily act of eating, and indeed, the sacredness of life itself. Because food and eating are sacred acts, so are all the activities and processes and forms of Nature, including the Earth and the land itself, with all its creatures and forms of life. When the Table functions as it should in human society, then the whole society, the whole culture, will function in a healthy and sustainable manner. If the Table as a place of sustenance and hospitality and generosity and reverence is lost, then the culture and social order of that Table is in precarious danger.

The industrial food system has pretty well demolished any sense of the sacredness of the Table in American society and in much of the modern world. There is a huge disconnect between the food we eat and the land and people and hands that raised that food, harvested it, processed it, commoditized it, and brought it to our tables, often from across the country or from foreign ports. With this disconnect between production and consumption, there can be little reverence felt or shown toward the food we eat, however spiritual we may be or however piously we may give thanks. Food is simply a commodity that might be marketed and prepared in novel ways and thus marveled over, but in the end, it can be thrown out into a landfill with no care or sense of loss and no awareness of how in our consumption and our garbage we are breaking the sacred cycle of life. We have no awareness or care for the land or sea that has produced our food, or for the people engaged in its production and processing. All this is a world away, not only culturally but often also geographically. We only become concerned when we begin to discover the ill-health such a secularized food system inevitably brings to us.

The industrial food system not only secularizes and commodifies food itself, but also the process of raising, tending, harvesting, processing, and preparing food. The people who raise the food are often alienated from the land. They are often workers who have no investment in the land or its health. They themselves are often oppressed victims of a food system whose bottom line is profit, and this applies also to the farmers in the industrialized agricultural system. If the land is being abused, if the food products are contaminated with poisons and genetically modified residues, if the workers are not being paid fairly, if farmers cannot receive a fair compensation for their crops, that's just the way the system works. Indeed, such a food system is not only not holy, it is demonic!

All this is why it is supremely important for rural communities and agrarian cultures to reclaim their divine vocation—raising food to sustain life! Obviously, this requires an agricultural system quite different from that which most farmers currently utilize. It requires an integrated agricultural system of plants and animals living symbiotically with each other and with the human community on the land. That means small farms, lots of farmers, lots of human labor, and lots of community participation in processing and marketing the produce of the land. It means that farmers will reclaim the religious rituals for planting and harvesting crops, and breeding and tending and slaughtering livestock, which is evident in traditional agrarian cultures around the world and which was also practiced by immigrant farmers of the Freeman community. It means that a local food system with direct producer/consumer links on the Community Supported Agriculture (CSA) model will become the primary venue for marketing the produce of the land, for if food is to regain its holy character, that must be as much the concern of the consumer in nearby urban centers as it is of the farmers who produce the food. For consumers to grasp the holiness of their food, they must put a face on the people who work on the land and visit the land from which their food comes.

It is the divine vocation of farmers and rural communities to raise food to sustain life—the lives of the farmers and their families first of all, and then the people who live in their community, and ultimately the lives of those who live in the larger urban society of the region. It is the loss of this divine vocation, more than anything else, that has torn apart the fabric of rural communities and agrarian cultures.

Rural churches and traditional religious and cultural leaders have a key role to play in the revitalization of rural communities and their agrarian cultures. These churches and leaders can *re-sacralize* the natural order, reviving or creating religious rituals appropriate to the seasonal work of the farm in their worship services, and providing such resources for farm families to do as they perform the work. In her book, *The Celtic Way of Prayer*, Esther De Waal describes the prayers used in traditional Irish society as the people of Ireland went about their daily activities of lighting the hearth fire, weaving, tending the flocks, and the myriad tasks that are involved in raising food to sustain life.[16]

Rural churches and their leaders can also provide the theological and cultural resources that laid the foundation for these agrarian cultures and rural communities. They can recreate the links that exist between what happens on Sunday at the Lord's Table, for instance, and what happens at the everyday domestic tables of people throughout the region. And rural churches, by virtue of their organization, can become catalysts to revitalize their communities through the adoption of agricultural practices required for a local food system. Since everything associated with the Table and food is sacred, it is appropriate for churches and religious leaders to be involved in every aspect of the food system.

Obviously, industrial agriculture and the industrial food system are not going to be changed overnight. It would be disruptive to the society as a whole if that were to happen, though with climate change and pandemics like the current coronavirus, that shift might happen quite fast and with considerable economic dislocation. However, both producers and consumers do not have to wait for new agricultural practices and a

---

16. De Waal, *Celtic Way of Prayer*, 74–93.

local food system in order to change the way they think about both food and their daily tasks. Farmers raising commodities for a global market or raising animals in CAFOs can realize that they too are engaged in a sacred task and let that realization work its way through the way they tend their crops and animals. Consumers can hold all the food products they buy sacredly and learn all that they can about how it was produced, where and by whom and with what practices and at what unseen costs.

It is in many ways ironic that life depends on life. Both as carnivores and as vegetarians, we all depend on other plant or animal species giving their lives for us. It is the only way we can live. And it is what makes food and everything having to do with food sacred. It is what makes agriculture a sacred vocation, and it is why the survival and health of agrarian cultures and rural communities depend on their making their livelihood a sacred vocation. Wendell Berry's essay, "The Gift of Good Land," concludes in this way: "To live, we must daily break the body and shed the blood of Creation. When we do this knowingly, lovingly, skillfully, reverently, it is a sacrament. When we do it ignorantly, greedily, clumsily, destructively, it is a desecration. In such desecration we condemn ourselves to spiritual and moral loneliness, and others to want."[17]

AFTERWORD

Despite the depredations suffered by agrarian cultures and rural communities throughout history and most intensively in the modern era, and despite the failures and mistakes and foolishness perpetrated by these local cultures and communities, including people like myself, I am optimistic about the agrarian cultures of the Freeman community and the future of agrarian cultures generally. There is in these local cultures a dynamic resilience that persists even when it seems that the dominant culture has *won* and local agrarian cultures are dead and gone.

This resilience, I believe, is rooted in the faith and heritage of these agrarian cultures. They may forget who they are for a season of time. They may seem to have acculturated entirely to the dominant, imperial, oppressive culture of the larger society. But always, the memory of their heritage and their faith persists, and as human society evolves and confronts crises like the current global climate change or the coronavirus pandemic, suddenly the old wisdom begins to inform these local

17. Berry, *The Gift*, 281.

cultures. New patterns and ways of life begin to emerge, not just like the old ways, but rooted in the wisdom of those old ways. We can see this development in rural communities throughout North America, and even more profoundly in the ways Native American First Nations are currently reviving and renewing their ancient cultural worldview to shape their communities in the twenty-first century.

The agrarian cultures that formed the Freeman community would seem to be near death. They were planted nearly 150 years ago by Russian-German immigrants in the 1870s, most of whom came here as faith communities. This corporate faith identity might have been the key to their survival in the difficult first years of their lives here on the Great Plains. It probably fed the growth and success of the community in the early and mid-twentieth century. And its near loss has led to the decline of the community as it was overshadowed by acculturation to the dominant culture of American society.

As the dominant culture of American society confronts and deals with the economic and ecological and energy crises of these decades, rural communities and their agrarian cultures have an opportunity to revitalize and renew the faith and heritage that informed their communal life for so many generations. I have a hunch that the Freeman community is in the process of recovering its agricultural vocation of raising food to sustain life. In the process, the community itself will be renewed and restored.

Bibliography

Ambrose, Stephen E. *Undaunted Courage: Meriwether Lewis, Thomas Jefferson, and the Opening of the American West.* New York: Simon & Schuster, 1997.
Barraclough, Geoffrey, ed. *Harper Collins Atlas of World History.* Rev. ed. Ann Arbor, MI: Borders, 1999.
Bartholomew, His All Holiness, Ecumenical Patriarch. *Encountering the Mystery: Understanding Orthodox Christianity Today.* New York: Doubleday, 2008.
Bayer. "How Can We Farm Better?" *National Geographic*, January 2019, 23.
Bell, Earl H. *Social Foundations of Human Behavior: Introduction to the Study of Sociology.* New York: Harper & Row, 1961.
Bender, Harold S. *The Anabaptist Vision,* Scottdale, PA: Herald, 1944.
Berry, Wendell. *The Gift of Good Land: Further Essays Cultural and Agricultural.* Berkeley, CA; Counterpoint, 1981.
———. *Hannah Coulter.* Berkeley, CA: Counterpoint, 2004.
———. *The Unsettling of America: Culture and Agriculture.* San Francisco: Sierra Club, 1977.
Bethesda Mennonite Church. *125th Celebration, Quasquicentennial, 1883-2008.* Heritage Hall Museum and Archives, Freeman, SD.
Boese, John A. *The Life Story of Grandfather Henry H. Buller, January 5, 1821-April 19, 1913.* Heritage Hall Museum and Archives, Freeman, SD.
———. *Loretta's Settlement.* Freeman, SD: Freeman Junior College, 1950.
———. *The Prussian-Polish Mennonites Settling in South Dakota 1874 and Soon After.* Freeman, SD: Pine Hill, 1967.
Bosch, William. *The German-Russians in Words and Pictures.* Self-published, CreateSpace, 2015.
Bose, B. A. *Johnny Schmidt: Son of a Dakota Pioneer.* Germans from Russia Heritage Collection. Rev. ed. Fargo, ND: North Dakota State University Libraries, 2002.
Bostick, Douglas W. *The History of Slavery in the South Carolina Lowcountry.* Charleston, SC: Charleston Postcard, 2014.
Brown, Gabe. *Dirt to Soil: One Family's Journey into Regenerative Agriculture.* White River Junction, VT: Chelsea Green, 2018.
Bryson, Bill. *A Short History of Nearly Everything.* New York: Broadway, 2004.
Carson, Rachel. *Silent Spring.* Greenwich, CT: Fawcett, 1962.
Center for Rural Affairs. "Center for Rural Affairs Newsletter." https://www.cfra.org.
Champagne, Duane, ed. *Native America: Portrait of the Peoples.* Detroit, MI: Visible Ink, 1994.

Church of the Brethren General Board. *This Land: Ours for a Season*. Elgin, IL: World Ministries Commission, 1974.

City of Freeman. "Freeman Community Development Corporation." https://cityoffreeman.org/fcdc.

City of Menno. *Menno: The First 100 Years, 1879–1979*. Freeman, SD: Pine Hill, 1979.

Cobb Jr., John B. *A Christian Natural Theology: Based on the Thought of Alfred North Whitehead*. Philadelphia: Westminster, 1965.

Crosby, Alfred W. *Ecological Imperialism: The Biological Expansion of Europe, 900–1900*. 2nd ed. Studies in Environment and History. New York: Cambridge University Press, 2004.

Dakota Rural Action. "Action Review." https://www.dakotarural.org.

Dale, Tom, and Vernon Gill Carter. *Topsoil and Civilization*. 2nd ed. Toronto: McClellan and Steward, 1961.

De Waal, Esther. *The Celtic Way of Prayer: The Recovery of the Religious Imagination*. New York: Doubleday, 1997.

Dismantling the Doctrine of Discovery. "Exhibit Timeline." https://doctrineofdiscoverymenno.files.wordpress.com/2015/06/dismantling.

———. "Fact Sheet." https://doctrineofdiscoverymenno.files.wordpress.com.

Driedger, Johann. "Farming Among the Mennonites in East and West Prussia, 1534–1945." *Mennonite Quarterly Review* 31, no. 1 (January 1957) 16–21.

Dyck, Cornelius J., ed. *An Introduction to Mennonite History: A Popular History of the Anabaptists and the Mennonites*. Scottdale, PA: Herald, 1967.

Evangelical Environmental Network. https://creationcare.org.

Flora, Cornelia Butler, et al. *Rural Communities: Legacy and Change*. 2nd ed. Boulder, CO: Westview, 2004.

Francis, Pope. *Laudato Si: On Care for Our Common Home*. Frederick, MD: Word Among Us Press, 2015.

Freeman Centennial Steering Committee. *Freeman Facts—Freeman Fiction: 1879–1979, Celebrating Our Centennial*. Freeman, SD: City of Freeman, 1979.

Garraty, John A., and Peter Gay, eds. *The Columbia History of the World*. New York: Harper & Row, 1972.

Gering, John J. *After Fifty Years: A Brief Discussion of the History and Activities of the Swiss-German Mennonites From Russia, Who Settled in South Dakota in 1874*. Freeman, SD: Pine Hill, 1924.

The Gilder Lehrman Institute of American History. "Doctrine of Discovery, 1493." https://ap.gilderlehrman.org/resource/doctrine-discovery-1493.

Graber, Jennifer. *The Gods of Indian Country: Religion and the Struggle for the American West*. New York: Oxford University Press, 2018.

Granberg-Michaelson, Wesley. *A Worldly Spirituality: The Call to Redeem Life on Earth*. San Francisco: Harper & Row, 1984.

Gries, John Paul. *Roadside Geology of South Dakota*. Missoula, MT: Mountain, 1996.

Hale, John R. *Age of Exploration*. Great Ages of Man. New York: Time-Life, 1974.

Harker, Ryan D., and Janeen Bertsche Johnson, eds. *Rooted and Grounded: Essays on Land and Christian Discipleship*. Eugene, OR: Pickwick, 2016.

Hartshorne, Charles. *The Divine Relativity: A Social Conception of God*. 1948. Reprint, New Haven, CT: Yale University Press, 1967.

The Heartland Project. *Strangers and Guests: Toward Community in the Heartland; A Regional Catholic Bishops' Statement on Land Issues*. 1980.

Heinrichs, Steve, ed. *Buffalo Shout, Salmon Cry: Conversations on Creation, Land Justice, and Life Together.* Waterloo, ON: Herald, 2013.

Hellerman, Joseph H. *The Ancient Church as Family.* Minneapolis: Fortress, 2001.

Hicks, John D., et al. *The Federal Union: A History of the United States to 1877.* 4th ed. Boston: Houghton Mifflin, 1964.

Hiebert, Clarence, ed. *Brothers in Deed to Brothers in Need: A Scrapbook about Mennonite Immigrants from Russia, 1870–885.* Newton, KS: Faith and Life, 1974.

Hofer, Norman. "Hutterite Colony or 'The Prairie.'" 2015. Heritage Hall Museum and Archives, Freeman, SD.

Hutterite Centennial Steering Committee. *History of the Hutterite Mennonites.* 1974. Reprint, Freeman, SD: Pine Hill, 1986.

Jackson, Wes. *Becoming Native to This Place.* Washington, DC: Counterpoint, 1996.

———. *New Roots for Agriculture.* San Francisco: Friends of the Earth, 1980.

Jackson, Wes, et al., eds. *Meeting the Expectations of the Land: Essays in Sustainable Agriculture and Stewardship.* San Francisco: North Point, 1984.

Jakeš, Petr. *Living Planet Earth.* Translated by Clare Krojzlová and Slavoš Kadečka. Prague, Czech Republic: Aventinum, 1994.

Jennewein, J. Leonard, and Jane Boorman, eds. *Dakota Panorama: A History of Dakota Territory.* 4th ed. Sioux Falls, SD: Brevet, 1988.

Jeschke, Marlin. *Rethinking Holy Land: A Study in Salvation Geography.* Scottdale, PA: Herald, 2005.

Jones, Ruth Richert. *Land of Their Own: From Russia to South Dakota: A Historical Novel.* Omaha, NE: Thorne Tree, 2002.

Juhnke, James C. *Vision, Doctrine, War: Mennonite Identity and Organization in America, 1890–930.* The Mennonite Experience in America 3. Scottdale, PA: Herald, 1989.

Jung, Shannon, et.al. *Rural Ministry: The Shape of the Renewal to Come.* Nashville: Abingdon, 1998.

Kaufman, S. Roy. "The Anatomy of a Rural Church." *The Mennonite* 14, no. 9 (September 2011) 16–19.

———. "Award-winning Farm Family Marches to the Beat of Different Drummer." *Freeman Courier*, February 15, 2015, 3.

———. Centennial Sermons and Talks. Papers. 2008. Heritage Hall Museum and Archives, Freeman, SD.

———. "Conventional Crops, Unconventional Practices." *Freeman Courier*, August 2, 2016, 8A.

———. "Grassland Farming." *Freeman Courier*, June 20, 2019, 3A.

———. *Healing God's Earth: Rural Community in the Context of Urban Civilization.* Eugene, OR: Wipf and Stock, 2013.

———. "A Local 'Local Food' Enterprise." *Freeman Courier*, May 26, 2016, 8A.

———. "Midwinter Grazing." *Freeman Courier*, January 5, 2017, 8B.

Kidwell, Clara Sue, et al. *A Native American Theology.* 2001. Reprint, Maryknoll, NY: Orbis, 2006.

Kingsolver, Barbara. *Animal, Vegetable, Miracle: A Year of Food Life.* New York: HarperCollins, 2007.

Kinsella, Steven R. *900 Miles from Nowhere: Voices from the Homestead Frontier.* St. Paul, MN: Minnesota Historical Society, 2006.

Krahn, Cornelius, ed. *From the Steppes to the Prairies (1874–1949)*. Newton, KS: Mennonite, 1949.

Krehbiel, H. P. *The History of the General Conference of the Mennonites of North America*. St. Louis, MO: A. Wilrusch & Son, 1898.

Land Stewardship Project. "Carbon's Crisis Management Potential." *Land Stewardship Letter* 37, no. 2 (2019) 8–9.

———. *Land Stewardship Letter*. https://www.landstewardshipproject.org.

———. "Opportunity Knocks." Review of *Look Who's Knockin'*, by Doug Nopar. *Land Stewardship Letter* 29, no. 1 (2011) 8–9.

Lavin, Stephen J., et al. *Atlas of the Great Plains*. Lincoln, NE: University of Nebraska Press, 2011.

Leopold, Aldo. *A Sand County Almanac*. 1949. Reprint, New York: Ballatine, 1966.

Leopold Center for Sustainable Agriculture. *Leopold Letter*. https://www.leopold.iastate.edu.

Meadows, Donella H., et al. *The Limits to Growth: A Report for the Club of Rome's Project on the Predicament of Mankind*. New York: Signet, 1972.

Meier, Johannes. "Beating the Big Dry: How an Australian cattle farm is fighting drought by reviving ancient landscapes." *Plough Quarterly* 20 (Spring 2019) 42–55.

Mendel, J. J. *History of Freeman from 1879 to 1958*. Freeman, SD: Pine Hill, 1958.

Mennonite Church and General Conference Mennonite Church. *Confession of Faith in a Mennonite Perspective*. Scottdale, PA: Herald, 1995.

Mennonite Creation Care Network. https://mennonitecreationcare.org.

Merriam Webster's Collegiate Dictionary.

Merrill, Richard, ed. *Radical Agriculture*. New York: New York University Press, 1976.

Meyer, Art, and Jocele Meyer. *Earth-keepers: Environmental Perspectives on Hunger, Poverty, and Injustice*. Scottdale, PA: Herald, 1991.

Moltmann, Jürgen. *God in Creation: A New Theology of Creation and the Spirit of God*. Translated by Margaret Kohl. San Francisco: Harper & Row, 1985.

Nolt, Stephen M. *A History of the Amish*. Intercourse, PA: Good Books, 1992.

Norris, Kathleen. *Dakota: A Spiritual Geography*. Boston: Houghton Mifflin, 1993.

Pares, Bernard. *A History of Russia*. 1926. Reprint, New York: Vintage, 1965.

Platt, LaVonne Godwin, ed. *Hope for the Family Farm: Trust God and Care for the Land*. Newton, KS: Faith and Life, 1987.

Polkinghorne, John. *The Faith of a Physicist: Reflections of a Bottom-Up Thinker*. Princeton, NJ: Princeton University Press, 1994.

Pollan, Michael. *The Omnivore's Dilemma: A Natural History of Four Meals*. New York: Penguin, 2006.

Rath, George. *The Black Sea Germans in the Dakotas*. Freeman, SD: Pine Hill, 1977.

Redekop, Calvin, ed. *Creation and the Environment: An Anabaptist Perspective on a Sustainable World*. Baltimore: Johns Hopkins University Press, 2000.

Robinson, Ron, with contributions by L. Adrien Hannus. *The Village on the Bluff: Prehistoric Farmers/Hunters of the James River Valley*. Sioux Falls, SD: Archeology Laboratory of Augustana College, 2011.

Rölvaag, O. E. *Giants in the Earth: A Saga of the Prairie*. Translated by Lincoln Colcord. 1927. Reprint, New York: Harper & Row, 1965.

Rural Revival. "Mission." https://ruralrevival.org.

———. "Proposal for a Community Farmland Trust." 2018. https://ruralrevival.org/2019/01/PROPOSAL-FOR-COMMUNITY-FARMLAND-TRUST.pdf.

Salatin, Joel. *Folks, This Ain't Normal: A Farmer's Advice for Happier Hens, Healthier People, and a Better World.* New York: Center Street, 2011.
Sale, Kirkpatrick. *Human Scale.* New York: Perigee, 1980.
Salem Mennonite Church. A Moment on Our Journey of Faith: Centennial Anniversary of the Salem Mennonite Church, Freeman, South Dakota, 1908–2008. Papers. Freeman, SD.
———. Yearbook and Directory. Papers. 2019. Freeman, SD.
Salem-Zion Mennonite Church. *Looking Back 100 Years: A Compilation of Events Before, During, and After the 75th and 100th Anniversaries of the Salem-Zion Mennonite Church of Freeman, South Dakota.* Freeman, SD: Pine Hill, 1980.
Sampson, R. Neil. *Farmland or Wasteland: A Time to Choose. Overcoming the Threat to America's Farm and Food Future.* Emmaus, PA: Rodale, 1981.
Sansom-Flood, Reneé, and Shirley A. Bernie. *Remember Your Relatives: Yankton Sioux Images, 1851–1904.* Marty, SD: Marty Indian School, 1985.
Savage, Candace. *Prairie: A Natural History.* Vancouver, BC: Greystone, 2004.
Schell, Herbert S. *History of South Dakota.* 4th rev. ed. Edited by John E. Miller. Pierre, SD: South Dakota State Historical Society Press, 2004.
Schmidt, Diena, ed. *The Northern District Conference, 1891–1991.* Freeman, SD: Pine Hill, 1991.
Schrag, Martin H. *The European History of the Swiss Mennonites from Volhynia.* 2nd ed. Edited by Harley J. Stucky. Newton, KS: Graphic Images, 1999.
Shaw, Mary Lou. "Fostering Healthy Soil for Better Health." *Farming Magazine* 19, no. 3 (Fall 2019) 41–43.
Shepherd, Mark. *Restoration Agriculture.* Austin, TX: Acres, USA, 2013.
Smith, C. Henry. *Smith's Story of the Mennonites.* 5th rev. ed. Edited by Cornelius Krahn. Newton, KS: Faith and Life, 1981.
Smith, Morgan. "Celebrating 95 Years," *Catholic Rural Life Magazine* 60, no. 4 (Fall 2018) 8–10.
Snyder, C. Arnold. *Anabaptist History and Theology: An Introduction.* Kitchener, ON: Pandora, 1995.
Stoddard, W. H., ed. *Turner County Pioneer History.* Reprint, Freeman, SD: Pine Hill, 1991.
Stoltzfus, Duane C. S. *Pacifists in Chains.* Baltimore: Johns Hopkins University Press, 2013.
Stucky, Harley J. *A Century of Russian Mennonite History in America: A Study in Cultural Interaction.* North Newton, KS: Mennonite, 1973.
Stumpp, Karl. *The German-Russians: Two Centuries of Pioneering.* Translated by Joseph S. Height. 3rd ed. Bonn, Germany: Edition Atlantic-Forum, 1966.
Swiss-German Centennial Committee. *The Swiss-Germans in South Dakota (From Volhynia to Dakota Territory, 1874–1974).* Freeman, SD: Pine Hill, 1974.
Thoreau, Henry David. *Thoreau: Walden and other writings.* Edited by Joseph Wood Krutch New York: Bantam, 1962.
Three Groups, One Story: The Journey that Built a South Dakota Community. Written by Robert Engbrecht et al. Five Core Media, 2018. DVD. Heritage Hall Museum and Archives, Freeman, SD.
Toews, Paul. *Mennonites in American Society, 1930–970: Modernity and the Persistence of Religious Community.* The Mennonite Experience in America 4. Scottdale, PA: Herald, 1996.

Treat, James, ed. *Native and Christian: Indigenous Voices on Religious Identity in the United States and Canada.* New York: Routledge, 1996.

Tschetter, Martha M. *The Descendants of Benjamin G. Boese to 1976.* 1976. Heritage Hall Museum and Archives, Freeman, SD.

Turner County South Dakota. *Directory of Land Owners and Rural Residents.* Larchwood, IA: County-Wide Directory, 2009.

United States Department of Agriculture. Census of Agriculture Historical Archives. "Summary County Tables for South Dakota for 1925, 1950, 1974, 2002." https://www.agcensus.mannlib.cornell.edu/AgCensus/homepage/do.

———. National Agricultural Statistics Service. "Table 1: County Summary Highlights, 2012." http://www.nass.usda.gov/Publications/AgCensus/2012.

———. National Agricultural Statistics Service. "Table 1: County Summary Highlights, 2017." http://www.nass.usda.gov/Publications/AgCensus/2017.0

Unruh, Abe J. *The Helpless Poles.* Grabill, IN: Courier, 1973.

Unruh, Abe J., and Verney Unruh. *Tobias A. Unruh: Biography, Diary, and Family Record, 1819–1969.* Unpublished family history and translation of the Tobias Unruh Diary of the 1873 delegation and the 1874 voyage to America. Heritage Hall Museum and Archives, Freeman, SD.

Unruh, John D. *A Century of Mennonites in Dakota: A Segment of the German Russians.* South Dakota Historical Collections 36. Reprint, 1972.

Unruh, John D., and Gary J. Waltner. *An Andreas Schrag Document with Some Implications.* Freeman, SD: printed by the authors, 1982.

Unruh, John D., and John D. Unruh Jr. "Daniel Unruh and the Mennonite Settlement in Dakota Territory." *Mennonite Quarterly Review* XLIX, no. 3 (July 1975) 203–16.

US Census Bureau. "Quick Facts for Turner and Hutchinson Counties." https://www.census.gov.quickfacts/fact/table/hutchinsoncountyturnercountySD.

US-Dakota War. "*Oceti Sakowin:* The Seven Council Fires." www.usdakotawar.org/history/dakota-homeland/oceti-sakowin-seven-council-fires.

van Braght, Thieleman J. *The Bloody Theatre; or Martyr's Mirror of the Defenseless Christians.* Reprint, Scottdale, PA: Herald, 1950.

Waldner, Marie J., and Marnette D. Ortman Hofer. *Many Hands, Minds and Hearts: A History of Freeman Junior College and Academy, 1900–2000.* Sioux Falls, SD: Pine Hill, 2000.

Wallbank, T. Walter, et al. *Civilization Past and Present.* 3rd ed. Chicago: Scott Foresman, 1955.

Waltner, Emil J. *Banished for Faith.* Freeman, SD: Pine Hill, 1968.

Waltner, Gary J. "Andreas D. Schrag: A Diary of a Visit to America, 1873." Unpublished paper presented to the Department of History, University of South Dakota, Vermillion, SD, 1966. Heritage Hall Museum and Archives, Freeman, SD.

———. "Hutterite Pottery." Oral presentation at Heritage Hall Museum and Archives, Freeman, SD, September 8, 2015.

———. "A Study of the Economic Conditions of the Swiss Mennonites of Dakota, 1874–1882." Unpublished paper for a course at Bethel College, North Newton, KS, 1961. Heritage Hall Museum and Archives, Freeman, SD.

Waltner, Jeremy. "Idea Men: Prairie-to-Plate: An Exclusive Report." *Freeman Courier,* August 22, 2019, 1, 3.

———. "Where the Buffalo Roam." *Freeman Courier,* July 23, 2015, 1–3.

Webb, Walter Prescott. *The Great Plains*. Reprint, Lincoln, NE: University of Nebraska Press, 1981.
Wells, H. G. *The Outline of History: Being a Plain History of Life and Mankind*. 2 vols. Rev. ed. Garden City, NY: Garden City, 1961.
Wessel, James. *Trading the Future: Farm Exports and the Concentration of Economic Power in Our Food Economy*. San Francisco: Institute for Food and Development Policy, 1983.
West Freeman Reformed/Lutheran Tour. Notes. 2016. Heritage Hall Museum and Archives, Freeman, SD.
Wikipedia. "Dakota Freie Presse." http://en.wikipedia.org/wiki/*Dakota_Freie_Presse*.
———. "Demographics of South Dakota." http://en.wikipedia.org/wiki/Demographics_of_South_Dakota.
———. "Freeman." https://en.wikipedia.org/wiki/Freeman_South_Dakota.
———. "Global Warming." https://en.wikipedia.org/wiki/Global_warming.
———. "Hutchinson County." http://en.wikipedia.org/wiki/Hutchinson_County_South_Dakota.
———. "Reaper" and "Reaper-Binder." http://en.wikipedia.org/wiki/reaper; http://en.wikipedia.org/wiki/reaper-binder.
———. "South Dakota." http://en.wikipedia.org/wiki/South_Dakota.
———. "Turner County." http://en.wikipedia.org/wiki/Turner_County_South_Dakota.
———. "United Nations Framework Convention on Climate Change." https://en.wikipedia.org/wiki/United_Nations_Framework_Conventon_Climate_Change.
Willers, Bill, ed. *Learning to Listen to the Land*. Washington, DC: Island, 1991.
Williams, William Appleman. *Empire as a Way of Life: An Essay on the Causes and Character of America's Present Predicament Along with a Few Thoughts About an Alternative*. New York: Oxford University Press, 1980.
Zinn, Howard. *A People's History of the United States*. New York: Harper & Row, 1980.

Index

Acculturation/assimilation, 130–31, 138–44, 242–43
    Challenge of being "in the world," 139, 238
    Citizenship, 140
    Loss of German language, 139–40
    Resistance to, 138
    Theological acculturation, 142
Age of Exploration, 21, 26–30
Agrarian cultures, 157–58
    As colonial agents of imperial powers, 64, 74, 75
    As new born infants, 95–96, 101–2
    As subsistence village economies, 103
    Challenges to, xii, 101, 135, 164–69, 237–38
    Character of, 43–45, 156–57, 241
    Cohesion and social stability of, 154–55
    Components of, 220–224
    Criteria for sustainable, 149
    Ethnocentrism of, 169–70, 182–84
    Growing out of their land base, 137, 154, 200, 227–28
    Mission of, 232–34
    Relationships within and between, 198–99, 220, 229–34
    Strategies of coping with dominant culture, 220, 235–36, 252–54
    Transition from one place to another, 44–45, 144–45
Agricultural task, raising food for urban communities, 237–38
    Reclaiming the, 200, 227, 256–60

Agriculture in the Freeman community, 144–48, 153–54
    New paradigms of, 196, 197, 206–9, 226–27
Agricultural Revolution and rise of civilization, 24–26
Anabaptism, 47–48
    Agrarian roots of, 46–48, 240–243
Anabaptist leaders
    Ammann, Jacob, 52
    Bender, Harold S., 47, 142
    Blaurock, George, 47
    Burkholder, J. Lawrence, 157
    Cornies, Johann, 60
    Fretz, J. Winfield, 157
    Funk, John F., 77, 78, 79, 92
    Gingerich, Melvin, 157
    Grebel, Conrad, 47
    Haury, S. S., 108
    Hoffman, Melchior, 55
    Hut, Hans, 58
    Hutter, Jacob, 58
    Manz, Felix, 47
    Philipps, Obbe and Dirk, 55
    Reist, Hans, 52
    Simons, Menno, 55
    Sprunger, Samuel F., 108
Anabaptist Mennonite Biblical Seminary, 214
Anthropic Principle, 18–19
Apocalyptic Era, 19–20
Authors
    Ambrose, Stephen F., 100
    Berry, Wendel, 43–44, 168, 260
    Bose, Ben, 147

Index

Authors (cont.)
  Brown, Gabe, 226
  Crosby, Alfred, 145
  Dale, Tom, and Vernon Gill Carter, 14
  Flora, Cornelia Butler and Jan, 180–88
  Granberg-Michaelson, Wesley, 213
  Hightower, Jim, 168
  Jackson, Wes, 15
  Kingsolver, Barbara, 209
  Moltmann, Jurgen, 213
  Norris, Kathleen, 148
  Polkinghorne, John, 18
  Pollan, Michael, 209
  Preheim, Lois Janzen, 178
  Rolvaag, O. E., 93
  Salatin, Joel, 15
  Sale, Kirkpatrick, 195
  Shepherd, Mark, 15
  Webb, Walter Prescott, 31
  Wessel, James, 165
  Williams, William Appleman, 25
  Zinn, Howard, 196

British colonization of North America, 27–28
Brothers in Deed to Brothers in Need, 79, 80

Carbon sequestration, 154, 212, 236
Catholic Rural Life, 157, 244
Center for Rural Affairs, 16, 206
Center for Theology and Land, 244
Changing attitudes in rural communities, 201–3
Childstown Township, 119, 120, 133, 175
Churches of the Freeman community, Formation of, 104–19
Churches of the Freeman community, Historic Russian-German
  Bethany Mennonite Church, 115–16
  Bethel Mennonite Church, 113
  Bethesda Mennonite Church, 111, 112
  Bethlehem Reformed Church, 117
  Brothersfield Mennonite Brethren Church, 113
  Evangelical Mennonite Brethren Church, 113
  German Reformed Bethany Church, 117
  Hutterdorf Church, 114
  Hutterthal Mennonite Church, 115
  Johannestal Reformed Church, 116–17
  Karlswalde German Old Mennonite Church (Schartner), 111, 112
  Krimmer Mennonite Brethren Church, 115
  Neu Hutterthal Mennonite Church, 114
  Salem Church, 106–7
  Salem Mennonite Brethren Church, 115
  Salem Mennonite Church, 107, 125, 135, 154–55, 172–73, 178–79, 204, 215
  Salem-Zion Mennonite Church, 107, 154–55, 173, 203, 215
  Silver Lake Mennonite Brethren Church, 113
  St. Paul Lutheran Church, 118, 121
  Trinity Lutheran Church, 118
  Union Church (*Grosse Kirche*), 111, 112
  Zion Church (*Schpitzige Kirche*), 106–7
  Zion Kassel Reformed Church, 117
  Zion Mennonite Church, 114–15
Civilian Public Service, 141, 155
Civilization, cities, urbanization, 14, 25–26
Climate change, global warming 154, 210–212, 260
  Framework Convention on Climate Change, 211
Commodification of nature, 161–62
Commons, 22–24, 250–251
Coronavirus pandemic, 19, 116, 260
Corporations in industrial agriculture, 166–67
Creation care, 213–15

Index

Crises of economy, energy, ecology, 194–96
Culture, 155, 184–86, 221–22

Dakota Freie Presse, 139
Dakota Rural Action, 16, 206
Dakota Territory, 39, 71–72, 90, 91
Dawes Allotment Act, 1887, 37–38
Demographic changes, 203–6
Doctrine of Discovery, 21, 28–30
Dominant cultures, 238, 241, 247, 251–52
    Relationships with, 223–24, 234–38, 252–54

Earth, Planet, 5, 18, 246
    Stewardship of, 249
Ecology, environment, 148, 176–77, 194, 195, 210–212, 225–26
Economy, 195
Education/educational institutions, 119–25, 127
Empires, imperialism, 25
Energy, 195
European pilgrimage of Russian-German groups, 48–62
    Heilbronn Lutheran, 62
    Hutterian sojourn, 58–62
    Johannestal Reformed, 62
    Kassel Reformed, 62–63
    Klein Kassel Reformed, 63
    Low German Mennonites, 55–58
    Swiss Volhynian journey, 48–54
Evangelical Environmental Network, 244–45
Exploratory delegation of 1873 to America, 71, 75–81
    Composition of delegation, 76
Explorers, 26–35
    La Salle, Rene Robert, 22, 32
    La Verendre family, 33

Faiths, religions
    Amish, 52, 105, 137, 164, 229
    Church of God in Christ, Holdeman, 88
    Eastern Orthodox, 243–44
    Evangelical Mennonite Brethren, 113, 124
    General Conference Mennonite Church, 108–9, 113, 114, 115, 124, 142, 214
    Hutterite, 53, 58–61, 88–89
    Krimmer Mennonite Brethren, 115, 124
    Lutheran, 118
    Mennonite, 55–56, 67, 213, 215
    Mennonite Brethren, 113, 124
    Mennonite Church USA, 178, 214
    Muslim, 245
    Orthodox Presbyterian Church, 117
    Reformed/Protestant/Evangelical, 47, 118, 244–45
    Roman Catholic, 244
    Seventh Day Adventist, 112
    Swiss Brethren, 52, 65–67
    Traditional, Native American, 245–46
Farms, farming, 131, 144–47, 153–54
    Percentage of households, 205
    Size of, 170–71
Food, sacredness of, 256–57, 260
Food system, local, 200, 237–38, 258–60
    Industrial, 257–58
Foodie phenomenon, 209–10
Freeman, City of, 9, 126–29, 139, 152, 182, 186
Freeman Courier, 128, 139, 202, 216
Freeman Jr. College and Academy, 121–25, 134, 178
    As a teacher-training school, 123, 125
Freeman Network for Justice and Peace, 233
Freeman, rural community of, 152
    Agrarian cultures of, 45–46
    Capital assets of, 180–89
    Cultural life of, 155, 184–86
    Decline of, 169–72
    Economically self-sufficient, 199–200
    Envisioning the future of, 197–200
    First formative years, 101–4
    Geographical location of, 8–9, 129, 234

Freeman, rural community of (cont.)
   Life cycle of, x, 223, 261
   Paradigmatic for rural communities, xi
   Portrait of, 149–56
   Relationship with Yankton Sioux, 233
French colonization of North America, 32–34
Fundamentalism/modernism, 125, 142–43. 170, 230, 243

Geography of southeast South Dakota, 10–11
German colonies in Russia, 43, 55–56, 63
Germans-from-Russia, Russian-Germans, ix, 74, 103, 164, 183
Germans-from-Russia groups around Freeman
   Heilbronn Lutheran, 62, 118
   Hutterian *Prairieleut*, 88–89, 113–16
   Johannestal Reformed, 62, 116
   Kassel Reformed, 62–63, 117
   Klein Kassel Reformed, 63. 117
   Molotschna Mennonites, 88, 109, 111
   Prussian-Polish Mennonites (Karlswalders), 82–88, 109, 111, 134–35
   Swiss Volhynian (Schweitzer) Amish, 82, 105–9, 136
      Amish or Mennonite? 108–9
   Their sojourn in European lands, 63–65
   Unique gifts of, 230–231
Global crises, 196, 197
Governmental agricultural policy, 165–66
Great American Desert, 11, 99
Great Depression, 134, 136–37
Great Plains, 6–7
   Imperial history of, 31–35
Heritage Hall Museum and Archives, 79. 103, 188, 221
Holocene Epoch, 9–10, 13, 16
Homestead Act of 1862, 38–39, 41, 71, 99–101, 197, 132
   As radical lend tenure policy, 131–32
   Provisions of, 38
Homesteading on the Great Plains, 98–101
   The first winter, 93–96
Horodischers, 105, 107
Human occupation of the Earth, 13
Hutchinson County, 9, 149–52
   Farms in, 170–72
   Population of, 149, 171, 205
Hutterite Colonies, 61, 88–89, 113–14

Ice Ages on the Great Plains, 7–8
Image of God, 17, 248
Immigration hymn, 84–85
Immigration of the 1870's, Russian-German, 85–90
   Communal nature of, 44, 90, 97
   Financial assistance for, 83
   Heritage of immigrants, 42
   In relation to Great Plains settlement, 43, 101
   Preparations for, 81–84
   Push and *pull* of immigration, 74–75
Imperial history and agrarian cultures, 40–41, 101
Industrial agriculture, 160–62
Industrial Revolution, 160–62, 165, 210
Incarnation, 4

Journey to America, 85–89

Krehbiel, Peter, poem, 65–66

Land, Creation of, 5
   Defining conditions of human use, 3
   Lessons it teaches, 13–16
Land Grant universities, 167–68
Land, Relationship with, 219, 224–29
   Prepared for human habitation, 16–19
Land Stewardship Project, 16, 185, 206
Land tenure/use, 159, 217, 227–29
   As communal, familial inheritance, 137
   Ethic of, 239, 246–50

Land tenure policy on the Great
    Plains, 131–33, 137
Land tenure practices in the
    Freeman community, 133–37
Land trusts, 217–18, 228–29
Legacy of, 185, 216
Traditional and contemporary,
    22–24
Landscapes, 10–11
    Changed by agriculture, 148, 181
    Symbiotic relationship with human
        community, ix, 44
Leaders/personalities of Freeman
    community
    Alberty, Louis N., 119
    Bachman, H. A., 116, 122
    Becker, Peter, 110, 111
    Boese, Abraham and Helena, 134,
        145, 147
    Boese, John, 135
    Buechler, Christ, 127
    Buller, Heinrich and Helena, 134–
        35, 144
    Buller, Jakob, 76, 92
    Childs, James, 119
    Droescher, John, 118
    Ewert, Wilhelm, 76
    Gering, John C., 128
    Gering, John J., 93, 95
    Kaufman, Christian, 105, 107, 120,
        121, 133–34
    Kaufman, Harry, 120, 134, 169, 201
    Kaufman, John C., 133–34, 142
    Kaufman, Joseph, 106
    Kaufman, Maynard, 201
    Kaufman, Peter, 105
    Mendel, J. J., 128, 139
    Mueller, Christian, 102, 105, 107
    Mueller, John C., 120
    Orth, Joseph, 116, 117
    Ortman, Friedrich C., 98, 121
    Schartner, Friedrich, 110, 111
    Schrag, Andreas, 72, 76, 78, 79, 90,
        92, 102, 108
    Schrag, Jacob R., 106, 107
    Schrag, Johann, 105, 106, 110, 111
    Schroder, P. R., 125, 142
    Stucky, Jacob, 76, 105–6
    Teichrieb, Henry, 117

Tieszen, Dirk, 96. 111
Tieszen, Dirk P., 111
Tschetter, Lorenz, 71, 76, 79
Tschetter, Paul, 71, 76, 79, 114
Unruh, Daniel, 57, 71, 72, 91–93,
    96, 110
Unruh, John D., 92, 96, 147, 152
Unruh, Tobias, 57, 71, 79, 90, 92,
    93, 109
Waldner, Fred, 126
Waldner, John, 115
Waltner, Emil, 46, 53, 65
Waltner, Gary, 94, 96
Wipf, John L., 115
Leopold Center for Sustainable
    Agriculture, 16
Lewis and Clark Expedition, 34, 99
Louisiana Purchase, 22, 34

Manifest Destiny, 28
Mennonite Aid Committees of
    1873/1874, 83–84, 102
Mennonite Central Committee/service
    organization, 204, 213, 214,
    255
Mennonite Creation Care Network, 214
Mennonite migrations to America in
    1870s, 86–87
Mennonite population of Turner and
    Hutchinson Counties, 152
Mennonite solidarity in the 1870s
    immigration, 80

Nationhood, nationality, 23
Native American First Nations, 4, 12,
    35–38
    Arikara, 12, 35
    Dakota Nations, *Oceti Sakowin*,
        35–36
    Disenfranchisement of, 37–38, 71,
        99
    Mandan, 12, 35
    Mound Builder cultures, 13
    Population of in South Dakota, 40
    Yankton Sioux, 35,38, 71, 73, 75,
        131, 233
Nature as teacher of agrarian cultures, 13
North America, Formation of, 8

Index

Pacifism/non-resistance, 140–43, 204, 240–241
Peasants' Wars of the 1520s., 48, 235
Place names related to local cultures
    Alsace, 49, 52, 53, 62
    Alwinz, Transylvania, 59
    Austerlitz, Czechoslovakia, 58
    Avon, SD, 57
    Beresan Settlement, Ukraine, 62
    Berne Canton, 49
    Crimea, 62
    Chortitza Colony, Ukraine, 55, 67
    Danzig, Prussia, 55
    Dubno, Volhynia, 54
    Edwardsdorf, Volhynia, 54
    Galicia, 52–54
    Glueckstaler Settlement, Ukraine, 62
    Heinrichsdorf, Ukraine, 57, 86
    Henderson, NE, 88, 124
    Holland, 55, 67
    Horodisch, Volhynia, 54
    Kansas, 54
    Karlswalde, Volhynia, 57, 87–88
    Kotosufka, Volhynia, 54, 86
    Lemburg (L'vov), Galicia, 53
    Michalin, Ukraine, 53, 56, 87
    Molotschna Colony, Ukraine, 55–56, 60
    Montbeliard, France, 53
    Moravia, 58
    Mountain Lake, MN, 78, 88, 91, 124
    New York, 85
    Nicholsburg, Czechoslovakia, 58
    Ostrog, Volhynia, 57
    Palatinate (Pfalz), 49, 52, 62
    Philadelphia, 85, 87
    Poland, 54, 74
    Prussia, 55, 67
    Red River, Pembina Valley, ND, 78, 90
    Rovno, Ukraine, 54
    Russia, 54
    Raditschewa, Ukraine, 60
    Sahorez, Ukraine, 54
    Switzerland, 47, 49
    Ukraine, 52
    Urszulin and Michelsdorf, Poland, 54
    Volhynia, 53–54, 56, 74
    Waldheim, Volhynia, 54
    Wischenka, Ukraine, 53, 60
    Wuerttemberg, 62
Portuguese explorations and colonization, 26–27
Prairie, 225–26
    Characteristics of, 6–7, 10–11
    Destruction of, 14
Prairieleut (Prairie People), 61, 72, 88–89
Prayer Walks in Childstown Township, 172–78
Private property, 132, 137

Railroads and the birth of Freeman, 98, 126–29
Religious faith in agrarian culture, 178–80, 240–246
    Co-opted to justify dominant cultures, 29, 244–45, 253–54
Religious leaders
    Alexander VI, Pope, 29
    Bartholomew, Patriarch, 244
    Frances, Pope, 244
    Luther, Martin, 47
    Nicholas V, Pope, 29
    Zwingli, Ulrich, 47
Reservations in South Dakota, 37
Rulers, Political
    Alexander I, Czar, 56, 73
    Alexander II, Czar, 71, 73
    Catherine the Great, Czarina, 43, 55, 64, 73
    Charles V, Emperor, 55
    Czartoryski, Prince, 53
    Ferdinand, Archduke, 58
    Grant, Ulysses S., President, 79
    Jefferson, Thomas, President, 34, 99
    Joseph II, Emperor, 52, 64
    Karl Ludwig, Prince, 52, 64
    Leonhard of Lichtenstein, 58
    Leopold Eberhard, 53, 64
    Lincoln, Abraham, President, 73
    Louis XIV, King, 53
    Lubanirsky, Prince, 57
    Marie Theresa, Empress, 59
    Marshall, John, Chief Justice, 30

Rumyantsov, Count, 60
Sealth, Chief, 245–46
Turner, John W., Dakota Territorial Member, 93
Rural communities, Attitudinal changes in, 201–3
    Capital in, 180–89
Rural congregations, Mission of, 198, 232–34, 243, 253–54
Rural crisis in America, 164–69, 178–79
    Failure of religious leadership in, 179–80
    Powers leading to, 165–69
Rural life movements, 157–58
Rural Revival, 16, 194, 207, 215–18
Russia, Empire of, 43, 73
Russianization policies, 73–74, 75–76

Scripture references
    1 Samuel, 8:20, 101, 252
    1 Samuel 13:19–22, 163
    Acts 2, 163
    Genesis 1, 17
    Genesis 1:26, 17
    Genesis 2:7, 17
    Genesis 2:15, 13, 249
    Genesis 2:18, 250
    Genesis 11, 163
    Genesis 12:6, 30
    Leviticus 25:23, 30, 229, 252
    Mark 5:1–20, 253
    Mark 6 and 8, 257
    Mark 15:41, 257
    Matthew 10:29–31, 248
    Numbers 13–14, 81
    Philippians 2:1–4, 254
    Psalm 24:1, 30
    Revelation 12–13, 169
Sod houses, 94–95
South Dakota Mennonite College, 98, 121, 139, 152

South Dakota, 39–40
    Exploration of, 33
    Population of, 152, 171
Spanish colonization of North America, 27, 31–33

Table, Lord's Table, 240, 256–57, 259–60
Technology, technocracy, 162–64, 194
Theology of creation care, 143, 213–15, 250
Towns and cities in the larger rural Freeman community, 198–99
Treaties with First Nations, 36–38
    Treaty of Laramie, 1968, 36, 99
    Treaty of Traverse des Sioux, 1851, 36, 100
    Yankton Cession of 1858, 36, 71, 73
Turkey Ridge, 8, 104, 107, 234
Turner County, 9, 38, 93, 136, 149–52
    Farms in, 170–72
    Population of, 149. 171, 205

United States, 79, 80
    As Mennonite promised land, 81
    As an imperial power, 101
    Expansion onto the Great Plains, 34–35

Wagner Area Horizons Team, 233
Waldheimers, 105, 107
Watersheds of the Freeman Community, 8
    James River, 8, 129, 234
    Mississippi Rover, 107
    Missouri River, 34
    Turkey Ridge Creek, 8, 129
    Vermillion Rivers, East and West, 8, 129, 234
    Wolf Creek, 8, 234